D0151934

# THE LONDON
# MONSTER

# THE LONDON
# MONSTER

## A SANGUINARY TALE

## JAN BONDESON

The MONSTER disappointed of his Afternoons Luncheon ... or Porridge Pots preferable to Cork Rumps.

UNIVERSITY OF PENNSYLVANIA PRESS

Philadelphia

Copyright © 2001 University of Pennsylvania Press
All rights reserved
Printed in the United States of America on acid-free paper

10 9 8 7 6 5 4 3 2

Published by
University of Pennsylvania Press
Philadelphia, Pennsylvania 19104-4011

Library of Congress Cataloging-in-Publication Data
Bondeson, Jan
    The London monster : a sanguinary tale / Jan Bondeson
        p.    cm.
    Includes bibliographical references and index.
    ISBN 0-8122-3576-2 (cloth : alk. paper)
    1. Williams, Renwick.    2. Williams, Renwick—Trials, litigation, etc.
3. Criminals—England—London—Biography.    4. Women—Crimes against—England—
London—History—18th century.    5. London (England)—History—18th century.
HV6248.W485 .B65    2000
364'.15/55/092—B21                                                      00-056789
                                                                              CIP

Terrific Fiend! Thou Monster fell!
Condemn'd in haunts profane to dwell,
Why quit thy solitary Home,
O'er wide Creation's paths to roam?
Pale Tyrant of the timid Heart . . .

Mrs. Mary Robinson, *Ode to Despair*

# CONTENTS

# THE CAST

**Catherine and Molly Alman.** Two of Rhynwick Williams's alibi witnesses. But were they telling the truth?

**John Julius Angerstein.** A wealthy philanthropist and art collector, who took a great interest in the bottoms and thighs of wounded ladies.

**Miss Barrs.** The devious daughter of a fruiterer, who pretended to be a Monster victim.

**Elizabeth and Frances Baughan.** Respectable young ladies; both victims of the Monster.

**Sir Francis Buller.** Also known as Judge Thumb. He presided at the first Monster trial, at the Old Bailey.

**John Coleman.** The Monster-catcher. Also known as the Catamite, the Dastard, Miss Porter's Puppy, and the Cowardly Fishmonger. A deeply flawed hero.

**"Captain" Crowder.** A robber and highwayman. Transported to Botany Bay.

**The Hon. Mr. Cuffe.** Brother of Viscount Netterville. Once accused of being the Monster by Charley Jones, alias Fat Phillis, a dangerous transvestite.

**Elizabeth Davis.** A washerwoman who refused to smell a nosegay, and who had her bottom cut by the Monster as a consequence.

**Mary Forster.** A "Greffe-Street Vestal" according to Theophilus Swift. Another Monster victim.

**Typhone Fournier.** A Frenchman with a silly name.

**"Sir" John Gallini.** A lecherous dancing-master; the tutor of Rhynwick Williams.

**Sarah Godfrey.** A beautiful lady assaulted by the London Monster.

**George Hanger.** A crony of the Prince of Wales. Depicted as the Monster on a well-known caricature drawing.

**Walter Hill.** A rowdy Lieutenant in the Navy, who once made a riot in the Tottenham Court Road, and was arrested as the Monster as a consequence.

**Newman Knowlys.** The barrister of Rhynwick Williams at the first trial.

**Colonel Charles Lennox.** Rake and duelist. He once nearly blew out the brains of the Duke of York. In another duel, he shot Theophilus Swift in the stomach. He later became Duke of Richmond, but was bitten by a young fox in Canada and died of hydrophobia shortly after.

**Macmanus.** A Bow Street Runner.

**William Mainwaring.** A corrupt Judge, who was Chairman of the Middlesex Sessions; nevertheless, he took pains to elucidate the Monster mystery, and left valuable notes regarding the second trial.

**Aimable Michelle,** alias Amabel Mitchell. An artificial flower-maker, and the former employer of the scapegrace Rhynwick Williams.

**Reine Michelle,** sister of the above. Another artificial flower-maker.

**Mrs. Miel.** An old lady who received a knock on the head in St. James's Street.

**Moses Murrant.** Another Bow Street Runner, who was once tricked by the Monster in Castle Street.

**Mr. Pearson.** Lived in Bond Street. Took an interest in ornamented chip-hats.

**Sir Arthur Leary Pigot.** The prosecuting attorney. A clever, experienced man.

**William Pitt.** The Prime Minister. Depicted as the Monster on a ribald drawing.

**Anne Porter.** The Beauty of the Bagnio. The charming young heroine of our tale, but a lady who may have had a colorful past.

**Sarah Porter.** Anne's sister, also a victim of the London Monster.

**Thomas Porter.** Father of Anne and Sarah. Keeper of Pero's Bagnio, a notorious den of vice in late eighteenth-century London, as alleged by Theophilus Swift.

**Elizabeth Porter.** Wife of the above. A strong, forceful woman, who once waved her fist in the Monster's face.

**Mr. Smith.** A man of mystery, living in South Moulton Street.

**Theophilus Swift.** The bad guy. An Irish lawyer, adventurer, duelist and pamphleteer. The Monster's Champion, and the Bane of the Wounded Ladies. My favorite in the cast.

**Deane Swift.** Son of Theophilus, and helped him to investigate the Monster mystery. Later sent down from Trinity College, Dublin, for kicking his tutor of mathematics.

**Captain Philip Thicknesse.** Also known as Lieutenant-Governor Gall-Stone. Accused of being the Monster on posters all over London.

**William Tuffing.** A wimpish ladies' hairdresser turned clothes salesman, who was nevertheless thought by some to be the London Monster.

**Lady Wallace.** A female playwright, of a violent temper, who once claimed to have been frightened by the Monster. She later tried to frame Amabel Mitchell as the Monster's accomplice.

**Kitty Wheeler.** A beautiful "Tavern Vestal," as alleged by Mr. Swift. Insulted by the Monster, and testified against him.

**"Parsloe" Wheeler.** Kitty's father. A tavern-keeper. Grappled with the Monster once, but had to release him. A rough character, and a possible arsonist.

**Joshua Williams.** A kinsman of Rhynwick Williams. Not the sharpest tool in the box.

**Rhynwick Williams.** A foul-mouthed little man with a big nose, who was obsessed with sex. Another artificial flower maker. A thoroughly despicable character. Was he the London Monster?

**Thomas Williams Junior.** Rhynwick's respectable brother, another apothecary.

**Thomas Williams Senior.** Rhynwick's father. A respectable Welsh apothecary who settled in London.

**Sir Sampson Wright.** A Bow Street Magistrate. Led the investigation of the Monster mystery.

**Extras.** Bow Street Runners and Patrols; Night watchmen; Monster hunters; Snobs; Swells; Pimps; Prostitutes; Bullies; Pickpockets; also the Augsburg Girl-Cutter, the Halifax Slasher, and Jack the Snipper.

# INTRODUCTION: THE COMING OF THE MONSTER

*From thorny wilds a Monster came,*
*that fill'd my soul with fear and shame;*
*The birds, forgetful of their mirth,*
*Droop'd at the sight, and fell to earth. . . .*
—*William Cowper,* Self-love and Truth Incompatible

ONE of the more enigmatic figures in the old Newgate Calendar is that of the London Monster of the 1790s. The strange crimes of this mysterious offender earned him distinction as a forerunner of Jack the Ripper.[1] Indeed, the alarm and terror caused by the Monster's wanton outrages against unprotected women were equal to the uproar after the Marr and Williamson murders in the Ratcliffe Highway in 1811, and the Ripper murders in 1888. The general alarm among London's women was without precedent. A certain John Williams was arrested for the Ratcliffe Highway murders, but later committed suicide under highly suspicious circumstances; later research has cast considerable doubt on whether he was the murderer.[2] As we know, no arrest was made for the Ripper crimes; despite the list of suspects paraded by imaginative writers, the case is still unsolved, and likely to remain so.[3] Through chance combined with vigilante effort (the police of 1790 were incapable of tackling the matter on their own) an arrest was finally made for the crimes of the London Monster: The young Welshman Rhynwick Williams was arrested as the Monster and committed to Newgate after a sensational trial at the Old Bailey. He was eloquently described in Henry Wilson and James Caulfield's *Wonderful Characters*: "His unnatural and unaccountable propensities in maliciously cutting and stabbing females whenever he found them unprotected, soon made him a terror to the metropolis: his behaviour was so revolting to the feelings, and carried with it such hellish appetite, and dreadful consequences, that the horror he spread, it is impossible to describe."[4]

Quite a few contemporaries believed that Rhynwick Williams was innocent. He was energetically defended by the eccentric Irish poet Theophilus Swift, a blood relation of the great Dean, who wrote a pamphlet depicting Williams as the innocent victim of an elaborate conspiracy. The wealthy philanthropist John Julius Angerstein, one of the founders of Lloyd's, had offered a reward of 100 pounds to the person who succeeded in capturing the London Monster; Swift claimed that this immense sum had induced several of the key witnesses to perjure themselves. Swift actually appeared as Williams's barrister in a farcical second trial.

Doubts concerning Williams's guilt have persisted. Andrew Knapp and William Baldwin's *New Newgate Calendar* (1826) remarks that Williams had a modestly solid alibi and that all were not convinced about his guilt, "believing that the female witnesses (a circumstance which we have shown too frequently to have happened) mistook the man who wounded and ill treated the prosecutrix."[5] Other writers have postulated that there never was a Monster, and that the 1790 phenomenon was a kind of mass hysteria[6]: the London Monster was a bogeyman in the tradition of Sawney Beane, the Scottish cannibal;[7] Spring-heeled Jack, the fire-breathing horror who mystified the Londoners;[8] or Sweeney Todd, the Demon Barber of Fleet Street.[9] They theorized that Williams was a scapegoat, a man who habitually pestered and insulted women on London streets and was unlucky enough to fall into the hands of the authorities. His trial could be likened to an exorcism: once Williams was committed to Newgate, the Monster attacks ceased.

My first acquaintance with the London Monster was made one day in 1996, when I was looking through some large late eighteenth-century scrapbooks in the British Library. The books had once been the property of Miss Sophia Sarah Banks, the sister of Sir Joseph Banks, the president of the Royal Society of London. Miss Banks collected handbills and broadsides relating to popular entertainments: ballooning, firework displays, and theatrical productions. More pertinent for my earlier book *The Feejee Mermaid* was a section on "learned pigs" and other eighteenth-century performing animals. The most intriguing discovery that day, however, was Miss Banks's scrapbook about the London Monster.[10] She had taken much interest in the Monster hunt and built up an extensive collection of newspaper clippings, prints, and manuscript material. She herself took an active part in the vigilante efforts to catch the Monster. At first, I believed Miss Banks's collection was the definitive account of the Monster mania that consumed London in the spring and summer of 1790, but this turned out to be very far from the truth. Not only was there a wealth of information about the Monster in various other newspapers not covered by Miss Banks, but not less than seven pamphlets had been written about the hunt for the elusive criminal and the indictment and trials of Rhynwick Williams. Three of these pamphlets were kept at the British Library; one had once been there but was a casualty of wartime action; three had never been held even by this famous library. Fortunately, copies of two of these very rare and valuable Monster pamphlets existed at the Free Library of Philadelphia.[11] Another vital clue to the Monster mystery was unearthed at the Public Record Office in Kew, in a dusty volume of reports on criminals. Also compelling was the amount of attention given to the Monster by London caricaturists: there were not less than twelve caricature prints on the subject, some of them praiseworthy attempts to present a likeness of the perpetrator to the public, others lewd fantasies about sharp rapiers piercing exposed female buttocks.

The majority of my research on the London Monster was carried out in the venerable North Library at the old British Museum, next to the famous Round Reading Room, which is now, alas, gone forever.[12] The final touches were added at the present-day abomination at St. Pancras, the monstrous ugliness of which might well have inspired my work further.

CHAPTER 1

# A MELANCHOLY OCCURRENCE IN ST. JAMES'S STREET

*If in the Park, as usual, my walk I should pursue,*
*And civilly accost a Miss—"My pretty, how do you do?"*
*So strange the times! Each Miss is sure my meaning to*
*    misconstrue,*
*And jumps and squeaks, and cries aloud—"O Heavens! Here's*
*    the MONSTER!*
*    You nasty thing.*
*    You'll surely swing!"*
*    And then she'll swear,*
*    Would make you stare,*
*She saw me ready to—O rare!*
*To stab her thro' the pocket-hole—exactly like the MONSTER.*
*                —Mr. Hook, "The Monster," a song presented to the*
*                                    proprietors of Vauxhall*

IF ONE wishes to go back in time more than two hundred years to study the daily life of the Londoners in 1790 and how it was disrupted by the terror and rage caused by the London Monster's crimes, the best resource to consult is the Burney newspaper collection at the British Library.[1] This collection was originally compiled by the Rev. Charles Burney, brother of the novelist Fanny Burney. The Burney Collection today exists on microfilm, and one thus does not get the agreeable smell and feel of the huge, bedraggled-looking tomes of old newspapers in the Colindale Newspaper Library. The year 1790 is reasonably well covered: long-defunct newspapers like the *Argus, World, Oracle,* and *Diary* depict the metropolis, soon to be threatened by the Monster in its midst, with many curious details. These late eighteenth-century newspapers were notoriously unreliable; many reports were inserted by interested parties or invented by unscrupulous journalists.[2] Yet this historical snapshot is untroubled by hindsight and "political correctness," as yet untinged by modern theories of historiography. After all, there are three elements to history—what actually happened, what people felt about it when it happened, and what people feel about it later.

The newspaper columns of the early 1790s devote a good deal of attention to the revolutionary activities in France, and there is much apprehension regarding the fate of the captive King Louis, Queen Marie Antoinette, and their poor children. The future of the revolutionary French republic is viewed with much concern that this kind of political extremism would not do Europe any good. The war between Sweden and Russia is another important story, and the warring galleys and gun sloops in the icy Baltic Sea are a recurring topic. The slave trade is also much debated: Most writers seem to be convinced that this barbaric practice should be abolished, but a notice in the *World* mentions without further comment that "At the sale of a Gentleman's effects lately in Jamaica, a Negro blacksmith was sold for two hundred and sixty pounds; the highest prize ever known to have been given."[3] The miraculous escape of Captain Bligh from the mutineers of the *Bounty* is a piece of hot news, surpassing even the arrest of Lieutenant John Frith, who had thrown a large stone at King George III. (The dastardly assailant is described as a man of genteel, but frantic appearance.)

The most popular sport of the time was boxing, and the activities of the notorious bruisers William Ward, Richard Humphries, and Daniel Mendoza were followed as avidly in the newspapers as those of today's heavyweights. The boxers would publish polite challenges to each other in the letter columns of the newspapers, often with barbs and teases attached to make the opponent more eager to accept the proposed fight. The lottery is another recurrent story, but it seems the late eighteenth-century players invested rather more heavily than present-day ticket buyers hoping for the big win: "the melancholy effects of insuring in the Lottery, may be seen in our streets every day, and the bitter cries of the Poor are incessant."[4] Many ruined servants stole property from their masters to feed their gambling habit and were turned out without a character reference, clothes, or bread: "Can it then be wondered that the Cities of London and Westminster should swarm with thieves and vagabonds?"

The late eighteenth-century morals were little better than those advertised by the tabloids today. In a much-publicized incident, a brewer's clerk bought another man's wife for a guinea, with her child into the bargain. The husband made his lady a most obsequious bow, wished her a good day, collected the payment, and left her. "Shame unto the morals and follies of the day!" thundered the *Public Advertiser.*[5] The *World* published a somewhat callous epitaph on a young lady who had thrown herself out of a window after her mother had forbidden her to wear stiffened stays:

Women, they tell us, have strange ways,
So Harriett pin'd for stiffen'd stays;
Till hopeless grown, and in the dumps,
For want of *Stays,* she took to *Jumps.*[6]

\*   \*   \*

These distant tales of a bygone time are not the complete story, however. The poverty of the lower classes of society was appalling, the ignorance among both high and low classes abysmal, and the barbarity of older times lurked just beneath the polite veneer of the "Age of Improvement." In 1780 London saw full-scale riots that had begun as an anti-Catholic demonstration led by the fanatical Lord George Gordon.[7] Things soon got out of hand as the mob marched on the Houses of Parliament. They harried the peers and members and smashed their coaches. Parts of the mob burned and looted Roman Catholic chapels, schools, and private houses; the police, the Lord Mayor, and even the military were powerless to intercede. In the late evening, Charles Burney, the newspaper collector, looked out of his observatory window (his house had formerly belonged to Sir Isaac Newton) and saw the whole of Leicester Fields illuminated by the many raging fires. What had begun as an anti-Catholic demonstration soon became a social protest: 60,000 rioters attacked the houses of the wealthy as well as the prisons, the banks, and the magistrate's house in Bow Street.[8] Armed with cutlasses, clubs, and poleaxes, the mob stormed Newgate Prison and freed 300 prisoners; they then set the prison alight, and proceeded to do the same at the Bridewell, King's Bench, and New Prisons. Not until the militia had been summoned and supplementary troops called in could the mob be confronted: after a violent onslaught on the Bank of England, there was a pitched battle, from which the rioters retired in confusion. Had many of them not been the worse for wear after pillaging the Holborn gin distilleries, the outcome might have been a yet more violent one.

London's population had risen from approximately 60,000 in the year 1500 to 400,000 in the mid-seventeenth century; it stood at nearly one million by the late 1700s. This growth gave the criminal underworld unique opportunities for vice and crime.[9] The crime rate rose appallingly high, with armies of burglars, pickpockets, footpads, and highwaymen at large in the metropolis and its vicinity. There were rookeries where the police hesitated to arrest any criminal because his friends and any other ruffian standing nearby were sure to fall upon them with bludgeons, knives, and axes, to free him by the use of force. The many alehouses, hotels, and seamen's hostels in London gave the brothels a roaring trade; the increasing wealth of the upper and upper middle classes attracted burglars; and the immense number of lanes, courts, and narrow alleyways gave street criminals great possibilities for concealment and anonymity. In 1782, after the American Revolution, robberies and burglaries increased, and pickpockets were more numerous than ever.[10] By 1784, Londoners were fearful of going outdoors after dark, even in the well-lit main streets, due to the threat from the violent footpads infesting the city.[11] Although the policing of London was notoriously lax and ineffective, the sheer number of crimes committed meant the prisons were nevertheless crammed full of villains of every description.

What could be done with all these criminals? The system of criminal law of this period, the Bloody Code, had originally contained just a few crimes punishable by execution, such as treason, murder, and rape, but throughout the eighteenth century, more than one hundred capital offenses had to be added. The moneyed classes felt inadequately protected in the absence of a regular police force; in a vain attempt to deter criminals, an increasing number of property crimes were made subject to the death penalty. By the 1790s there were more than two hundred capital offenses that were punishable by death. It was a capital offense to steal a sheep, to pickpocket more than a shilling, to illegally cut down trees in an orchard, to break the border of a fish pond so as to allow the fish to escape, or to break a pane of glass in a winter's evening with intent to steal. But the objective of the criminal law was to frighten and deter the potential criminal, and at the same time the number of capital statutes had been increasing in the mid-eighteenth century, the number of executions had been decreasing. An increasing proportion of the convicted felons had instead been deported to the American penal colonies. But after the American Revolution, this was no longer possible, and the prison hulks on the Thames and the penitentiaries for hard labor were woefully inadequate both as crime deterrents and as a way to get rid of the villains. After the crime wave in the early and mid-1780s, an increasing number of prisoners were executed, sometimes for very insignificant crimes. It was not until the Botany Bay penal colony in Australia was founded in 1786, and the first fleet of prisoners was sent there the year after, that the overpopulated prison system was able to recover.[12]

The rising scale of punishment in the 1780s and 1790s meant that minor property offenders were whipped and/or imprisoned in houses of correction for six to nine months.[13] More serious thieves, housebreakers, and pickpockets were usually transported to penal colonies. Finally, murderers, highway robbers, arsonists, and hardened burglars and robbers were hanged. Late eighteenth-century justice was overwhelmingly concerned with property, and pickpockets could be hanged after stealing trifling amounts. In December 1789, fourteen-year-old Thomas Morgan and twelve-year-old James Smith were convicted of stealing seven silk handkerchiefs from a shop; they were sentenced to death.[14] On the other hand, many rapists walked free because their victims were disbelieved. In general, women were considered untrustworthy witnesses, and a lower class woman in particular had little chance of winning a case against a gentleman of some social distinction.[15]

Visitors to London, and many of the less fastidious Londoners, regarded public executions as major attractions. When, in 1789, a housebreaker named William Skitch was executed, the *Times* reporter on the scene recounted that the rope slipped off the gallows and Skitch's body fell heavily to the ground. The crowd was moved by the condemned man's predicament, but Skitch simply stood up and said to the executioner and his assistant, who were getting another rope ready: "Good people, be not hurried; I can wait a little." Another writer in the same newspaper found it a melancholy contrast that from 1775 until 1787 just six people had been executed in Amsterdam and Utrecht, while during the same period of time 624 prisoners convicted at the Old Bailey had been hanged at Tyburn or Newgate.[16] In 1790, a humanitarian writer in the *Gentleman's Magazine* blasted the laws of England as cruel, unjust, and useless. The number of people strung up on the gallows was sufficient proof that the laws were cruel; the fact that the same punishment was inflicted on the parricide as on a starving wretch who took three shillings on the highway proved they were unjust; and the frequency and multiplicity of serious crimes offered ample evidence that they were useless as a deterrent.[17]

Long prison sentences were rare, and were reserved for "special cases," for example, a woman of good family who had murdered her child and who was protected from the gallows and transportation by family influence. A considerable percentage of London's prisoners were debtors, some of whom were incarcerated for protracted periods of time until their debts were settled. The pillory was irregularly used for crimes thought particularly heinous. To be pilloried for a sexual offense could literally be a death sentence in itself.[18] When, in early 1790, two homosexual valets (caught "in the act") were put in the pillory, an enormous mob gathered to see them punished. The mob did not arrive empty-handed. A punning newspaper reporter was delighted to find that the valet named *Bacon* was pelted heavily with *eggs*. Potatoes, stones, and brickbats were showered over the two blood-spattered wretches in the pillory; the police took cover from the torrent of missiles; and the two valets were barely extricated from the pillory alive.[19]

*        *        *

In London of 1790, several debating societies met to discuss the burning questions of the day. They had many female members, and some catered almost exclusively for the fair sex; thus it is somewhat surprising that one of the questions for late 1789 was whether women had no soul.[20] During this time, women were regarded as defective men: little interested in public concerns, they were weak, imbecile creatures fit only for gossip and embroidery. In one newspaper comment prompted by the debate about the souls of women, a disgruntled man wrote that women who attended debating societies would be better employed at needle and thread.[21] A question in another debating society was whether "the tender sensibility of the female heart lessened or increased the happiness of the fair sex."[22] The 1780s and early 1790s were the height of the culture of sensibility.[23] While courage and cleverness were seen as male attributes, kindness, attentiveness and delicacy belonged to the female sex. It was widely believed that a woman's weaker, finer nerves made her more timid and tenderhearted, liable to vapors and hysterical paroxysms when faced with strong emotions. It became fashionable among the ladies to weep, faint, and go off in hysterics at the slightest provocation as evidence of their refined, delicate nerves. The ideal woman in contemporary fiction was a pale, helpless, timorous creature with a nervous system strung as high as a violin. A banging door, a violent gust of wind, a peal of thunder, or the appearance of a toad or a mouse was enough to send her into hysterics. The contrast between the predatory male gallant, strong, fierce and sexual, and the innocent, passive young heroine who suffers endless crises of nerves, was particularly marked in the Gothic novels of Mrs. Radcliffe and her various imitators which were enormously popular in the 1790s—not least among female readers.[24]

The sexual world of London of 1790 was male dominated. The chastity of a young woman before marriage was considered of paramount importance. A woman's life after marriage was dull and respectable: she gave birth, took care of the household, and obeyed her husband in everything.[25]

Young men had a more interesting time. Sexuality was on public view everywhere in the metropolis: there were erotic novels, lewd songs, and por-
nographic prints in abundance.[26] The most prominent feature in the female
dress of the time was the décolletage. The newspapers advertised brothels,
aphrodisiacs, and cures for venereal disease, and Jack Harris's popular
*Whoremonger's Guide to London* listed a directory of prostitutes that
detailed addresses, physical characteristics, and "specialties."

Sexual exploitation of maidservants was common; the image of the
chambermaid as sexual fodder for the young master is a cliché, but it has its
basis in reality. Even very young girl servants were raped or seduced by
libertines who were aroused by pedophilia or fearful of venereal disease.[27]
Actresses, dancers, and serving girls in the taverns were considered sexually "easy"; some played along with the morals of the time and preferred to
be well-kept mistresses of a string of reasonably attractive men to exploitation as a domestic servant or "respectable" wife.

There were brothels in every part of town. Mrs. Hayes's Seraglio in
Pall Mall was famous for a live show with naked dancers of both sexes.
At Mother Wisebourne's house off the Strand, girls were said to cost 250
pounds a night. London at this time was home to 10,000 prostitutes who
openly plied their trade in the streets, markets, and theaters. The district
between Charing Cross and Drury Lane, and well into Soho, was the favorite haunt of these prostitutes. The Covent Garden area was particularly
notorious: There, in addition to regular brothels, were many alehouses
where prostitutes were available and a number of "bagnios," brothels dis-
guised as bathhouses, some of which were veritable dens of vice and catered to varied sexual tastes. One constabulary raid on Covent Garden
resulted in the arrest of twenty-two prostitutes, two of whom turned out to
be men dressed as women.[28]

If the sexuality of London of 1790 was earthy and abandoned, the
popular amusements were of a corresponding vigor and brutality. Upper
class rakes spent their time at racecourses and gaming parlors, bet on
pugilists, and caroused around the streets, fighting, drinking, and whor-
ing. One newspaper report states that it was a popular pastime of the
"bloods"—the young hooligans about town—to blacken the faces of elderly,
respectable people who passed through the West End, using a long brush
and a bucket full of a mixture of eggs and lampblack.[29] The common man of
1790 did not much care for a public reading from the works of Shakespeare,
or indeed anything that hinted of intellectual activity, as long as there was
hope of going down to the pub to have a jug of ale while watching a badger

with its tail nailed to the floor being harried by three fierce fox terriers. Several rat pits in the city allowed bets to be made as to how many rats a dog could kill in a certain number of minutes.[30] After a couple of sacks of squirming rats had been poured into the pit, an evil-looking cur was introduced in their midst to begin his gory work of destruction. When sewer rats were used, lady visitors used perfumed handkerchiefs to counteract the rodents' pungent smell. The champion dog Billy reportedly could kill one hundred rats in five minutes. His fellow champion Jacko once piled up one thousand corpses in an hour and forty minutes, but there were allegations that the rats had been drugged with laudanum beforehand. Henry Mayhew once spoke to a costermonger who sometimes took the dog's place, leaping down into the pit and killing the rats with his teeth: his face was badly scarred from the bites of the infuriated rodents. In March 1790, after a bet had been agreed to, a man drank five quarts of ale and then masticated and swallowed the earthen mug; he died two days later.[31] In January 1790, after another bet had been agreed upon in a public house near Windsor, a man ate a living cat, tearing it to pieces with his teeth and leaving only the bones "as the memorials of the exercise of a brutal appetite, and the degradation of human nature."[32] A few weeks later, the newspapers reported that the Windsor cat eater had once more revealed his brutality: suddenly and without reason he hacked off his own right hand with a bill hook.[33] The reason he gave was that he was "disinclined to work" and hoped the overseers of the parish would provide for him in his maimed condition. This sinister outbreak of brutality in early 1790, heralding the coming of the Monster, even spread to the animal kingdom: "A Poney seized a sheep, and bit and kicked it till it died. The Poney then separated the head from the neck, and devoured near two quarters of the sheep."[34]

* * *

At least at the outset, a sinister event in early 1790 was the queen's birthday on January 19. To celebrate the day, flags were up everywhere, church bells were rung, and guns were fired. The illuminations on the main streets were more numerous than on any previous royal birth night: the theaters on Drury Lane were splendidly lit, and the gunsmith's shop at Ludgate's Hill displayed a brilliant storefront with a transparency of the queen.[35] The *World* published an exhaustive feature about the dresses of the ladies. The queen and princesses were soberly dressed and could not compete with such extravagant fashionables as the countesses of Westmoreland and

Warwick and Lady Elizabeth Waldegrave, who were glittering with diamonds and fitted out according to the latest fashions. A huge crowd, some in the ballroom and some in the galleries, as befitted their respective social stations, had admired the dazzling crowd of courtiers and nobles. The prince of Wales made a brief appearance at the ball, wearing a Mazarine coat emblazoned with silver, before going out to his normal rakehelly nocturnal pursuits. The Princess Mary, her majesty's fourth daughter, made her first public appearance in the ballroom that night.

Among the crowd assembled in the galleries, consisting mainly of those who were not quite considered gentlefolk, were twenty-one-year-old Miss Anne Porter and her nineteen-year-old sister Sarah. Their father, Thomas Porter, did not belong to the nobility or gentry, nor was he of an old and respected family; he was a contented, relatively well-to-do member of the lower middle class who kept a combined hotel, tavern, and cold-bath establishment called Pero's Bagnio, at No. 63 St. James's Street. This bagnio had existed since 1699; it was named for an early owner, a Frenchman named Peyrault.[36] Unlike the rowdy bagnios of Covent Garden, Pero's was a reasonably respectable establishment, and if it served as a concealed brothel, that fact was kept well hidden. The area of St. James's was at this time not as fashionable as it had been in Restoration days, but at least the vicinity of St. James's Palace was still prosperous, and Pero's Bagnio was likely to have attracted a good deal of clientele from the gentleman's clubs nearby.[37] Thomas Porter was prosperous enough to give his six children a good education. He also was not unwilling to give his four daughters, of whom Anne and Sarah were the two eldest, some experience of fashionable life. The Porter girls were all pretty and vivacious, and this was not the first time they had visited a ball. They liked to dance and were regular visitors to various dancing parties and assembly rooms, chaperoned, of course, to keep them out of mischief. But it was not just in the ribald novels of the time that a chaperone might be careless in her duty, or persuaded to let her young charges wander off by a bribe from the girl's wealthy admirer.

The pleasure-loving Anne and Sarah would have liked to stay at the ball as long as possible, but the queen retired early, at eleven o'clock, and the others followed her. Reluctantly, the two Misses Porter left the ballroom gallery. Their father had arranged to escort them home at twelve, but they were tired and did not want to stand about for an entire hour waiting for him. After consulting their chaperone, a stockily built, middle-aged lady named Mrs. Miel, Anne and Sarah decided to walk the short distance home to Pero's Bagnio, without waiting for any male companion to protect them.[38]

Neither of them was fully at ease with the situation, however; they set out on their short walk with some trepidation, for this was the time when the London Monster was known to prowl the dark streets of the metropolis.

*  *  *

To begin with, the Porters and their companion made swift progress. It was a quarter past eleven, but due to the festivities of the day, the streets were brightly lit and there were still quite a few people about. When they had come about halfway up St. James's Street, and could see the bagnio just a few houses away, Anne and Sarah believed themselves safe. Some men carrying a sedan chair approached them, calling out "By your leave!" and the ladies moved aside. This cry apparently alerted a man who had been lurking nearby. He went up to Sarah Porter and stared her hard in the face. As the sedan bearers walked away, he cried out "Oh ho! Is that you!" and struck her a violent blow on the back of the head. Sarah pitched forward with the force of the blow, but managed to keep her footing. She ran toward Pero's Bagnio as fast as she could. To alert her sister and Mrs. Miel, she cried out, "For God's sake, Nancy, make haste! Can't you see that—that *wretch* behind!" They all made a dash for the front door of the bagnio: the terrified Sarah in front, Mrs. Miel panting to keep up, and Anne bringing up the rear. Anne Porter had not quite heard what her sister had said, except that they should all make haste, and was not aware of the danger she was in.

The man did not, at first, pursue them, but as Sarah Porter was banging on the door of the bagnio to get in, he suddenly ran up and struck Anne Porter on the hip. It did not hurt much; she only felt "a strange sensation." Turning round to see who or what had struck her, she saw a man in an odd posture, with his legs stretched out. The man walked on to the next house, without any hurry, and then once more returned, to gloat at the sight of the terrified ladies. He stared Anne full in the face and grinned at her. He stood close behind them as John Porter, Anne and Sarah's brother, finally opened the front door; in a wild stampede, the ladies rushed past him into the house. Their mysterious assailant remained standing outside looking at them, and made no attempt to run away. John Porter asked Sarah whether this gentleman was in their company, preparing to invite him inside. Sarah replied, "No; shut the door against the fellow," little knowing what had happened to her sister. Anne now complained about a sharp pain in her hip, and nearly fainted when she saw and felt that her dress was completely soaked with blood on one side. Blood dripped down from the garment and formed a growing pool on the floor. The London Monster had struck again!

*Miss Ann Porter,*

*Who was so Barbarously treated by the Monster.*

Figure 1. Miss Anne Porter as she was portrayed in *New Lady's Magazine*, July 1790. Reproduced by permission from the British Library.

The entire Porter family came rushing along, full of concern for poor Anne. When Mr. Porter saw that his daughter had been dangerously wounded, he sent a couple of servants after her assailant, but the Monster had absconded in time. A local practitioner, Surgeon Tomkins of Park Place, was promptly sent for. As he dressed the wound, which was situated on the outside and back of Anne's thigh and buttock, he found it to be more than six inches long and three inches deep in the middle. Apparently, the incision had been made with a particularly sharp instrument. A few days after his daughters had been assaulted, Thomas Porter went to the Bow Street public office—the name of the main London police station in 1790—to lodge a complaint about the attack. Sarah came with him; according to the record, she described her assailant as at least six feet tall, thinly built, with light brown hair and a large nose. He appeared to be about thirty years old.[39] It is not clear whether this was Sarah's own observation or a composite view of the observations made of the Monster that fateful evening; it is likely that John Porter, Mrs. Miel, and Anne Porter herself had also seen him. Later, indeed, Sarah told Nicholas Bond, one of the Bow Street magistrates, that she herself was quite unable to describe the man who attacked her,[40] and when her sister Anne was asked to describe the Monster for a newspaper account, all she could volunteer was that he had a very pale and fair complexion.[41]

*   *   *

The organization of the London police of 1790 merits a brief discourse here, since it features prominently in the story of the Monster and his strange crimes.[42] At this time, the metropolis was divided into parishes, each one responsible for its own policing arrangements. If a parish chose to keep any police force at all, it was usually comprised of tradesmen who served as constables for a year each; they were on duty every fifteenth day, armed with staves and lanterns. Many tradesmen resented serving as part-time policemen and would hire substitutes; this would have been fine had the substitutes been vigorous men, but in reality, they were often elderly workhouse inmates.

In addition, each parish had a force of night watchmen: Westminster, for example, had three hundred, spread among its nine parishes.[43] Led by an elderly night beadle, these watchmen each had a beat to patrol; they also manned the watch houses, where prisoners could be confined until removed by a constable. Each watchman was armed with a staff, a lantern, and a rattle, the latter to be used to give the alarm if anything untoward occurred on his beat. The watchmen called out the time at regular intervals, sometimes adding the comforting reassurance that all was well.

But in practice, this picture of orderliness was far from reality. The watchman's salary was a meager one and the working hours singularly unattractive; the watchmen were recruited among the elderly, the destitute, and the wretches who inhabited the workhouses. Contemporary newspaper accounts say that their rattles served as a rallying call to criminals; there were also unkind comparisons between the cracking sound of the rattles, the cracking joints of the elderly watchmen, and their old weather-cracked voices calling out the time. The inefficiency of these watchmen was well known to the authorities, but very little was done about it. Not infrequently, they abandoned their beats to sit in a drunken stupor in their watch house. The more vicious of these old men took bribes from prostitutes and burglars to leave their activities alone. There were even instances of watchmen serving in league with burglars: the watchman would arrest some house-owner on a trumped-up charge; then, the victim would come home after a miserable night at the watch house to find his house emptied of valuables, which the burglar had been able to remove in complete safety! Significantly, the parish of St. James and Marylebone, which recruited its watchmen from the war invalids and old soldiers of the Chelsea Hospital, was well known for the efficiency of its night watchman patrols; these tough old invalids were a force far superior to the corrupt and decrepit watchmen usually employed in the metropolis.

In 1785, there was great debate over whether there should be a police reform: a new bill proposed that London should be subdivided into nine divisions, each of which should have its own public office and magistrate, and a force of 25 fit and able men, properly armed and with far wider powers than the parish constables. These professional policemen would be able to arrest any person in possession of articles presumed to be stolen and to enter licensed premises without a warrant. The Gordon riots had demonstrated the meaning of mob rule to the London authorities, and one of the aims of the new system was to have a reliable anti-riot police force in the capital. But the old-fashioned Surrey and Middlesex justices defended the old system, and they were supported by the Sheriffs of London. In particular, the influential Judge William Mainwaring, M.P., a chairman of the Middlesex Quarter Sessions, condemned the bill as inexpedient and unnecessary.[44] As a result of a combination of professional jealousy and the sincere belief that a professional police force would undermine the long-established voluntary system, the bill was rejected.

The sad result was that in 1790 the police force patrolling the streets of London was little different, in terms of organization and efficiency, from that of 1690. The only major difference was the existence of the Bow Street

Figure 2. A view of St. James's Street in 1800. On the right can be seen the west side of the street, with Brooks's Club as the first building. Just after the street is No. 61; No. 62 is the house with the large bow windows and tall chimney. Immediately behind it, hidden by the bay windows in this engraving, is Pero's Bagnio and the entry to the narrow stable yard behind it. From the author's collection.

Figure 3. Pero's Bagnio, a drawing made after the year 1800, when the establishment had been taken over by Francis Fenton. It still carried its old name and was probably not greatly changed from the time it had been run by the Porter family. Reproduced courtesy of the Wellcome Trust.

public office, the center of the London detective police. Founded by Sir
Thomas de Veil in 1740, it became justly famous during the time of Henry
Fielding and his brother John, both of whom served as Bow Street magistrates. Sir John Fielding was succeeded by Mr. Sampson Wright in 1782.[45]
At Bow Street, a set of unbiased, honorable magistrates directed various
criminal investigations. Their police detectives—the Bow Street Runners—
had no distinctive uniform, but they often wore red waistcoats and carried
truncheons bearing a metal crest to show their authority. There were not
very many Runners—just six or eight at a time—but they were tough and
resilient thief takers, and they often worked with extensive networks of
informants who kept them abreast of the actions of the criminal underworld. Under the Runners were the Bow Street patrols: ordinary policemen
who formed a much-needed core force to combat riots and civil unrest.

Upon visiting the Bow Street public office, Thomas Porter was astonished to discover from Sir Sampson Wright, the magistrate on duty, that
four other ladies had also been attacked by a mysterious assailant on the
evening of the queen's birthday.[46] A Miss Toussaint, who had like Anne
Porter been in the gallery at St. James's Palace, was returning home with
her mother, her sister, and two other ladies. As they proceeded toward their
home in Sackville Street, a man came up to them and began a highly inde-
corous conversation. His words were so extremely foul and improper that
the ladies ran away, helter-skelter. But the man pursued them, and was seen
to strike at Miss Toussaint several times. When they reached their home,
the ladies were aghast to find that Miss Toussaint's dress had been badly
slashed with a sharp instrument. She herself was unhurt, thanks to her
strong whalebone stays.

At half past eleven the same evening, Mrs. Harlow, a lady bookseller,
was walking up St. James's Street with a gentleman friend. Just outside
Brooks's Club, she received a blow from a man who stood against a chair.
When she came home, she noticed that every layer of her clothes had been
cut through, but she herself sustained no injury. The same evening, Mrs.
Burney, the wife of Captain Burney, also had her clothes cut by an unknown person.

The fourth of these outrages took place outside the house of a fashionable lady, the Hon. Mrs. Walpole, in Dover Street. A young lady named Miss
Felton had been cut through the pocket hole of her dress with such force
that the dress was completely shredded and an apple in her pocket split.
There was a rumor at the time that Mrs. Walpole herself had been cut, and
that she had been saved from the Monster's rapier by the apple in her
pocket. A poem in her honor appeared in one of the major newspapers:

To Mrs. R. Walpole,
On her escape from the Stab of the MONSTER, by an Apple in her
    pocket:

The Apple was, in days of yore,
An Agent to the Devil,
When EVE was tempted to explore
The sense of Good and Evil.

But present Chronicles can give
An instance quite uncommon,
How that which ruin'd mother EVE,
Hath sav'd a modern woman.[47]

# CHAPTER 2

# A MONSTER ON THE PROWL

*My nose is really somewhat short—but what's the use of that?*
*The MONSTER, too, is monstrous thin, and I am monstrous fat:*
*But not a word the Lady hears, determin'd to misconstrue,*
*And up to Bow-street I'm convey'd, to try if I'm the MONSTER.*
*Of such a snare,*
*Ye Beaux beware!*
*Or chuse a Maid*
*Who will not swear*
*She saw me ready to—O rare!*
*To stab her thro' the pocket-hole—exactly like the MONSTER.*
                    *—Mr. Hook, "The Monster," a song presented to the*
                                          *Proprietors of Vauxhall*

THOMAS Porter's report of the Monster's assault on his daughters is likely to have aroused some trepidation among the Bow Street magistrates, since it was now apparent that something quite serious was afoot. Since May 1788, there had been an alarming series of attacks on women in the streets of central London, many of them following the same pattern as those on the queen's birthday. Mrs. Maria Smyth, the pretty young wife of Dr. Smyth, of Stephen Street, Rathbone Place, had the dubious honor of being the Monster's first recorded victim.[1] Early on a Sunday evening, in the middle of May 1788, she was walking on Fleet Street when she was approached by a thin, vulgar-looking man with very ugly legs and feet. He was rather below medium height, with a villainous, narrow face; he wore a cocked hat slapped on one side of his head. In a remarkable voice, "in which there seemed to be a *tremulous eagerness*," he accosted Mrs. Smyth, speaking to her in a highly shocking and indecent manner. When she did not answer, he kept stalking her, using the same foul language, until she arrived at her destination, a house in Johnson's Court, just off Fleet Street. She asked him to go about his business and stop following her, but he simply stood there grinning and made no reply. Mrs. Smyth knocked hard on the door of the house, but the man suddenly jumped up on the step beside her. Just as the door opened, he struck her a violent blow beneath her left breast, and followed up with another blow to her left thigh. The assailant did not run away, but just stood looking at her with perfect composure, until the swooning Mrs. Smyth was helped inside. The thigh wound, fortunately, proved to be slight, and the blood flow was easily stopped by the application of some balsam. The weapon used was presumed to have been a sharp instrument, like a lancet or a penknife; there were marks from a similar sharp implement on her stays from the blow to her chest. Maria Smyth was a fragile, nervous woman, and in 1790 she claimed that the Monster's savage attack, and the ensuing wound, bruise and terror, had made her severely ill; she had been confined to her bed for many months, and her life had been despaired of not less than seven times.

In the summer of 1788, Mrs. Franklin, a recently married young lady, was insulted by a small, thin, big-nosed man who accosted her with grossly indecent language. Mrs. Franklin was the daughter of a tavern keeper in St. James's Street, a rough character known as "Parsloe" Wheeler. Coincidentally, Parsloe's other daughter, Miss Kitty Wheeler, described as "a fine, lively, spirited, beautiful young lady," had a similar experience in 1789, while in the Ranelagh pleasure garden in Chelsea, the night after the Spanish ambassador's gala. Kitty's father had left to get their carriage to go home. Suddenly, a small man with a long nose and face, regular features, and curly hair approached her and spoke to her using indecent language. Frightened, she called out to some gentlemen nearby for protection. The man quickly made himself scarce. A few days later, the same man made another attempt as Kitty Wheeler was walking in St. James's Park with her sister, but Miss Wheeler's instincts again proved sharper than those of the Monster's other victims. She called out to her father that the same man who had insulted her at the Ranelagh was again following her. Parsloe advised his daughters to walk on ahead while he kept an eye on them; if the fellow came up and insulted them, he would interfere.

In Bennet Street, the Monster again spoke to the girls, in the same indecent manner, but Parsloe Wheeler tackled him from behind and brought him down to the ground. The man was shaken like a rat by the irate tavern keeper, but the noise of the fight alerted a rough crowd. Parsloe was not particularly well liked, and they sided with the attacker. The tavern keeper was unwilling to let go of his prey, but the mob was becoming more and more dangerous, and Kitty Wheeler finally persuaded him to release the man, fearing that her father might be seriously injured by the crowd. She had little thanks for this action, however, since she afterward several times observed the Monster standing in front of their house, where he made use of his usual impertinent expressions to her and her sisters.[2]

In May 1789, Mrs. Sarah Godfrey, a beautiful lady of fashion living in Charlotte Street, was accosted by a man of medium build, aged about thirty. Dressed in black, his hair well dressed, he had the appearance of a gentleman and wore a cocked hat. Without speaking, he followed Mrs. Godfrey from Bond Street into Leicester Square, then into Piccadilly, walking sometimes before her, sometimes behind her, and sometimes by her side. When she stepped into the doorway of an upholsterer's shop in Piccadilly, he came up to her and made a very indecent proposal. She did not reply, but merely went into the shop. When she came out, her persistent and foul-mouthed "admirer" was waiting outside. He did not speak to her again, but stalked her all the way to Charlotte Street, sometimes walking behind her, sometimes just in front of her. Just as she stepped on the first step to walk through her front door, the man came up to her very rapidly and stabbed her in the upper part of her thigh with a sharp instrument. He then walked away as if nothing at all had happened. Mrs. Godfrey fell and lay bleeding in the street; before she had recovered her senses, the Monster was gone.[3]

Four months later, a young lady named Miss Mary Forster was returning from a visit to the Haymarket Theatre when she was accosted by a slender man, about five feet six or seven inches tall, with regular features and a long nose. He seemed agitated and had "something of an eagerness of countenance." He first offered to call her a coach, and then to see her safely home, but she was distrustful of his intentions and declined. Miss Forster contemplated calling for assistance from two workmen who were standing nearby, but decided to walk home without creating any alarm. Her strange admirer followed close behind her, and at times advanced to stare her directly in the face in an impertinent manner. Miss Forster declined his attempts at opening a conversation. When they had reached Dean Street, near St. Anne's Church in Soho, the man suddenly "uttered very indecent, scandalous language, such as shocked and amazed her; and, after a horrid oath, he struck her upon the hip." At first, Miss Forster was not even aware that she had been wounded, but she called out to the two workmen nearby, and they chased after the man, who ran down King Street. The Monster was too quick for them, however, and they could not overtake him.

Mary Forster now felt a pain in her hip, and was unable to walk home. She was helped by two gentlemen passersby. As soon as she arrived at her home, she fainted. Her clothes were drenched through with blood; as a result of her wound she had lost nearly a quart of blood. Miss Forster was later able to give an excellent description of the Monster, which agreed well with those of Mrs. Franklin and Kitty Wheeler; it appeared likely that these three ladies, at least, had been attacked by the same man.

Mary Forster also volunteered the information that she had seen this unprepossessing character several times before, lounging about in the theaters and public assembly rooms. Indeed, shortly after she was wounded, she had another encounter with him, this time in the Covent Garden Theatre. As she sat in her box with another lady, she saw a man she thought resembled the Monster enter one of the other boxes. When the man perceived that he was being observed, he went out with an enraged look at Miss Forster, and shut the door with great violence. Miss Forster alerted some gentlemen, who ran after the man and caught him in the lobby; there was a scuffle "which produced some disturbance." The gentlemen did not want to miss the play, however, and they appealed to the box-attendants of the theater to arrest him. The attendants refused, since there was no warrant to detain him. No one, alas, thought to send a man to Bow Street to fetch one of the Runners. The Monster put on his best behavior and managed to persuade the gentlemen to let him go, after he had given them his address. Miss Forster, believing herself free of the man after she had seen him being collared in the lobby, was horrified to see him leap out in front of her as she left the theater. He did not attack, but scowled at her as he passed—so close that he almost could touch her dress.[4]

* * *

The London Monster's next victim was Jermyn Street resident Miss Ann Frost, described in accounts as "a tall genteel girl, with a pair of fine black eyes, an elegant person, brisk, lively, and agreeable." On November 9, 1789 (Lord Mayor's day), she was returning from a late night gathering when a man accosted her on the street, using "very shocking and indecent" language. Miss Frost tried to get rid of him, but he followed her to her home in Jermyn Street, where he struck her on the hip just as she knocked at the door. Fortunately, she was not hurt, although her clothes were cut through. She described the Monster in a similar way to Mrs. Franklin, Miss Wheeler, and Mary Forster: a thin, middle-sized individual with regular features and a long nose. She added that she would know his voice if she ever heard it again.[5]

Not long afterward, Miss Ann Morley was assaulted in Whitehall on a Sunday evening. She was walking with another young lady when a man dressed in black, at least six feet tall, pale and sallow, left a woman with whom he had been talking and followed them. He walked first on one side of them and then on the other, and then violently shoved between them and struck Miss Morley on the hip. She called out, "Good God!" He then struck her again and remained standing near her, staring in her face. Miss Morley screamed, "Good God, that man has struck me twice!" The man then struck her a third time before walking away, composedly.

Just a few days later, a man described as very tall, dressed in black with long ruffles, attacked Miss Eleanor Dodson near Charing Cross. He cut her in the hip with a sharp instrument believed to have been the blade of a penknife or a long lancet.[6]

The next victims were the sisters Elizabeth and Frances Baughan, described as "two very agreeable, genteel young ladies, blue eyes, fair complexion; one is of the middle size, the other smaller and very pretty, sensible, candid, and open: they were both dressed in blue silk." On the evening of December 7, 1789, at about a quarter past seven o'clock, they were passing along Bridge Street, Westminster, when they noticed a short man following them closely. He was grumbling to himself in an odd manner. Suddenly, he came up to them and said "Blast you, is that you!" into Frances Baughan's ear. The sisters did not reply to this uncouth greeting, and tried to avoid him, but he persistently stalked them through the streets, all the while addressing them in obscene, insulting language. When they came into Parliament Street, the sisters began to run, but the Monster ran after them and struck at them several times. As the terrified girls stopped, the Monster stood looking at them composedly, before walking off unhurriedly. The sisters found that their dresses had been badly slashed, and that they both had been slightly wounded by the man's rapier. Their description of the Monster agreed well with that given by Miss Wheeler, Mrs. Franklin, and Ann Frost. Interestingly, Frances Baughan said that both she and her sister had seen the Monster several times before, the first time about two years earlier, and that it was his habit to come up to them in the street and insult them. Once, in Green Park, this strange character had behaved so obnoxiously that an enraged Frances Baughan had slapped his face.[7]

*   *   *

After the Baughan attacks, the Monster apparently somewhat changed his modus operandi but he continued to wreak havoc in the metropolis. From January 1790 onward, his outrages increased. One day in late January, Mrs. Allan, the daughter-in-law of a plumber in Piccadilly, was taking a walk with her mother and sister when she observed a man with a small parcel in his hand following them at a distance. In the court leading from Piccadilly into Vine Street, the man pushed hard against Mrs. Allan and nearly sent her sprawling. She first thought it had been an accident, but when she came home she found that her gown and the rest of her clothes were very badly cut. A certain Mrs. Drummond had an even more disagreeable experience. She was visiting the theater when she observed a short man with a narrow face and prominent nose bustling about her in a disagreeable manner. When she came out from the play, she was mortified to find that her gown and petticoat were totally in shreds. Her handkerchief and even her hair had been cut and hacked by the Monster.[8]

In late January, the maidservant of Mrs. Gordon was standing outside her mistress's house when a man suddenly and without provocation grasped her from behind and violently kicked her buttocks with his knee several times, "damning her all the while." When she recovered from her terror and surprise, she found that she was "dreadfully wounded" by some very sharp instrument that must have been fastened to the Monster's knee.[9]

In the middle of March, a similar attack was made upon Mrs. Charlotte Payne, the lady's maid of the countess of Howe. Mrs. Payne was a middle-aged, conventional lady, plain in appearance and unexceptional in dress. When, one Sunday evening, she was walking along Brook Street on her way to Lord Howe's house, she was surprised by a well-dressed man in dark clothes, wearing a cocked hat with a cockade, who approached her and offered to see her home. Although he looked the perfect gentleman, the prim lady's maid did not honor his immodest proposal with an answer. The man took no notice of her disapproval, but continued to walk with her along Bond Street and Grafton Street, "making love to her all the way with a rather uncommon energy," even after she asked him to leave her. At Lord Howe's door, she begged her "admirer" to go away, but as she was going in the man grabbed her from behind and violently kicked her up the steps with his knee, "making use of the most horrid language and imprecations all the time." One of his expressions was "Damn you, you bitch, I would enjoy a particular pleasure in murdering you, and in shedding your blood!" Fortunately for Mrs. Payne, the door was opened by another servant of Lord Howe's, and with a final, resounding kick in the backside, the Monster sent her careening toward the servant.

It took some time for Mrs. Payne to recover, and when the other servants went off in pursuit of her mysterious assailant, he was nowhere to be found. Some of Mrs. Payne's wounds were quite deep, and they may have become infected. Several newspapers reported that she had died from her wounds, but this report was later contradicted: Charlotte Payne was still alive, but continued "in a state of extreme danger."[10]

Not long after the attack on Mrs. Payne, a Mrs. Blaney was stabbed in the thigh outside her door in Bury Street by a man she described as about thirty-five years old, tall, stout, and gentlemanly looking, with a very dark complexion.[11]

The Monster soon hit upon another tactic in his campaign to strike terror into London's female population. About the same time as the attack on Mrs. Payne, a servant girl was approached by a man in Holborn. He asked her to smell a large nosegay in his hand, and she complied. A moment later, she noticed a sharp pain in her nose, which, needless to say, she hastily withdrew from the nosegay. The Monster, who had stabbed her in the nose with a sharp instrument concealed in the nosegay, walked away with much composure.

One evening in April, just before dusk, another servant girl, who was going about on her mistress's business, had the misfortune to be overtaken by four men in the Strand. One of them had a nosegay, and asked her to smell it, but she declined, since the flowers looked artificial. The man kept pestering her, however; to get clear of him and the others, she agreed to smell the nosegay. As it was held to her face, she was wounded just under the eye by a very sharp instrument. The men, laughing loudly, immediately made off, leaving the terrified girl standing in the street, her face bleeding copiously.[12]

*   *   *

By early April, Londoners had begun to despair about the ability of the Bow Street police to catch the Monster. Although Thomas Porter had lodged a complaint at Bow Street after his daughters had been assaulted, he had also requested that it be investigated quietly, so the Monster's activities on January 18 had not been widely reported in the newspapers. The attacks on Mrs. Payne and Mrs. Blaney in March were widely publicized, however, and more than one newspaper writer compared these crimes with other attacks on women during the previous two years. In the *Morning Chronicle* of April 3, the attack on Mrs. Blaney was considered another outrage by "the miscreant whom we have noticed more than once for similar instances of brutality." Letters, both anonymous and signed, were sent to the daily newspapers: Some deplored the lack of police activity and called for vigilante action; others actually accused the Runners of being in league with the

Monster. Mr. Andrew Franklin, husband of Mrs. Franklin, who had been stalked and insulted by the Monster, was among the first to raise the alarm.[13]

One anonymous letter came from a man who claimed that he had once been brought before the Bow Street magistrates and accused of being the Monster. He now boldly declared that he knew the Monster's true identity, and that this criminal was a gentleman of some rank, and a lawyer active in the Temple. Although the accused man was well known to the Bow Street magistrates, they did not arrest him. Six days later, Sir Sampson Wright and Mr. Nicholas Bond wrote that, as a result of an anonymous letter sent to them, the gentleman in question had been taken to Bow Street. Anne Porter and several other victims were brought to see him, and unanimously declared that he had not the slightest resemblance to the man who had wounded them.[14]

Dr. William Smyth, the husband of the first woman to be cut by the Monster, in May 1788, was shocked to observe the parallels between the attack on his wife, Maria, "during which she very nearly lost her life," and these new outrages. He sent a letter to the *Morning Chronicle* asking for the addresses of Mrs. Blaney and other recently wounded ladies. Mrs. Smyth and Mrs. Blaney met and compared their experiences: the conclusion was that they had almost certainly been wounded by different men. Later, as a result of the doctor's detective work, twelve other victims came forward. Dr. Smyth was outraged that the Monster had been able to evade detection for so long, and joined in the call for vigilante action.[15]

On April 14, Maria Smyth was attending a public auction. Her consternation can be imagined when she suddenly saw the man who had assaulted her sitting nearby! She managed to keep calm and inform her husband, who was sitting beside her. He also acted quite rationally, and after the auction, followed the man to his home in Great Queen Street. The man turned out to be William Tuffing, a former ladies' hairdresser, who now worked as a clothes salesman.

Dr. Smyth acted very prudently (some Monster hunters said too prudently). He first sent for Anne Porter and tried to organize a clandestine operation in which his wife and she would enter Tuffing's shop and point him out as the Monster. But Dr. Smyth changed his mind, and instead decided to inform Mr. Justice Addington, of Bow Street, planning to perform a full-scale confrontation when Tuffing was brought to Bow Street. Meanwhile, he personally called on many of the Monster's victims, of whom Mrs. Blaney, Mrs. Newman, Miss Toussaint, Miss Felton, Mrs. Godfrey, and the Misses Baughan promised to turn up.

On her own initiative, however, Anne Porter went to Tuffing's shop beforehand (this was just at the time when a large reward had been posted for the arrest of the Monster, which may well have prompted her action). She declared that he was not the man who had cut her, although he bore a strong resemblance to him.[16] Tuffing, meanwhile, denied the charge, and declared that he had never seen Mrs. Smyth before in his life. The little man wept and moaned, lamenting his hard fate and that of his family. He was not strong and could not bear life in prison, even for a couple of days.

At the larger confrontation held at the Bow Street public office on April 19, a considerable crowd of people, among them the duke of Gloucester and several other notables, assembled to see the suspected Monster face his victims. But none of the wounded ladies except Mrs. Smyth could identify Tuffing as the man who had cut or frightened them. Seeing them testify, one newspaper reporter wrote that these ladies had been "wounded by some MONSTER (for such the perpetrator of such horrid deed must be, as there was not one but laid strong claims to beauty)."[17] Dr. Smyth repeatedly urged his wife (as he had often done before) to be cautious and consider the consequences of her actions, but she remained adamant that Tuffing was the man. The *Oracle* reporter, however, doubted Mrs. Smyth's reliability, since she was a very nervous lady and the crime had been committed two years earlier. Furthermore, William Tuffing had never been convicted of any crime; he had a very good character and was a married man with a young family. Mrs. Smyth did not give any reason why she had fixed on William Tuffing; she also volunteered the information that, three or four months earlier, she had seen Tuffing at another public auction but had not mentioned her suspicion to Dr. Smyth or any other person.

After many character witnesses had appeared in Tuffing's behalf, and all the other victims had declared themselves convinced that Tuffing was innocent, Mrs. Smyth "then *thought* only, that he was like the person."[18] William Tuffing again wept, lamenting that his family would become destitute if he were to be held in prison much longer. Dramatically, just at this moment, a Bow Street Runner brought the news that, while Tuffing was being examined, a servant maid had been cut by the Monster.[19] Mr. Justice Addington committed Tuffing for trial, but allowed him to post bail so that he could still support his family. There is no record of Tuffing ever being tried; fortunately for him, his plight was ended by the sensational events of early June.

# CHAPTER 3

# THE ANGERSTEIN REWARD

*And when before the Justices, what justice 'tis to see*
*Of MONSTERS there, already charg'd—two hundred good as me!*
*For every Miss, thro' all the town, this scheme can aptly*
*    construe*
*'Tis "touch and take": so if you touch, she takes you for the*
*    MONSTER.*
*'Gainst such a league,*
*Adieu INTRIGUE!*
*For here, ye fair!*
*I truly swear,*
*You'll find me ready to—O rare!*
*But not to stab—the pocket-hole, for I am not the MONSTER.*
*                    —Mr. Hook, "The Monster," a song presented to the*
*                                    Proprietors of Vauxhall*

BY EARLY April 1790, the Monster business had caught the interest of the wealthy Lloyd's insurance broker John Julius Angerstein. Angerstein had been born in Russia in 1734. According to the official accounts of his life,[1] he was the son of the German Dr. Henry Angerstein; the doctor certainly brought him up as his son, although one source states that he was actually the natural son of the English merchant Andrew Poulett Thomson and Empress Anne of Russia.[2] John Julius Angerstein had come to London in 1749 as an office boy. He worked as a broker at Lloyd's Coffee-house, as it was then called, from 1756 onward, and was instrumental in establishing it as a great insurance house.

Angerstein was intrigued by the Monster's long catalog of crimes against London women and did much to collate the annals of the attacks. In addition to the cases known by the Bow Street magistrates or those discovered by Dr. Smyth, there were quite a few others: as the newspapers

Figure 4. *John Julius Angerstein, Esq.*, portrait by his friend Sir Thomas Lawrence. From the author's collection.

were full of the Monster's activities, many women came forward to report their encounters with this brutal character. Angerstein personally visited each of the victims to get their eyewitness accounts of the Monster attacks. He was aghast to find that there had been, from May 1788 until April 1790, not fewer than 30 attacks on unaccompanied women in the metropolis. Angerstein took copious notes of the various accounts of the Monster and his modus operandi; he also noted the dress and appearance of the ladies and the details of their wounds. He was by no means unsusceptible to feminine charms—indeed, an uncharitable individual might suspect that his frequent visits to these beautiful women were not prompted by philanthropy alone. Miss Toussaint, whose clothes had been cut by the Monster on January 18, was described as "young, about or rather below the middle size, with dark hair, fine large black eyes, her face rather full and plump, a good agreeable countenance, lively, pleasant, and very pretty." Sarah Porter was not quite Mr. Angerstein's type: she was only "mild, genteel, and rather handsome," but her sister Anne met with his full approval: she was "young, below the middle size, with fine black eyes, good skin, fine teeth, lively, sensible, delicate, and very pretty."[3]

Angerstein wrote that, if it was an act of utmost cowardice for a man of superior strength to attack and beat up a weak and defenseless person of his own sex, then what to make of the Monster's offenses? To attack unsuspecting women with a sharp weapon that seemed to have been manufactured specifically for this inhuman purpose was a crime "rendered still more atrocious by the insult that generally accompanies the outrage, and by the savage delight he enjoys in the terror, pain, and distress of the lovely victim!" No woman was safe from this villain. Although the Monster had, in 1788 and 1789, mainly confined his attacks to elegant, good-looking women, his lust for blood had increased, and by 1790 age, deformities, or even indigence was no protection against his diabolical attacks.[4]

\* \* \*

At a meeting in Lloyd's Coffee-house, on April 15, 1790, Angerstein opened a subscription to raise a reward for the person who apprehended "that INHUMAN MONSTER, whoever he may be, who has of late so frequently wounded several young women." Angerstein himself donated five guineas, and nineteen other gentlemen immediately did the same; two more impecunious gentlemen donated two pounds two shillings each, one of them anonymously. The next day, the newspapers were full of the sensational news. The Bow Street public office made it known that anyone who apprehended the Mon-

ster or gave information to Sir Sampson Wright that led to his arrest would
have a claim to fifty pounds, delivered by Angerstein upon the man's commitment to prison; the further sum of fifty pounds would be awarded upon
his conviction.[5] The advertisements also gave a description of the Monster:

> He appears to be about 30 years of age, of middle size, a little pock
> marked, of a pale complexion, large nose, light brown hair tied in a queue,
> cut short and frizzed low at the sides, is sometimes dressed in black,
> and sometimes in a shabby blue coat, sometimes wears straw-coloured
> breeches, with half-boots laced up before, sometimes wears a cocked hat,
> and at other times a round hat, with a very high top, and generally carries a
> Wangee cane in his hand.

A large poster with details of the reward and the description of the Monster
was printed at Angerstein's expense and stuck up on walls all over London.[6]

Fifty pounds was a princely sum at that time, and after Angerstein's
reward had been advertised on April 16, the Monster hunt was on. Numerous amateur detectives were on the lookout for anything suspicious,
and the Bow Street police received a torrent of information: one person had
had blood on his clothes, another had stayed out late a certain evening, a
third had acted suspiciously, and so forth. All these informants were of
course eager to get their hands on the reward. Even worse, the more impetuous Monster hunters themselves made citizen's arrests of various suspicious characters. One Monster hunter arrested his employer after beating
him; another took his brother-in-law into custody and brought him to Bow
Street. One lunatic arrested a butcher, at gunpoint, after finding a bloody
knife in his pocket. The number of individuals brought before the magistrates soon exceeded twenty, and there was absolutely no evidence against
any of them: Anne Porter and the other victims could not identify them, and
it was apparent that many of these arrests had been prompted by greed and
mischief alone.[7]

Even the official police force was led astray by Angerstein's reward. On
the evening of Monday April 19, a party of Runners belonging to the Poland
Street public office arrested a distinguished gentleman outside Devonshire
House; they accused him of being the Monster and took him to the watch
house, where he was confined all night. The morning after, the man was
taken before Justice Read's office by the exultant Runners, who hoped that
he would be committed to prison and the reward would be theirs. Several
victims were sent for, but none of them could identify him; furthermore, the
judge noted that the man, although definitely a suspicious character, did not
at all answer the description of the Monster issued on posters all over Lon-

*Public-Office, Bow-Street, Thurſday, 29th April,* 1790.

# One Hundred Pounds
## R E W A R D.

SEVERAL LADIES having of late been inhumanly cut and maimed by a PERSON anſwering the following Deſcription: Whoever will apprehend him or give ſuch Information to Sir *SAMPSON WRIGHT*, at the above Office, as may be the Means of his being apprehended, ſhall *immediately upon his Commitment to Priſon*, receive FIFTY POUNDS from Mr. ANGERSTEIN, of Pall-Mall; and the farther Sum of FIFTY POUNDS *upon his Conviction.*

N. B. HE appears to be about 30 Years of Age, of a middle Size, rather thin made, a little Pock-marked, of a pale Complexion, large Noſe, light brown Hair, tied in a Queue, cut ſhort and frizzed low at the Sides; is ſometimes *dreſſed* in *black*, and ſometimes in a ſhabby *blue* Coat, ſometimes wears *Straw coloured* Breeches, with half Boots, *laced up before*; ſometimes wears a *cocked* Hat, and at other Times a *round* Hat, with a very high Top, and generally carries a *Wangee* Cane in his Hand.

☞ A LL Servants are recommended to take Notice if any Man has ſtaid at home without apparent Cauſe, within theſe few Days, during Day light. All Waſherwomen and Servants ſhould take Notice of any Blood on a Man's Handkerchief or Linen, as the *Wretch* generally fetches Blood when he ſtrikes. All Servants ſhould examine if any Man carries ſharp Weapons about him, and if there is any Blood thereon, particularly Tucks; and Maid Servants are to be told that a Tuck is generally at the Head of a Stick, which comes out by a ſudden Jerk. All *CUTLERS* are deſired to watch if any Man anſwering the above Deſcription is deſirous of having his Weapon of attack very ſharp.

Printed by J. MOORE, No. 134, Drury-Lane.

Figure 5. Angerstein's first Monster poster, dated April 29, 1790. Reproduced by permission from the British Library.

don. The gentleman was freed, and the *Times* was full of censure against the impetuous Runners, who it said themselves deserved to be prosecuted for this wrongful arrest. Although the gentleman, whose name was not mentioned, had "certainly on a former occasion appeared in a suspicious light before the public," this was no reason to drag him off to prison with no evidence at all.[8] In the same article, the wisdom of Angerstein and the other generous gentlemen of Lloyd's Coffee-house was questioned: the immense reward they had posted would evidently open a wide field for imposition and perjury. One *Times* journalist found it mysterious that, although Miss Porter had sworn that William Tuffing was not the Monster, she had not come forward with a description of the man who had cut her; was she keeping this information to herself in the hope of pointing out the right man and claiming the reward?

Angerstein continued his efforts, however: in a new advertisement dated April 29, headed "One Hundred Pounds Reward," all servants were urged to take notice if some person had stayed at home for no apparent reason, hiding from the Monster hunters scouring the streets, or if they observed a sharp weapon about the house. All washerwomen were to take notice if a man came to them with blood on his clothes, and all cutlers were to report customers who wanted to have a weapon of attack made very sharp. At this time, it was an extraordinary step to entice servants to report on their masters; that such a stratagem, resembling those of the French revolutionaries, was at all contemplated is proof of the intensity of feeling arisen by the Monster's crimes.

In the meantime, the Monster had continued his one-man vendetta against London's female inhabitants. In mid-April, Mrs. Susannah Thompson, described by Angerstein as a "plain woman, with every proper appearance of a tradesman's wife," went out to visit an acquaintance in Princess Street. A man, whom she could not afterward describe, came up to her and, after having made several improper proposals, struck her violently on the hip. She found that her clothes had been cut through, and the skin underneath slightly wounded.[9] Mrs. Harlow, the bookseller who had been one of the Monster's five victims on January 18, was again attacked in April. When she was walking in the Pall Mall, a very tall man with a genteel appearance followed her very closely. Suddenly, he pushed her violently against the house wall and nearly threw her off her feet. When she came home, she again found that all her clothes had been badly cut and that she herself was slightly wounded.[10]

Just after eight o'clock in the morning of April 19, a servant girl, Rebecca Lohr (unflatteringly described by Angerstein as being "about twenty years of age, middle sized, very plain, long nose, thin face, and a pale complexion") went out to buy some rolls. Opposite the oil shop in the Strand, next to Charing Cross, a man came up to her and took her hand; having read about the Monster, she snatched her hand away from him. The man then clawed her on the arm, from the elbow down to the hand, with some very sharp instrument that appeared to be fastened to his hand. He clawed her other arm in the same manner before running off. Miss Lohr staggered into a baker's shop, bleeding profusely. The blood flowing from the wound—apparently quite deep—was not stanched until after midday. Miss Lohr had been so terrified by the unprovoked assault that she could not give a description of the Monster, except to note that he was wearing blue and white stockings.[11]

The next victim was Jane Hurd, "a stout well-grown young woman" in the service of Mrs. Jefferson, a lady of quality living in Edgeware Row. At half past eight in the evening of April 26, Mrs. Jefferson sent Miss Hurd out for some radishes. Just as she returned and was standing at Mrs. Jefferson's door, a man came up, laid hold of her arm, and said "Now, who shall treat with a glass of gin first, you or I?" She replied "Go along you nasty fellow!" and pushed him off. He swore at her, then struck her violently on the breast. When Miss Hurd screamed, the Monster ran off. Mrs. Jefferson helped her into the house, where it was found that the attacker had delivered his slash with enough force to cut through the strong whalebone of her stays and divide an iron wire, giving her a wound nearly two inches long. She described the Monster as stout and middle-sized, with a full face and a large nose; he wore a greatcoat.[12] A few days later, the Monster offered a young woman in Salisbury Square a nosegay to smell "in which was concealed a knife, and [he] took that opportunity to wound her in the face with it."[13]

In late April, there were several other mysterious assaults on women, all of which were, in the gathering hysteria, blamed on the Monster. In late April, a servant girl in Greville Street and another one in Holborn had their clothes cut by mysterious assailants; one of these was described as a very tall man dressed in black. In the Strand, a girl was frightened by a man shouting "Buh!" in her face; another maidservant, in Silver Street, received a punch in the face through a doorway, for no apparent reason, and was knocked out cold.[14] On April 30, a tall, foreign-looking Monster dressed in a brown greatcoat and a round hat pushed a woman in a crowded marketplace as she tried to avoid him; he then forcibly struck another woman who was in his way. A man followed him as he made his escape, but this individual was "timid of making any alarm," and the Monster escaped.[15]

Angerstein's efforts nearly paid off on May 4. Dr. Bush, a young and vigorous medical practitioner, was returning from the house of a patient when he observed a man pursuing a well-dressed woman on the pavement opposite. The doctor knew about the Monster from Angerstein's posters and did not hesitate to intervene. As he raced toward the woman, who appeared nearly overcome with fright and fatigue, the assailant followed her onto a porch and attempted to stab her. The doctor took his stout cane and directed a blow toward the attacker's head, but the man nimbly dodged away. Shoving a shiny object into his waistcoat pocket, he quickly ran off.

Dr. Bush attended to the woman, who told him that she served as cook to Mr. J. Sullivan. The Monster had followed her from St. James's Street onto Arlington Street, accosting her with obscene language the whole way. When two gentleman's servants came along, the doctor ordered one of them to remain with the lady and the other to help him pursue the Monster. The two ran after the man, who had obviously believed himself secure, and caught up with him at the corner of St. James's Street and Piccadilly. Just as the doctor was about to seize the Monster, another man grabbed *him* and accused him of being the Monster. A large and threatening mob soon gathered, convinced the doctor was the criminal. In vain the doctor attempted to persuade them at least to take both him and the man he had chased into custody. Finally, the victim came along and called out to the mob that Dr. Bush was not the Monster but her protector.

Dr. Bush suspected that the muscular ruffian who had seized him was in fact the Monster's accomplice. He offered to stand as a witness against the elusive Monster, who once more had escaped capture.[16]

\* \* \*

When the Monster struck again, on May 5, his choice of victim was surprising. Mrs. Elizabeth Davis was the wife of a laboring man, and by no means attractive. She was described by Angerstein, whose eulogies to the wounded beauties have previously been quoted, by the highly uncomplimentary words that she was "about forty years old, short, thick, and perfectly plain: her dress too corresponded with her person and business, which is that of a washer-woman (some degrees below a laundress), being a threadbare cloak, which had been red, and the rest of her clothing in the same style." At about ten o'clock in the evening, Mrs. Davis was returning home after a long day's work washing clothes. In Chancery Lane, a man approached her and inquired where she was going. At first she tried to ignore him, but he repeated his question several times; at length, she replied that she was going home. As they passed along Holborn, the man pulled out a large nosegay and asked, "Are not these pretty flowers?" "Yes, sir," Mrs. Davis replied meekly, although she thought the flowers did not look real. The Monster flourished his nosegay in an enticing manner and asked, "Will you smell at it?" but she refused. The man repeated his request with some urgency and shoved the nosegay into her face saying, "If these flowers were not pretty, for the time of year!" Mrs. Davis pushed them away, saying they looked artificial. Without saying anything further, the Monster furiously seized her by the throat, pulled from his coat a short stick, and struck her across the left thigh with it. As Mrs. Davis cried out, "Murder!," the man struck her on the breast with his left hand, then hurriedly ran off.[17]

Mrs. Davis was very much alarmed, especially when she came home to find that her thigh had been badly slashed. She yelled and banged on the door of her lodgings for some time before Mrs. Gamson, her landlady, could be induced to open it at such a late hour; when the suspicious landlady had finally undone the locks, Mrs. Davis almost fell into the room. She fainted, and medical attendants were sent for. Mr. Davis suspected that the Monster had been at work, and a representative of the Bow Street Runners was also summoned. When the Runner asked Mrs. Davis, once she had regained consciousness, to describe the man who had wounded her, she was surprised and even a little flattered that she had been the subject of the Monster's attentions: he only cut the nobility, she said, and she was but a washerwoman. She described the Monster as tall and gentlemanly-looking: he wore a greatcoat, an elegant striped waistcoat, and a high cocked hat with a cockade. He wore "his hair frized at the sides in a bush, plaited behind and turned up."

The same evening, a man exactly fitting this description was detected by a night watchman, who followed him through the streets of London. The watchman, however, did not give much thought to whether the criminal observed him or not. When the man knocked on the door of a house near Castle Street, Lincoln's Inn Fields, the watchman presumed this was his home address, and hurried to Bow Street to relay the information.

The following day, the watchman, Elizabeth Davis, and Runner Moses Murrant of Bow Street went to Castle Street to ferret out the Monster. Every person in the house was viewed by Mrs. Davis, but she declared that none of them bore even the slightest resemblance to the man who had wounded her. The watchman was nonplussed, but Runner Murrant discovered from a maidservant that someone had indeed been knocking at the door at the time in question; but when the girl had gone downstairs to answer the knock the street was empty. Runner Murrant and Sir Sampson Wright sagely deduced that the Monster must have noticed that he was being followed and "made use of the above stratagem to avoid being apprehended." They concluded that they were dealing with a criminal of superior intelligence and cunning, who had "twice escaped in a most wonderful way; but surely, from the enormity of his offences, he cannot long elude that punishment he justly merits, and we hope very soon to announce his being in custody."

This dismal story tells us much about the detecting ability of the 1790 police organization in London; even more remarkably, the report of it was actually published in the newspapers as an *encouraging* sign of police activity in the search for the Monster.[18]

*  *  *

On May 5, the same Wednesday night Elizabeth Davis had been assaulted, a maidservant named Jane Read was sent by her mistress to fetch some brandy at a public house in Glanville Street. On her way home, she was accosted by a man who asked her where she lived, then followed her to her master's door. There, he drew from under his coat an instrument that looked like a large knife or dagger; upon seeing it, Miss Read shrieked aloud and fainted. Mrs. McKenzie, her mistress, heard a loud double knock on the door, and went to answer it; she found the girl in a fit, her hand clenched on the knocker.[19] The girl, who had not received even a scratch from this supposed attack, "remained in fits all that night, and the following day."

On the evening of Friday, May 7, Lieutenant Walter Hill R.N. left his landlady's house to go make merry in the alehouses. He was soon gloriously drunk and stayed out well past midnight. When he finally reeled back toward his lodgings, something or someone at the door of a Mr. Grimes in Tottenham Court Road must have caught his fancy; he stood banging on this door for quite some time, shouting. Rowdy nocturnal behavior was not unknown in this neighborhood, then as well as now, but Lieutenant Hill had gone too far. Mr. Grimes went down to confront him, and an angry altercation ensued, which was finally resolved by the arrival of two stout night watchmen, who took Lieutenant Hill into custody. These watchmen were not blundering fools like the one who had bungled the pursuit of the Monster after he had cut Elizabeth Davis a few days earlier. They had been instructed to be exceptionally careful in the region of Tottenham Court Road, where two women had recently been cut. The capture of Lieutenant Hill was heralded by some as the end of the Monster's reign of terror.

On Saturday morning, the lieutenant probably sobered up considerably when he heard that he was suspected of being the London Monster.[20] On Monday, May 10, he was brought before the magistrates at the Litchfield rotation office. The session was a farcical one, even by Monster standards. First, Jane Read, the young woman who claimed to have been threatened by the Monster a few days before, was brought in. When she saw Walter Hill, she gave a shriek and nearly collapsed; her friends had to revive her with smelling salts. The magistrates, trying to preserve whatever dignity remained in the proceedings, sternly asked her why she had nearly fainted when she saw the prisoner. "Because he looked so like the Monster who nearly stabbed me!" she replied. They then asked if she could swear that Lieutenant Hill was the London Monster. No, she certainly would not, since he was not the man. The magistrates were perplexed. "I said he was *like* the Monster, not that he *was* the Monster," Miss Read explained. Shortly after this statement she was removed, but, to the dismay of anyone hoping to uphold the dignity of the law, a rowdy, garrulous old fishwoman took her place. Like Jane Read, she had been more frightened than hurt in a recent incident; she embarked on a long, meandering tale about how she had met a man with a "strange countenance" in Windmill Street; he had spoken to her, and she was so frightened by his "countenance" that she had turned back and run away. On being questioned, she admitted that the prisoner did not bear the least resemblance to the man she had seen. The magistrate dismissed her—swearing a terrible oath as he did so.

The *World* reporter despaired of female common sense after these two witnesses had been examined. He described the proceedings as a complete farce, and warned that these volatile, capricious creatures should not be allowed to corrupt justice with their unreliable testimony.[21] It was a shocking thing, he wrote, that any histrionic, featherbrained woman had been given the power to denounce someone as the Monster; clearly, these women acted merely out of impulse and had no concern whatsoever about the consequences of their actions.

Anne and Sarah Porter, who gave testimony at these proceedings, were also criticized: "Two Ladies thought he was like the man, (tho' they afterwards did not think he was the man)." The Porters described the man who had wounded them as having a brown coat. Lieutenant Hill's lodgings were searched, and the sailor was found to have a brown coat as well as a blue one. This was considered very damning evidence, and Hill was committed for reexamination to Clerkenwell Prison.

The *World*'s misogynist journalist painted a generally dark picture of the proceedings: indeed, according to him, it was a common danger for any innocent man to be taken as the Monster and clapped into prison. In fairness to the women examined, however, it should be noted that the other daily papers mentioned little about such things; the *Morning Herald* even stated that the Misses Porter and several other ladies had firmly declared that the prisoner was not the wretch who had wounded them.[22]

On May 11, Lieutenant Hill was again examined at the Litchfield Street public office. Jane Read was kept on a shorter rein this time and had less scope for her histrionics: she had to declare that although Walter Hill was like the man who had frightened her, she could definitely not swear to his identity. Although Mrs. Granger, the woman who owned the house in front of which the Lieutenant had made a riot, objected, Walter Hill was discharged.[23]

*    *    *

Until early May, John Julius Angerstein and his supporters had firmly believed that there was only one Monster. But as he was collecting descriptions of other, earlier Monster assaults, it must have struck him as odd that the descriptions of the culprit varied so greatly. Mrs. Chippingdale, the lady's maid of Viscountess Malden, had been approached in St. James's Place by a pale, thin, middle-sized man, who made filthy proposals and then stabbed her in the thigh when she tried to ignore him. A maidservant attacked at about the same time was certain that her assailant had been a tall, stout officer, dressed in his uniform. Miss Eleanor Dodson, who had been wounded in November 1789, was certain that the Monster was very tall, six feet at least, and that he had been elegantly dressed in a suit of black clothes with extremely long ruffles.[24]

In a new poster, issued on Friday, May 7, Angerstein reviewed the Monster's latest ravages. On the previous Friday night, the Monster had attacked a woman in Vigo Lane; he was dressed in a blue greatcoat with a lighter-colored coat underneath, a cocked hat, and held a cane in his hand. On Saturday night, he had abused and cut Mary Carter, a servant of one of the messengers of the marquess of Salisbury, in Conduit Street. As she was walking home with some beer for her master, a tall man, dressed in dark brown clothes and with a round hat over his face, had come up to her and insisted upon seeing her home. When she refused, he seized hold of her arm and began to use very indecent language. When she came to her master's door, the Monster "swore, damn'd, used horrid imprecations, and struck her a violent blow on the side, then looked at her and went away." Mary Carter had been saved from injury by her strong stays, although her gown had been badly cut. Two days later, on Monday night, she again went out to

*Pall-Mall,* 7*th May,* 1790.

# Mr. ANGERSTEIN
# Informs the Public,

THAT from the Information he has received of the PERSON who fince *Friday* laft, has affaulted and wounded feveral Women, there is great Reafon to fear that more than *ONE of thofe WRETCHES* infeft the Streets; it is therefore thought Neceffary to give the following Defcription of *ONE* who, within this Week, has committed many Acts of *Cruelty* upon Women.

HE is generally defcribed to be a Perfon upwards of fix Feet high, thin made, and thin vifaged; full Eyes, a large Nofe, and is marked with the Small-pox on his Cheek Bones. On *Friday Night* laft, when he affaulted a Woman in *Vigo Lane,* he was dreffed in a blue great Coat, with a light coloured Coat under it; light coloured Waiftcoat; cocked Hat; and had a Stick in his Hand. On *Saturday Night* and *Monday Night* laft, when he wounded a young Woman in *Conduit Street,* he was dreffed in dark brown Clothes, and wore a round Hat flapped over his Face. On *Tuefday Evening,* between feven and eight o'Clock, when he wounded a Woman in *Marybone Street,* he wore a black Coat, white Stockings, and half Boots; and upon one of his Stockings was a Spot of Blood; a round Hat with a high Crown; his Hair platted behind, and frizzed at the Sides; at this Time he had a DAGGER about fourteen Inches long. And on *Wednefday Night,* when he wounded a poor Woman in *Holborn,* he wore a drab coloured furtout Coat, which reached juft below his Knees; ftriped Waiftcoat; white Stockings; a cocked Hat, with a high Brim, and a Cockade; his Hair frizzed at the Sides, in a Bufh; platted and turned up behind; and had a Nofegay in his Hand.

PRINTED BY J. MOORE, No. 134, DRURY-LANE.

Figure 6. Angerstein's second Monster poster, dated May 7, 1790. Reproduced by permission from the British Library.

get beer for her master, and the same man was waiting for her. He seized hold of her and held her mouth to prevent her from screaming, then proceeded to cut, or rather claw, the fleshy part of one of her arms with a strange instrument fastened to his hand. She struggled hard and managed to break free; as she reached her home, she saw that her arm was cut in thirty or forty places and bled considerably. Angerstein was again surprised at the Monster's choice of victim: although Mary Carter was just nineteen years old, she was very plain, with a pale and sickly countenance. He was also surprised by her description of her attacker as very tall, at least six feet in height; some people who had pursued the Monster agreed with this description. A watchman walking up Great George Street had observed a remarkably tall man go by him very fast up the street toward the square, but did not consider this in any way suspicious or connect it with the Monster hunt.[25]

On Tuesday evening, the Monster continued to wreak havoc. As Jane Hooper, a fair, good-looking serving girl, was walking along Vigo Lane toward Bond Street, a man passed by her and struck her with something on her thigh. Miss Hooper immediately thought of the Monster and nearly fainted. She reeled into the shop of Mr. Trenchard, at No. 22 Bond Street, and fell headlong onto the floor. On examination, it was found that she did not have a scratch on her, but that all her clothes were cut through. She could not give any description of the man, whether as a result of her extreme fright or the concussion she sustained.[26] Later the same evening, the Monster, wearing a black coat, white stockings, and half-boots, had wounded a woman in Marylebone Street; on one of his stockings was a spot of blood. He wore a round hat with a high crown, and his hair was frizzed at the sides; in his hand was a fearsome-looking dagger about fourteen inches long.[27] During the attack on Elizabeth Davis, on Wednesday, he had worn a drab-colored surtout coat and a cocked hat with a cockade. On Thursday morning, as early as eight o'clock, the servant girl of Mr. Vickery, in Cheapside, was scratched, or clawed, by a sharp instrument fastened to the hand of a very short, shabbily dressed man, who immediately went away. His diabolical instrument appeared to have at least five prongs or blades.[28]

To digest this highly conflicting mass of evidence would have required the expertise of Sherlock Holmes himself. John Julius Angerstein probably regretted that he had ever meddled in the Monster business, but it was now too late for him to withdraw. The offer of a reward only seemed to have whetted the Monster's appetite for novel sanguinary outrages. Some imaginative Monster hunters theorized that this fiend wore several coats and surtouts, one over the other, so as to be able to discard one of them at will to avoid suspicion. He also had a very large wardrobe of hats, waistcoats, and other accessories to disguise his appearance; from this fact, it was apparent that he must be not only a criminal mastermind, but also a gentleman of considerable means. It was speculated that the Monster sometimes wore shoes with very high, stilt-like heels so as to appear very tall, and that he possessed a collection of wigs and theatrical props, which he used to alter his appearance. A journalist in the *Times* reminded the public that the actor Charles Price had used seven sorts of false noses, and that the Monster probably did, too: "we would advise all those hardy English Hercules's who are determined to rid London of such a wretch, to pull him hard by the nose!"[29]

Angerstein eschewed such idle speculation, however, and in his poster of May 7 warned that "there is great Reason to fear that more than *ONE of those WRETCHES* infest the Streets." At least four or five very different descriptions had been given by the presumed Monster victims, varying with regard to stature, complexion, and hair color, not counting the multiple descriptions of his clothes. He also concluded that "these unnatural men, these MONSTERS, certainly have some mode of communicating with each other: which evidently appears from the exact similarity of their attacks, as well as from the savage pleasure and delight each of them seems to enjoy in the terror, pain, and distress of the fair unfortunate victims whom they wound."[30] Angerstein freely admitted that his reward had not yet served its purpose: the cunning of the Monsters had enabled them to evade not only the regular police, but also the multitude of vigilantes aroused by the offer of a reward. There was no reason to withdraw the reward, however, since it had at least served to thoroughly alert the Londoners to the danger that threatened the female inhabitants of the metropolis, who were at the mercy of a ruthless gang of Monsters. In a postscript, Angerstein added another idea: the Monster must live in a house where the servants could not read; otherwise, he would have been captured long ago, since all London was looking for him. All tradesmen's servants and baker's boys were urged to spread the word about this fiend in human shape to the illiterate serving-girls they visited; an extra twenty pounds were offered if this information would lead to the apprehension of the Monster.

The same day Angerstein's new poster was pasted on the London walls, several inhabitants of St. Pancras held an emergency meeting at the Percy Coffee-house. It was clear to them that the watchmen were wholly incapable of dealing with the threat posed by the Monsters, and fifteen gentlemen undertook to patrol the streets of the south division of St. Pancras between half an hour before sunset and eleven o'clock at night. (They

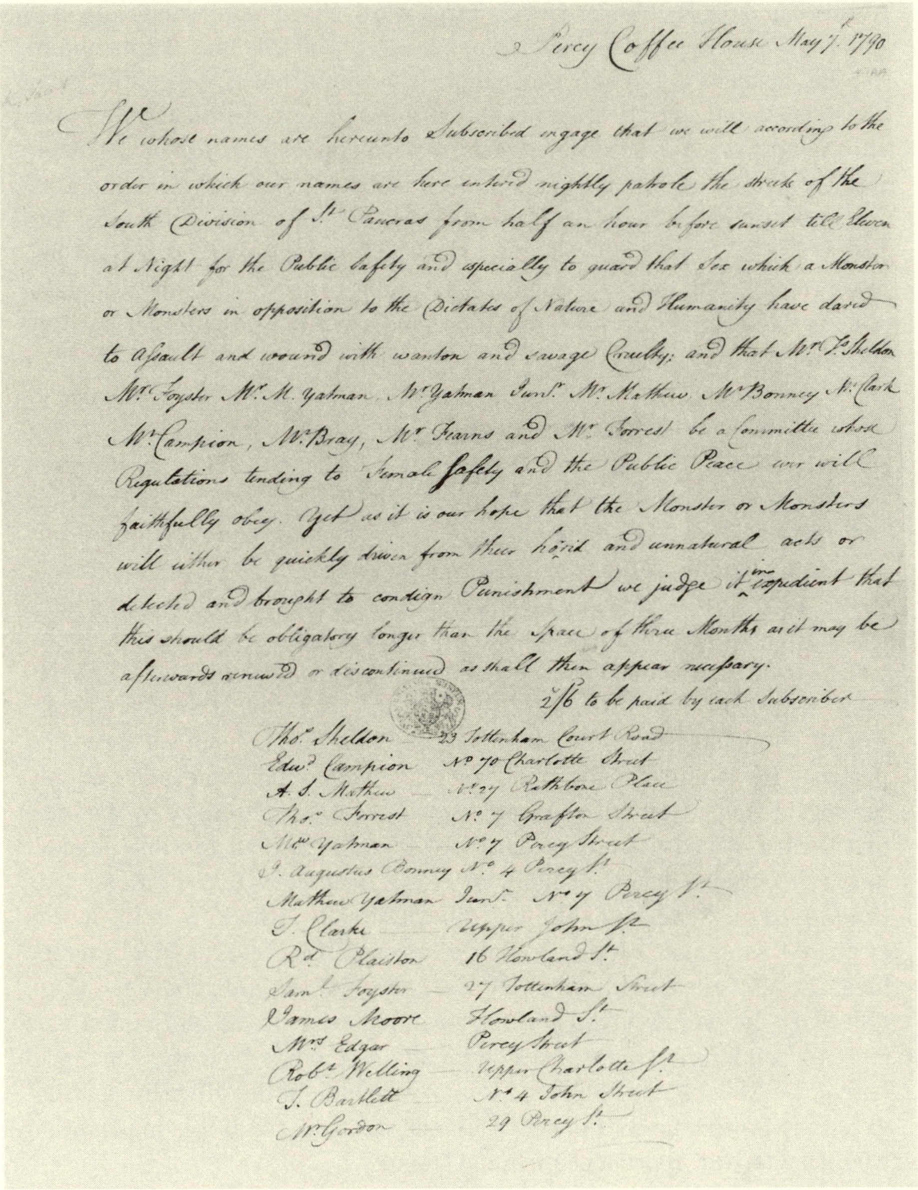

Percy Coffee House May 7th 1790

We whose names are hereunto Subscribed engage that we will according to the order in which our names are here entered nightly patrole the streets of the South Division of St. Pancras from half an hour before sunset till Eleven at Night for the Public Safety and especially to guard that Sex which a Monster or Monsters in opposition to the Dictates of Nature and Humanity have dared to Assault and wound with wanton and savage Cruelty; and that Mr. T. Sheldon Mr. Foyster Mr. M. Yatman Mr. Yatman Junr. Mr. Mathew Mr. Bonney Mr. Clark Mr. Campion, Mr. Bray, Mr. Fearns and Mr. Forrest be a Committee whose Regulations tending to Female Safety and the Public Peace we will faithfully obey. Yet as it is our hope that the Monster or Monsters will either be quickly driven from their horrid and unnatural acts or detected and brought to condign Punishment we judge it inexpedient that this should be obligatory longer than the Space of three Months as it may be afterwards renewed or discontinued as shall then appear necessary.

2/6 to be paid by each Subscriber

Thos. Sheldon — 23 Tottenham Court Road
Edwd. Campion — No 70 Charlotte Street
A. S. Mathew — No. 27 Rathbone Place
Thos. Forrest — No. 7 Grafton Street
Mw. Yatman — No. 7 Percy Street
J. Augustus Bonney No. 4 Percy St.
Mathew Yatman Junr. — No. 7 Percy St.
T. Clarke — Upper John St.
Rd. Plaiston — 16 Howland St.
Saml. Foyster — 27 Tottenham Street
James Moore — Howland St.
Mrs. Edgar — Percy Street
Robt. Welling — Upper Charlotte St.
T. Bartlett — No. 4 John Street
Mr. Gordon — 29 Percy St.

Figure 7. The original list of subscribers at the forming of the St. Pancras Monster patrol at the Percy Coffee-house, May 7, 1790. From Miss Banks's Monster scrapbook in the British Library. Reproduced by permission.

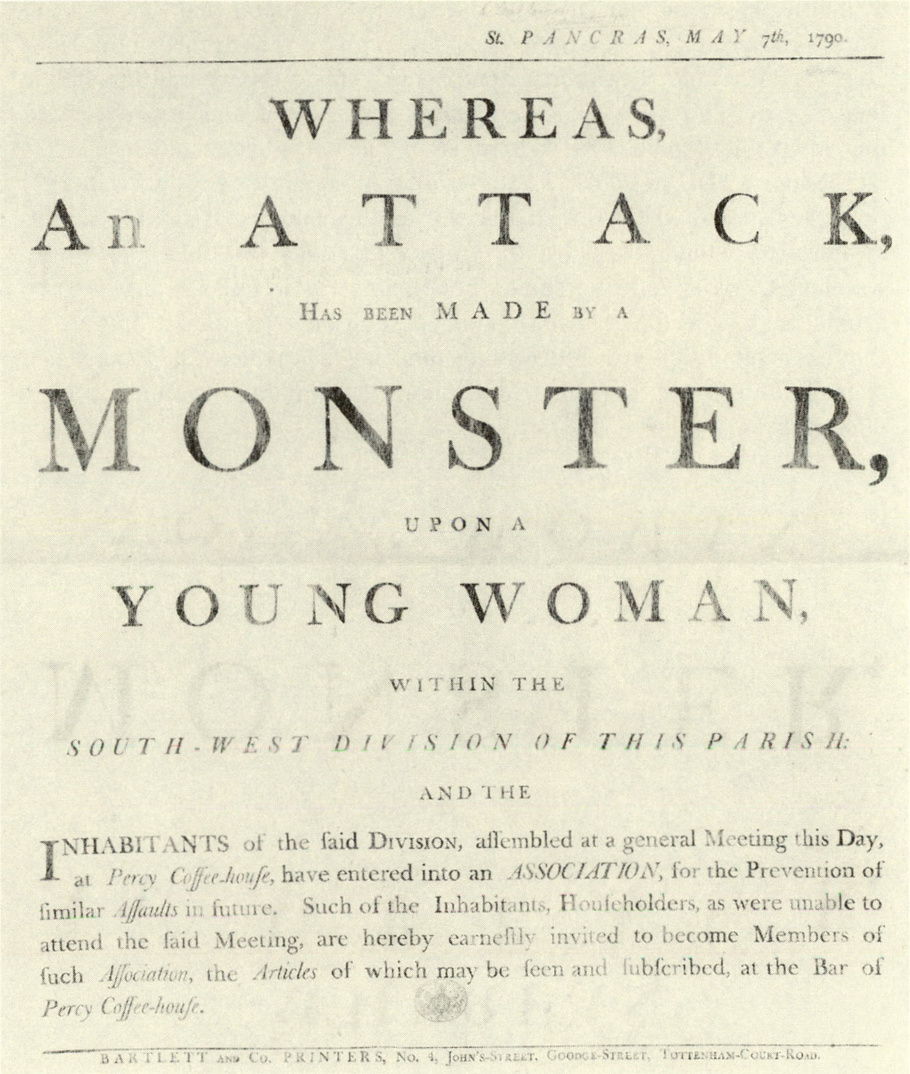

St. *PANCRAS, MAY* 7th, 1790.

# WHEREAS,

# An ATTACK,

HAS BEEN M A D E BY A

# MONSTER,

UPON A

# YOUNG WOMAN,

WITHIN THE

*SOUTH-WEST DIVISION OF THIS PARISH;*

AND THE

INHABITANTS of the faid DIVISION, affembled at a general Meeting this Day, at *Percy Coffee-houfe,* have entered into an *ASSOCIATION,* for the Prevention of fimilar *Affaults* in future. Such of the Inhabitants, Houfeholders, as were unable to attend the faid Meeting, are hereby earneftly invited to become Members of fuch *Affociation,* the *Articles* of which may be feen and fubfcribed, at the Bar of *Percy Coffee-houfe.*

BARTLETT AND CO. PRINTERS, No. 4, JOHN'S-STREET, GOODGE-STREET, TOTTENHAM-COURT-ROAD.

Figure 8. The first poster of the St. Pancras Monster patrol. From Miss Banks's Monster scrapbook in the British Library. Reproduced by permission.

evidently presumed that any lady who ventured out after that time was not worth protecting.) A subscription was taken up for the capture of the Monster, and a set of "Regulations tending to Female Safety and the Public Peace" drawn up. On May 7, they had a poster of their own printed and pasted up, with the heading "Whereas an Attack has been made by a MONSTER upon a YOUNG WOMAN," to recruit new vigilantes and subscribers.[31] Some newspaper writers applauded the venture and urged that this auxiliary force be extended to patrol the entire metropolis. Instead of the elderly watchmen, whose habit of calling out the time at regular intervals gave criminals an excellent idea of what part of their beat was safe to operate in, they envisioned a force of active young men, armed to the teeth, dressed in a special uniform, and wearing padded shoes for stalking the Monster more effectively.

CHAPTER 4

# MONSTER MANIA

*Good Angerstein,*
*Be not so keen,*
*For WOMEN still will roam:—*
*Nor wounds nor death,*
*'Till stopp'd their breath—*
Can keep our WIVES at HOME.
—*A poem by "Benedict," in the* World, *June 17, 1790*

IN MID-May, London was in a turmoil. In the *Oracle,* yet another journalist was complaining about the authorities' laxity in tackling the Monster or Monsters. The terror caused by the mysterious assailant, noted the writer, was now such that women hardly dared to venture outdoors after dark: "It is really distressing to walk our streets towards evening. Every woman we meet regards us with distrust, shrinks sideling from our touch, and expects a poignard to pierce what gallantry and manhood consider as sacred."[1]

John Julius Angerstein himself gave a similar account.[2] His reward had brought no other result than that several innocent people had been arrested, and sometimes beaten up by vigilantes, before being hauled off to Bow Street. In spite of the large posters bearing the heading "The MONSTER" pasted up at the corner of every street all over the metropolis, new accounts of fresh victims appeared almost daily. Angerstein's eloquent description of London in May 1790 is worth quoting verbatim:

The magistrates were much harassed; all the town, and especially the women were exceedingly alarmed; and the whole business appeared the more extraordinary and astonishing, as every day brought fresh accounts of new victims to the horrid attacks of these ruffians, notwithstanding the bills offering high rewards for their apprehension were pasted up at every corner of every street all over the metropolis.

It became dangerous for a man even to walk along the streets alone, as merely calling or pointing out some person as THE MONSTER, to the people passing, was sufficient to endanger his life; and many were robbed, and extremely abused, by this means.

No man of gallantry dared to approach a lady in the streets after dark, for fear of alarming her susceptible nature.

There was a total suspension of all street amours.

The gentle salutations and the gay blandishments of the *peripathetic* [sic] beauties, the soft, easy, accommodating fair ones, were all over; and gloomy jealousy and dark distrust appeared on every female brow.

The whole order of things was changed. It was not safe for a gentleman to walk the streets, unless under the *protection* of a lady.

The German naturalist Georg Forster was in London at the height of the Monster mania. In his diary he left an interesting sketch, dated May 12, 1790.[3] For the past four weeks, all London had been talking about the Monster:

The newspapers are full of him; the playwrights entertain audiences with his exploits from the stage; the ladies are afraid of him; the mob gives every pedestrian a keen look in case he is the Monster; all the walls are covered with posters advertising a reward for the apprehension of the Monster; a fund has been opened to finance the hunt; Mrs. Smith, a society lady, has shot him with a pistol behind the ear; he disguises himself, goes about in various different guises, wounding beautiful women with specially invented instruments, with hooks hidden in bouquets of flowers, with knitting pins, etc.

There were rumors, he stated, that the Monster or Monsters, these tigers lusting for the blood of women, were intent on destroying the entire female sex, or at least the beautiful portion of it. There were also rumors that the Monster was an evil spirit who could make himself invisible to evade detection; that he was a master of disguise who could change his appearance at will; or that he was an insane nobleman who had vowed to maim every beautiful woman in London. The German chronicler J. W. von Archenholtz, another resident of London, was aware that some ribald prints made fun of the Monster business; nevertheless, he asserted that the miscreant really did exist, since he had personally spoken to some of the ladies he had assaulted; their descriptions of his language and conduct were "sufficient to impress the most callous mind with horror!"[4]

There were, at this time, anti-Monster vigilante associations in both Westminster and St. Pancras, but they had succeeded only in arresting several innocent people. The prince of Wales had himself vowed to detect and expose the identity of the Monster; whether he actually made any attempt to do so is unknown.[5] An appeal was made to the Knights of the Order of the Bath, who were bound by their oath to defend all women and maidens.[6] There were frequent calls for a special Monster police force to be recruited, to patrol all the streets of London between seven and eleven o'clock in the evenings. The women of London did not trust even these well-organized guardians, nor had they any faith in the Runners or watchmen. At the height of the Monster mania, several ladies instead turned to the London braziers for protection: they were fitted with copper cuirasses or petticoats to shield them against his darting rapier.[7] Less financially well-endowed ladies had to be content with having cork-rumps[8] or even a large porridge pot fitted beneath their voluminous clothing to protect their *derrières* against the Monster's cutting implements.

At this time, the Westminster Forum debating society regularly arranged debates on the most interesting topics of the day. A committee of ladies had for some time tried to arrange a question to be put concerning the London Monster, but only after the intervention of a prominent advocate for the abolition of slavery could they come up with an atrocity that paralleled those of the Monster. The May 1790 question was "Who is the Greater Disgrace to Humanity, the Monster, who has lately cut so many women in London, or the Slave-trading Wretches, who drag the Unhappy Female African from her family and native country?" The outcome of this debate is not known but, considering the prevailing mood in London, anyone backing the Monster as the "Greater Disgrace" would probably have the odds in his favor. It is known, however, that there were several speakers and a full house that included many Monster hunters seeking new clues as to his identity; Monster victims, who basked in the glory of having been the subject of the Monster's attentions; and supporters of Distressed Female Africans.[9]

Monster mania also allowed the other criminal elements in London to capitalize on the situation. On May 10, a gang of pickpockets attacked a wealthy gentleman near Holborn.[10] They hustled him and took his watch, money, and hat, but the robbed man showed some spirit and attempted to run after them. The pickpockets called out, "It's the Monster, he has just cut a woman." Their plan worked brilliantly: they got away, but the gentleman had to run away along the London streets, pursued by an ever-growing mob of roughs and toughs who shouted, "The Monster! The Monster!" Finally they caught him after a furious chase; he was knocked down, pummeled, and surrounded by a howling mob of several hundred people. He would probably have lost his life had not some gentlemen of his acquaintance seen him being manhandled in the street. They broke into the mob and rescued him, dragging his limp body into the Gray's Inn coffeehouse. The mob was soon reinforced by other amateur Monster hunters, however, who believed that the Monster's wealthy accomplices had rescued him from justice. The furious mob, which now numbered nearly a thousand, charged the coffeehouse, but the gentlemen managed to hail a hackney coach and escape to the Brown Bear, a well-known public house situated just opposite the public office in Bow Street. The mob followed and attacked the pub. They broke every window, yelling and cursing all the while. At nine o'clock in the evening, after the siege of the Brown Bear had been going on for some hours, the gentleman's saviors managed to convey him, in disguise, to the Bow Street public office. The mob was still in the street outside and would have massacred him had they seen him. Sir Sampson Wright lamented that the perpetrators of the original daring assault and robbery were to go unpunished, but he was at least able to give the gentleman protection against the mob until it had dispersed.

Other low-life elements also benefited from the Monster mania. At least one man was convicted of calling out "The Monster!" as an enemy went by, to enjoy seeing him beaten by the street mob. In early May, a drunken gentleman returning from an alehouse had his pockets picked and was pushed into the gutter by a gang of thieves. By calling out "The Monster!" they alerted a furious mob, from which the gentleman barely escaped alive. A braggart who called himself Mr. Jon Pieters told the *World* on May 14 that his sister-in-law had been attacked by the Monster, and that she had shot him in the neck with one of Pieters's own pistols. This afterward proved to be a lie, published under an assumed name.[11] On May 17, a certain Mr. Heather was crossing Tower Hill at about nine in the evening when he observed a well-dressed woman lying on the ground. Her gown and apron were bloodstained, and she said that a very tall man had just wounded her with some sharp instrument; she begged his assistance to get her to a coach waiting nearby. After she had been driven off, the gallant Mr. Heather found, to his dismay, that she had picked his pockets of his watch and three guineas.[12]

In spite of the Monster mania, young gallants still went strolling about the London streets, ogling the ladies. But the ladies of easy virtue, formerly so accommodating, now shrunk with terror at their approach. One young man thought of a solution. He formed the "No Monster" club, comprised of himself and several friends who were above suspicion. They all wore cardboard "No Monster" badges on the lapels of their coats, and were soon seen sauntering about Oxford Street. Whether this club had any success is unknown, but the newspapers derided this latest fad. The *St. James's Gazette* wrote that "The distressed Beauties of Great-Britain present their grateful compliments to *No Monster*, and return him many thanks for reminding them of those noble and valorous knights who are sworn to defend all maidens and widows in want of protection." The *Gazette* found it deplorable that the "No Monster" club did not, through cowardice or "want of chivalry," have as its aim the capture of this elusive criminal.[13]

At Astley's Theatre, a new theatrical piece called *The Monster* had been getting full houses since late April; the play was a full-scale adaptation of the career of the London Monster, with musical interludes. Pretty actresses had their buttocks pricked by his rapiers and their noses wounded by his fiendish nosegay. The final song always produced unbounded applause:

When the Monster is taken in the fact,
We'll have him tried by the Coventry Act,
The Black Act,
The Coventry Act![14]

On one instance, an intoxicated Irish sailor jumped out of the gallery and, with a stout oak stick in his hand, dashed forward to give the actor playing the Monster a good drubbing. Stage personnel dropped the curtain hastily.[15] The only way the Drury Lane Theatre could compete with this hit was to produce a Monster entertainment of its own. On May 11, a monologue entitled *The Monster Discovered* opened, but it failed to attain the popularity of Astley's play.[16]

\*   \*   \*

In early May, there was much newspaper interest in the tragic story of Miss Barrs, "a very fine girl, daughter to a Fruiterer in Great Mary-le-bone-street," who had twice been cut by the Monster.[17] On Sunday, May 2, a man had approached her in the most obscene manner, and later stabbed her in the thigh. Not content with this outrage, he came back the next day and cut her in the other thigh. According to the *World,* the wounded girl was confined to her bed. She became a celebrity for a few heady days, and the fruiterer's shop was busier than ever as well-to-do Londoners rushed to visit the Monster's latest victim. Ladies of fashion heard her tale with a frisson of horror: would they themselves be the next victims? Bloods and gallants ogled the fair sufferer with many appreciative comments about the Monster's taste in choosing his victims.

The *World* of May 14 reported, however, that "the account of Miss B. of Marylebon-street, which appeared in all the Newspapers, having been twice wounded by the *Monster"* was a complete fabrication. The Select Vestry of Marylebone Parish had inquired into the matter, after some kindhearted parishioners had appealed for the injured Miss Barrs to obtain financial compensation. A commission led by the duke of Portland and Lord Somers inquired into the circumstances, and one gentleman immediately suspected a fraud. Miss Barrs was sent for, and her cut clothes and the slight wound in her calf were closely examined. Although the cuts in her petticoat and stockings were three inches long, her wound was just one inch long, and its appearance would suggest that she had scratched herself, rather than having been injured by some sharp instrument. Her account of the attacks was equivocal and contradictory, and the Select Vestry "was of but one opinion, namely that SHE WAS AN IMPOSTOR." They could only presume that her purpose in this fraud had been to procure compassion and money from those engaged in the Monster hunt.[18] Miss Barrs was evidently not alone in trying this caper. The *World* of May 15 condemned this disgraceful business: "Girls pretending to be maimed, who never were touched, are new kinds of MONSTERS, that should be as severely punished as the real one, who gave occasion to the reward."[19]

The *Times* used the Barrs story to launch a frontal attack on the Monster mania that was rampant throughout London. The Monster, their writer claimed, was fiction deriving from the pickpockets who used sharp instruments to cut ladies' pockets and steal their contents. Some pickpockets were clumsy in handling these weapons and cut not only the pocket but also the skin of their victim. This, claimed the *Times,* was the true origin of the Monster legend, which had put London in such turmoil. At a recent meeting of the Companies of Surgeons and Apothecaries, in fact, the Monster was one of the prevailing topics of conversation. When the many distinguished surgeons present were asked if they had ever attended a Monster victim, the answer was "Not one!"[20] It had been proven by repeated testimonies, the journalist claimed, that several women had fraudulently reported themselves to be wounded by the Monster in hopes of sharing Mr. Angerstein's reward. The public had been unnecessarily alarmed by the Monster mania that had ensued, and the reporter saw it as his public duty to point out the frauds of Miss Barrs and others. Ending on a lighthearted note, the newspaperman presumed that Miss Barrs had been scheming to attract customers to her father's shop, but "such is the force of truth, that the flimzy veil of deceit, is easily seen through." Indeed, "the serpent has taken *another* form to tempt mankind to eat an *apple*! If it was not too much like *fun,* we might be induced to say, she has really *Barred* the doors against all customers."[21]

\*   \*   \*

In mid-May, there were several attacks on women, all blamed on the Monster but less convincing than the earlier outrages. On May 11, a lady had her clothes cut as she passed by the Bank, and the Monster, aware that he was being pursued, turned into the Stock Exchange, where he quickly eluded detection.[22] Some days later, there was a great outcry near St. Bride's Church after a man dressed as a beggar, who had previously knocked and rang at several doors nearby, was captured after attempting to stab a woman. The man turned out to be an imbecile, maimed sailor, incapable of articulate speech.[23] Mary Fisher, the wife of a coal meter, who kept a cook's shop in Pye Street, was described by Mr. Angerstein as "a very plain, poor, middle-sized old woman, turned of forty, and very meanly dressed."[24] As she was walking past Charing Cross about eleven o'clock at night, with a basket of eggs under one arm and a piece of beef under the other, she saw three men coming toward her. She kept out of their way, fearing that they would break her eggs just for the fun of it, but one of them instead suddenly struck her in the face with some sharp instrument and knocked her down. Her face was badly cut, but she struggled to her feet to curse her assailants; one of them retraced his steps and knocked her down again. The three men, laughing loudly, made off.

Four days later, Mrs. Smyth, the first Monster victim, who had accused William Tuffing, was again attacked.[25] As she was returning from Covent Garden market with her maid, three well-dressed gentlemen came up to her when she was looking at the goods in a shop window. The unsuspecting Mrs. Smyth received a blow in the face; the three men laughed and walked away. Mrs. Smyth described the main culprit as a man about forty years old, tall, stout, and full faced, with abundant fair hair like a wig, and a round hat. His two companions appeared smaller and younger. A rather more typical Monster outrage was described a week later: a beautiful girl passing along the Pall Mall in the evening was stabbed several times and cut under the chin by the Monster's nosegay.[26]

As the uproar in town continued, several spurious cases appeared in the newspapers. Even Angerstein's friends joked and bantered, telling him that he was chasing a mere phantom.[27] A reporter in the *St. James's Gazette* confessed that he was "a little *sceptical* with respect to the many reports of the *Cutting Monster* or *Monsters*." He suspected that malice and mischief had combined to build up a formidable hysteria, and agreed that the Monster mania had resulted from the actions of a few blundering pickpockets.[28] A journalist in the *Public Ledger* went even further. He asserted that there did not exist, and never had existed, a London Monster.[29] The entire affair was the result of a few ladies being wounded by pickpockets using sharp instruments: "there is nothing *monstrous* here, unless the monstrous impudence of a pickpocket." The journalist saw it as his duty to free London from the Monster; the only people to have anything to gain from this fiction were the pickpockets themselves and the married men of London. The former could easily elude pursuit by calling out "The Monster!" and pointing at their victim; the latter for keeping their wives at home. The Monster provided them with an excellent excuse. Even Georg Forster had lost faith in the Monster: "the Monster is nothing more nor less than a phantom invented to amuse the bored inhabitants of London town. A pickpocket who may have learnt to turn pockets inside out and empty them with the aid of an instrument, might perhaps have injured a woman, while picking her pocket in this manner; and this insignificant incident created the story of a Monster enraged with feminine beauty."[30]

Angerstein was adamant, however, and gathered the entire company of Monster victims to give testimony to the *Public Ledger* a few days after the offending article appeared. The editor was forced to admit that these women had indeed been attacked, and that their attacker was no mere pickpocket. In two halfhearted apologies to Angerstein and the victims, the *Public Ledger* conceded that the Monster, or Monsters, did exist.[31] But Angerstein was next taken to task by another audacious journalist, who had his own theories about the Monster hunt in the *Gazetteer*.[32] Angerstein, he wrote, had been a fool to issue such a high reward for the arrest of the Monster: By May 17, at least thirty innocent men had been apprehended and charged as a result of the work of avaricious Monster hunters keen for the reward. All that Angerstein's interference had achieved was to slow down the detective work of the magistrates of Bow Street; the journalist asserted that if they had been allowed to work undisturbed by Monster hunters and crazy vigilantes, the Bow Street police would have captured the Monster in two days. Much of Angerstein's personal prestige was invested in the Monster hunt, and he must have been aware that some people in London society, like Horace Walpole, Mrs. Thrale, and their friends at Strawberry Hill, openly ridiculed his exertions as a crimefighter. Mrs. Thrale wrote in her diary that:

all this Spring a man has gone about London Streets in dark Evenings stabbing pretty girls if he could catch one walking alone; to which Enormity was added by the Perpetrator some expressions of a peculiar Cast; cruel, indecent, & undeserved. The Offence was first complained of, & then taken up with a high Hand by a rich Merch.ᵗ John Julius Angerstein of Pallmall, who offered a large reward for the fellow's discovery. This brought forward our natural Spirit of Derision, & the Ladies' Champion became a subject of Ridicule to all the Merry Fellows,—& most of all, to those who visited at Strawberry Hill whence all the Pasquinades came forth to laugh, & sett the

whole town o'laughing at poor Angerstein, whose Quixotism was represented on the Summer stages of London with great effect.[33]

\*    \*    \*

In May 1790, after the attack on the British trading station at Nootka Sound,
the Royal Navy began to arm in expectation of a war with Spain. Throughout this month, press gangs scoured the streets to recruit sailors; their
main tools of persuasion were strong bludgeons, and many a London tough
woke up with a headache, lying in a seaman's hammock on the lower deck
of a ship of the line. According to Angerstein, "a hot press, which continued
for many days and nights, cleared the town of disorderly and suspected
characters."[34] The cessation of the Monster's activities in late May suggested that he had been hauled aboard a man-of-war and was now a sailor
on his way to wreak havoc among the Spanish señoritas. One skeptical
*Times* journalist went so far as to ask, "Where is the MONSTER? Has the
Spanish war destroyed him, or Miss *Barrs* put him to flight?—or is he, as a
*wonder* of the day,—with Stone Eater, Learned Pig, Muny Begum, Polish
Dwarf, Irish Giant, and Cock-Lane Ghost, gone forever to sleep?"[35]

Angerstein and the other Monster hunters considered it too early to
celebrate, however; this clever master-criminal was probably hiding from
the press gangs, ready to resume his reign of terror as soon as the threat
had abated. In early June, they had to admit that the Monster was no longer
an active threat: there had been no typical attacks on women since early
May. The alarm was still up, however, and any woman frightened by a
threatening drunk or ugly beggar was likely to cry out "The Monster!" The
consequences of this could be dire, as shown by one newspaper report: On
the evening of June 4, a drunken young man was seized by some Holborn
Monster hunters after an outcry had been made. The vigilantes brought him
before the Bow Street magistrates, but he made a good account of himself
and did not resemble the original description of the Monster. Sir Sampson
Wright could not let him leave the public office, however, since a large and
furious mob had gathered outside, and he feared that they might tear the
man to pieces.[36]

In early June, a man accused of being the Monster was kept all night in
the watchhouse of the parish of St. Margaret, Westminster. This man had
picked up a girl in the street and invited her to a public house. He then
invited her to smell a large artificial nosegay he was carrying, but as she
took hold of it, she felt something prick her hand. She went away and told
some of her friends, and they concluded that he must have been the Mon-

ster. Her friends alerted the watchmen, who went back to the public house, where the man was still waiting for his female acquaintance, and took him into custody. The next day, the man was interrogated, but he was able to show to their satisfaction that the girl had in fact pricked her hand with the wire used to bind the artificial flowers together, and he was discharged.[37]

At about the same time, the pseudonymous Humphrey Henpeck wrote a joking letter to the *Diary,* claiming that the Monster mania was the plot of several husbands in London Westminster attempting to keep their wives at home. The idea of a bloodthirsty party of Monsters stalking the streets was enough to achieve this purpose, but the gentlemen had since relented, since the domestic ill-humor of their wives had proved too much for them, and they now declared that there was no such thing as the Monster.[38]

Now newspapers began publishing the doubtful instances of Monster activity with ribald and incredulous editorial commentary. One newsworthy story of late May 1790 concerned Egalantine Lady Wallace, the sister of the duchess of Gordon.[39] An eccentric playwright and poetess, she had, a few months earlier, divorced her husband on account of his cruelty. Lady Wallace's biographer describes her as "a boisterous hoyden in her youth, and a woman of violent temper in her maturer years"; she was in fact summoned at least twice for assaulting people who had annoyed her. In 1788, her play *The Ton* was enacted at the Covent Garden Theatre, but the booing of the audience was so loud that the actors could barely be heard; after a number of bottles and heavy missiles had landed on the stage, the entire party of actors fled. In 1789, Lady Wallace left London in disgust when her play *The Whim* was prohibited by the censor. She went to Paris, where she was arrested as an English agent and narrowly escaped with her life.

On May 27, 1790, Lady Wallace made a great outcry: the Monster had come up to her carriage and paid her compliments and afterward tried to enter the carriage. Had her friend Captain Monroe not interceded and put the Monster to flight, she would have joined the ranks of Anne Porter and the other injured beauties. From now on, she would always keep a brace of pocket pistols with her. A journalist for the *Times* was unimpressed, however. He suggested that the presumed attacker must have been a disappointed theater patron who had observed her sitting in the carriage looking through some *old* books to find *new* jokes for her plays. Even more insultingly, he concluded that "The Monster at last appears, but leaves cherry-cheeked chambermaids for Lady Wallace, a *monstrous* beauty."

Another remarkable story, occurring at about the same time, was that of "Fat Phillis." Two young gentlemen, Viscount Netterville and his brother, the Hon. Mr. Cuffe, had gone to the theater, where a very disreputable

character, Charley Jones, alias Vaughan, alias "Fat Phillis," whooped, hal-
loed, and made every sign of being a close acquaintance of Cuffe, who
claimed he had never seen him before. Fat Phillis pressed against Cuffe in
an indecent manner several times, to the great embarrassment of the two
prudish young gentlemen, who finally left their seats in confusion. Fat Phillis followed them out into the street, along with his companion, George
Smith, and another young man. Fat Phillis collared Cuffe and threatened to
call the watch, accusing Cuffe of making an improper proposal to the lad. He
suggested that the two gentlemen pay him a fee to avoid being prosecuted;
when they refused, Fat Phillis threatened to call out "The Monster!" and set
the mob on the two gentlemen. The brothers tore away and tried to reach
Netterville's house nearby. Just outside the house, Cuffe made a defiant
gesture and was promptly knocked down and pummeled by Fat Phillis. Lord
Netterville managed to drag his brother's limp body indoors and immediately sent servants to the Bow Street public office to report the incident to
the authorities. Runner Moses Murrant promptly appeared and arrested
the three men. When the gang was brought before Sir Sampson Wright, it
was recorded that "Charley Jones, alias Vaughan, is known to the Officers
of this Police. He continually frequents Masquerades, and always goes in a
Female Habit. He, as well as his companion, are extremely effeminate, and
Vaughan was much painted."[40]

In 1790, there was a flourishing market for satirical prints dealing
with famous or notorious people or with sensational recent events.[41] The
Monster mania naturally inspired several popular prints.[42] The earliest of
these was Isaac Cruikshanks's *The Monster Cutting a Lady,* issued on
May 1. The image of the Monster in this print was based on a drawing by one
of his victims, and it had been approved by two other victims. A lady holding
a large muff is attacked by the Monster, who grabs her by the right arm and
cuts her behind several times; the slits in her dress are stained with blood.
Behind her is a street door in Pall Mall marked "Angersteein," and one of
the Monster reward handbills can be seen pasted on the house wall. The
purpose of this caricature was not only to assist in the Monster-hunt, but
also to imply that in spite of Angerstein's reward, the Monster had cut one
of his victims just by his front door.

The second compartment in this print shows a scantily clad woman
standing before a kneeling brazier who is hammering together the back
seams of a short copper petticoat. A placard on the wall says: "Ladies
Bottoms covered on the most Reasonable Terms and kept in repair by the
year by Anti:Monster." In the shop window are three copper petticoats of
increasing size, intended, in turn, for young ladies of 15, ladies of 30, and

Figure 9. *The Monster Cutting a Lady,* print by Isaac Cruikshanks published May 1, 1790. The face and figure of the Monster were reconstructed from the evidence of several victims who afterward approved of the drawing, thinking it a good likeness. Note the diabolical spikes on the Monster's knees; this was after the ferocious attack on Mrs. Payne. Also note the door marked "Angersteein" and the Monster reward poster pasted on the wall. Reproduced by permission of the British Library.

Figure 10. *Copper Bottoms to Prevent being Cut,* print by Isaac Cruikshanks, published May 1, 1790. Reproduced by permission of the British Museum.

Figure 11. *The Monster going to take his Afternoons Luncheon,* etching by James Gillray, published May 10, 1790. One of several caricatures depicting the Monster as an ogre. Reproduced courtesy of the Wellcome Trust.

very fat ladies. The ribald note struck by this image was improved upon by other caricaturists. In James Gillray's *The Monster disappointed of his Afternoon Luncheon, or Porridge Potts preferable to Cork Rumps,* which was issued on May 10, the Monster is depicted as an ogre lifting up a shapely young lady. He roars in dismay when he sees that her buttocks are protected by a round, shallow pot. In another version of this print, the pot was erased, and the Monster can be seen ready to plunge his knife and fork into the lady's exposed buttocks.

Six days later, on May 16, the anonymous print *Old Maids dreaming of the Monster* was published. Here, two old maids dream that an attack by the Monster will prove that they are still young and attractive, since it was the Monster's habit to attack only fashionable, beautiful young women. The Monster suddenly appears in the guise of a grotesque, three-headed ogre, with the devil seated on his middle head. One of the old maids hastily tries to get out of bed, but steps in the chamberpot by mistake.

Two days later the anonymous print *Glaucus and Scylla, or The Monster in Full Cry,* appeared. Here, the immensely fat Miss Jeffries, one of the queen's ladies in waiting, is pursued by the Monster in the shape of George Hanger, one of the cronies of the prince of Wales. Hanger is depicted with a tail and clawed, deformed legs; he aims to prick her buttocks with a long spike attached to the end of his bludgeon. A man lying on the ground tries to pull him back by the tail, and William Pitt races up to the right, armed with a warming pan, to save her honor from this monstrous assailant. In the background can be seen one of the posters of the St. Pancras Monster Patrol, beginning "Whereas an attack was made on a young lady of this parish by a MONSTER. . . ."

On May 20, James Gillray's *Swearing to the Cutting Monster, or a Scene in Bow Street* was published. This print shows one of the wounded victims pulling her skirts up and revealing all to the Bow Street magistrates. Gillray was in fact a neighbor of the Porters in St. James's Street, and the print was probably inspired by newspaper reports of the sisters and other Monster victims giving evidence at Bow Street. Sir Sampson Wright, in his hat and spectacles, takes a closer look at the lady's posterior; the men on either side of him are the other justices William Addington and Nicholas Bond. The Monster at the dock bears a marked resemblance to the controversial politician Charles James Fox.

On May 29, the anonymous print *The Monster Detected* was published in the midst of the Monster mania. Accompanying verses relate that a certain devil was allowed to come to earth on condition that he marry a beautiful virgin. To test her virginity,

A little Dagger with a Tube, was fill'd
With Juice of Plants, which such a Liquor yield
That when to Womans velvet flesh apply'd
It makes no Entrance if a Maid is try'd.

The implication is that the great scarcity of virgins in London made it necessary for the devil to stab dozens of women, thus giving rise to the Monster mania.

On June 5, another Monster poster made its appearance on the London walls. It very much resembled those posted by Angerstein, but unlike them it positively identified the Monster as Captain Philip Thicknesse, an elderly controversialist. Thicknesse had libeled and blackmailed many people during his lengthy career, and numerous enemies were eager for revenge. Thicknesse himself suspected Captain John Crookshanks for libeling him

*OLD MAIDS DREAMING OF THE MONSTER.*

Figure 12. *Old Maids dreaming of the Monster,* anonymous satirical print that ridiculed the Monster's propensity for attacking fashionable, beautiful young women, published May 16, 1790. From the author's collection.

Figure 13. *Glaucus and Scylla, or The Monster in Full Cry*, satirical print by Isaac Cruikshanks, published May 18, 1790. From the author's collection.

Figure 14. *Swearing to the Cutting Monster; or a Scene in Bow Street*, ribald engraving by James Gillray, published May 20, 1790, showing one of the wounded ladies revealing all to the Bow Street magistrates. Sir Sampson Wright, in his hat and spectacles, takes a closer look; the men on either side of him are William Addington and Nicholas Bond. The Monster at the dock bears a marked resemblance to the controversial politician Charles James Fox. From the author's collection.

Figure 15. *The Monster Detected!*, satirical print, with verses, published May 29, 1790, in the midst of the Monster mania. The verses relate that a certain Devil was allowed to come to earth on condition that he marry a beautiful virgin. The ribald conclusion is that the great scarcity of virgins in London makes it necessary for the Devil to stab dozens of women, thus giving rise to the Monster mania. Reproduced by permission of the British Museum.

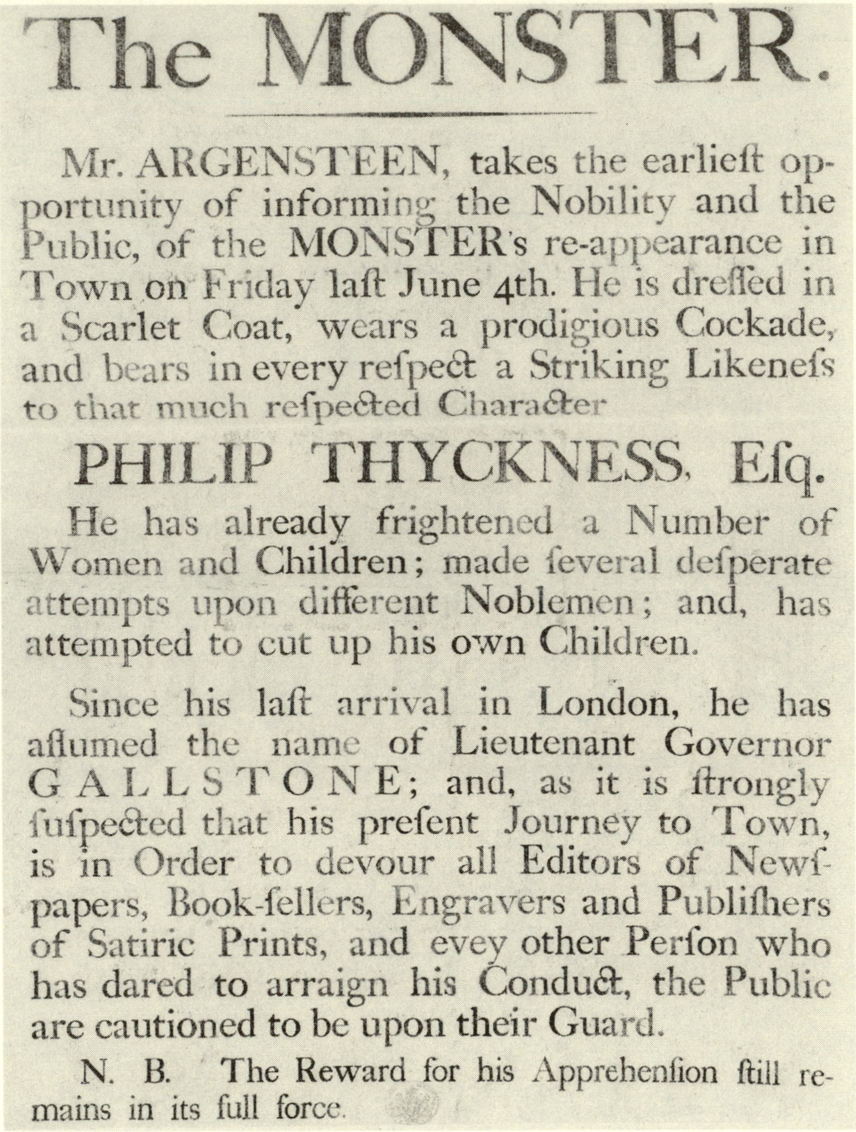

# The MONSTER.

Mr. ARGENSTEEN, takes the earlieſt opportunity of informing the Nobility and the Public, of the MONSTER's re-appearance in Town on Friday laſt June 4th. He is dreſſed in a Scarlet Coat, wears a prodigious Cockade, and bears in every reſpect a Striking Likeneſs to that much reſpected Character

## PHILIP THYCKNESS, Eſq.

He has already frightened a Number of Women and Children; made ſeveral deſperate attempts upon different Noblemen; and, has attempted to cut up his own Children.

Since his laſt arrival in London, he has aſſumed the name of Lieutenant Governor G A L L S T O N E; and, as it is ſtrongly ſuſpected that his preſent Journey to Town, is in Order to devour all Editors of Newſpapers, Book-ſellers, Engravers and Publiſhers of Satiric Prints, and evey other Perſon who has dared to arraign his Conduct, the Public are cautioned to be upon their Guard.

N. B. The Reward for his Apprehenſion ſtill remains in its full force.

Figure 16. Captain Thicknesse is accused of being the Monster in this spoof on Angerstein's posters, which appeared June 5, 1790. From Miss Banks's Monster scrapbook in the British Library, reproduced by permission.

Figure 17. *Monstrous Assassin or the Coward turn'd Bill-sticker,* a satirical print by Isaac Cruikshanks. Here Thicknesse gets his own back. Reproduced by permission from the British Library.

as the Monster. The two were old enemies: after Thicknesse had accused Crookshanks of cowardice and called him "a broken, deaf, and lame Sea-Duck," the eighty-two-year-old Crookshanks had challenged him to a duel, but Thicknesse declined to fight him. As revenge, Crookshanks apparently gave libelous information about Thicknesse to the caricaturist James Gillray, and had the faked Monster posters pasted up all over town.[43]

Thicknesse was left fuming with rage. He in turn commissioned another caricature, *Monstrous Assassin or the Coward turn'd Bill Sticker.* It depicts the lame Crookshanks as he supervises the bill-pasting operation, with the caption, "This is not the Captain *Straitshanks* who was Broke for Cowardice, & who afterwards Offered to Enter into the French Service . . . & who has kept his wife & two Children upon 13 pounds a year in Wales till the youngest Child is 44 years of age."[44]

CHAPTER 5

# THE ARREST OF RHYNWICK WILLIAMS

*Good Angerstein*
*Is not too keen;*
*For women ought to roam*
*At perfect ease,*
*Where'er they please*
*And Monsters keep at home.*
—"An Answer to the Monster," *in the* Gazetteer, *June 24, 1790*

AFTER she had eaten her evening meal on Sunday, June 13, 1790, Anne Porter wanted to take a walk in St. James's Park. She was accompanied by her mother, two of her sisters, and the twenty-year-old fishmonger John Henry Coleman. Coleman, evidently an admirer of Miss Porter, had his shop in Gray's Inn Passage. In *Bailey's London Dictionary* of 1790, he styled himself "Fishmonger to the Prince of Wales"; one would suppose that the prince's penchant for consuming vast amounts of oysters and deviled white-bait must have done his business much good.

As the Porter group strolled along, the topic of conversation turned, not surprisingly, to the Monster and his cowardly assault on the sisters. Anne Porter declared that just a week earlier she had actually seen the Monster again, but her fright deprived her of the power of acting rationally and calling out that he was the man all London was seeking. The Monster had stood outside her window, grimacing at her and using his customary foul language, before she observed him and alerted some servants. They ran off after the man, but he had easily dodged his bumbling pursuers, escaping into the narrow alleys nearby. Coleman earnestly begged the Porters that, if any of them set eyes on the Monster in the passing crowd, they should immediately point him out. A few minutes later, Anne Porter was seen to stagger and to call out, with much agitation, "There he is—the *Wretch*!" She appeared to have fainted, but Coleman nevertheless pulled her toward a group of people, imploring her to point out the Monster among them. With her last reserve of energy, she did so, saying "That's him, in blue and buff!" before falling into the arms of her sisters, like a heroine in one of the novels of Mrs. Radcliffe.[1]

Coleman, at first, did nothing at all. Considering the prevailing mood in London, a man of energy might have brought the man down with a rugby tackle before the admiring eyes of the Porters, singing out "Tally-ho! The Monster!" Like the manly, forthright heroes of the gothic novels he must have read, he would then have basked in the glory of all sundry: Monster hunters, police, magistrates, and last but not least all the ladies of the metropolis. However, the Gray's Inn fishmonger was not a man of action, but a timid and unadventurous character. It is likely that he was frightened that, like his paramour, he would soon get a taste of the Monster's rapier. Instead of challenging the man, Coleman quietly crept after him as he left the park, down Spring Gardens, and as far as the Admiralty, where the man turned down a narrow passage.

The suspect first very steadfastly looked up at a particular house, then turned sharply about to stare directly at Coleman. Unnerved by the man's steely glare, Coleman nearly gave up the pursuit. The man then very quickly walked down the alley and turned back into Spring Gardens. After some deliberation, Coleman followed him at a safe distance. The suspect appeared confused and made no effort to run away. Coleman gradually became bolder, particularly as the man was just five feet, six inches in height and did not look particularly strong. As they moved onto Cockspur Street and along Pall Mall, Coleman followed him like a shadow, just a yard behind.

In St. James's Street, Coleman was relieved to meet a fellow fishmonger. After a brief discussion, the two hurried after the man, but their prey turned sharply onto Bolton Street, where he knocked at the door of a house and was admitted. Coleman and his colleague were at a loss how to proceed. The two fishmongers stood outside for a couple of minutes, debating whether to follow the man into the house. They eventually found this course of action imprudent, and Coleman's friend left him, preferring to ply his trade than to chase a dangerous criminal through the streets. Coleman indecisively hung about outside. Had his quarry stayed indoors or bolted through the back door, he would have been safe. But after Coleman had waited about three or four minutes, the man came out through the front door and walked quickly back into Piccadilly. He walked past Pero's Bagnio, down St. James's Street, and stopped abruptly at a china shop at the corner of Pall Mall, where he knocked sharply at the door. Although the shop was about to close, a servant opened the door, and the suspect was seen to ask him a number of questions.

\* \* \*

As the man left the shop and went up St. James's Street, Coleman approached the servant, who was busy shuttering the shop's windows, and asked him whether he knew the man's name; the china-shop assistant did not know the name, or would not say. Coleman, who had hoped to obtain the man's name without having to tackle a possibly formidable criminal, raced ahead to catch up with the man, who was disappearing into the crowds in Piccadilly. He was probably acutely aware that if Miss Porter found out that he had followed the man she had pointed out as the Monster around London for half an hour without even trying to challenge the criminal, he would not stand highly in her favor. Even worse, the professional and amateur Monster hunters, police, and journalists would jeer and mock his conduct.

As Coleman followed the suspect through the darkening London streets, he desperately pondered how to stop the man and find out his name and address. To shout out, "He's the Monster!" would now be futile, since the streets were becoming empty, and the man would find it easy to run away. Then, Coleman thought of a way to get the man's name and address: to insult him and provoke him into a quarrel. To achieve this, Coleman overtook the man, turned round and walked straight at him, looking him straight in the face in an insulting manner. When he stopped at a house in Bond Street to knock at the door, Coleman crept up near him and said in what he presumed to be a highly insulting manner: "Why, this is an empty house, what do you knock here for?" The suspect, who now appeared very unlike a sinister, brutal criminal, meekly begged his pardon and said that he had believed the house to be inhabited by a gentleman of his acquaintance by the name of Pearce. He then rushed off toward Oxford Street. Coleman walked close behind, and tried to behave as obnoxiously as possible. At one point he actually peeped over the man's shoulder and called out "Buh!" at the top of his voice.

The suspect merely quickened his pace as the exasperated Coleman "continued his gestures of offence; nay, made a feint to square at him."[2] The man passed safely onto Oxford Street, sharply turned down South Moulton Street, knocked at the door of a house and was swiftly admitted. Once more, the fishmonger stood outside pondering what to do. After some minutes, he gathered what remained of his wits and courage and knocked at the door. A servant opened, and introduced him to a pitch-dark parlor, where two men awaited him in silence: one of them turned out to be Mr. Smith, the owner of the house; the other was the suspect.

For once, Coleman behaved coolly and rationally. He took Smith aside and asked him the name and address of the other man. Smith was astonished and at first refused, but Coleman firmly said that he was determined to find out who he was. Smith said that the man was an old school fellow of his, and that Coleman must assign his reasons if he wanted any kind of information. The fishmonger replied that he would give his reasons when he saw the man, and demanded that some candles be brought in. Coleman's relief when Smith meekly ordered his servant to fetch some candles can easily be imagined; surely, it must have been the most exciting moment in his life when he had faced two unknown men, one of whom he believed to be a dangerous and desperate criminal, in the dark room. He again demanded the man's name and address, and declared that, since he suspected that Smith's visitor had grossly insulted a lady of his acquaintance in St. James's Park, he was fully determined to have satisfaction.

The suspect suggested that he go to a coffeehouse nearby and wait for Coleman to bring the ladies there, but the fishmonger replied that he thought a coffeehouse a very improper place for ladies to visit. Smith called for pen and ink, and wrote, at his companion's direction, "Mr. Williams, No. 52, Jermyn Street." Significantly, the word "Monster" had not been mentioned in the conversation, and all three men became visibly more relaxed as Coleman pocketed the paper and gave his own name and address to the suspect.

The situation then again descended into farce. Suddenly, at the flicker of a candle, Coleman leaned forward and exclaimed, "Good God, Williams, I think I know you!" The mysterious Williams replied, "I think I know *you*!" It turned out that the two had previously met several times at certain assembly rooms and public houses, among the throng of young London pleasure-seekers. Coleman even recollected that Williams had formerly been a theater violinist, and that his brother was a well-known London apothecary. Both were astounded that they had not recognized each other during their mad chase through the London streets. Knowing that Williams, or at least his brother the apothecary, was a respectable person, made Coleman even more reluctant to try to arrest him. Happy to have come so creditably out of his encounter, the fishmonger took his farewell to Smith and Williams and started walking back toward Pero's Bagnio, to meet Anne and Sarah Porter and break what he imagined would be the good news that he had met the Monster and knew his identity.

Suddenly, as he was walking down Bond Street, his sluggish brain still working over the sensational recent events, Coleman was struck, as by a thunderbolt, with the realization that a man capable of attacking and stabbing at least thirty women would not stop short of giving a *false* name and address to his pursuer!

\* \* \*

Distraught, Coleman raced back to Smith's house, but this gentleman told him gleefully, one would imagine, that their mutual acquaintance had left some minutes ago. For about ten minutes, Coleman ran around the dark streets like a man possessed, looking everywhere for the elusive Monster. Giving up, he ran back onto St. James's Street where, at the top of the street, completely by accident, he almost ran into the mysterious Williams. The man did not try to run away, but merely said, "We meet again." After some gasping for breath, Coleman blurted out, "Yes, Williams, we meet again. . . . I think Williams I have some knowledge about you—did we not meet at a Ball in King-Street, Covent Garden?" Once Williams answered in the affirmative, Coleman suggested that, since they were actually old acquaintances, he no longer was certain that Williams really was the man who had insulted his lady friends; perhaps they should visit the ladies in question to have him cleared of this accusation? Williams objected that it was very late, but Coleman pointed out that their house was nearby, and Williams then came along without demur.

When Sarah Porter and her sister Martha saw Coleman and Wilson approaching Pero's Bagnio, they crossed the street and hastily rushed inside. When Williams perceived where they were going, he called out, "Why, that is Mr. Porter's!" Without further ado, they went in through the front door and into the parlor where the ladies were sitting. The moment Williams came into the room, Anne and Sarah Porter clasped their hands together, screamed, "Good God, that is the *Wretch!*" and fainted away. Surveying their recumbent forms, Williams turned to Coleman and said, "The conduct of the Ladies, Sir, is extremely odd; I hope they do not take me for that Person who is advertised." Coleman coolly told him that they certainly did.

Williams protested his innocence and asked leave to send for his mother and sister. He also claimed that he had been working the entire evening of the queen's birthday, when Anne Porter had been cut, and asked to be allowed to fetch some of his coworkers, who could easily prove his alibi. Coleman did not move to restrain him as he got up to leave, but

Figure 18. Rhynwick Williams as portrayed in *New Lady's Magazine*, July 1790.
Reproduced by permission from the British Library.

Mrs. Elizabeth Porter, Anne's and Sarah's mother, did. A strong and active woman who served as the chief bath attendant at Pero's Bagnio, she promptly collared Williams and waved her huge red fist in his face. She swore that if the Monster moved a muscle she would give him ample reason to be sorry for it. Williams sank back into his chair.[3]

A servant was sent to the Bow Street public office, and after about an hour, Runner John Macmanus, a grizzled veteran who had acted as the bodyguard of George III, after the attempt on his life by the madwoman Margaret Nicholson in 1786, arrived at the Porter residence. Macmanus took Williams into custody, and he was committed to the New Prison, Clerkenwell. The man gave his name as Mr. Rhynwick Williams and his trade as an artificial flower maker. Macmanus also promptly searched Williams's lodgings. The address given earlier proved not to be correct. Rhynwick Williams did not live at No. 52 Jermyn Street, but his mother and sister lived nearby, in Duke Street. His own lodgings were at a dismal-looking alehouse, where six men lay every night in three contiguous beds in the same small room. Both premises were searched by Runner Macmanus; at the alehouse, a suitcase containing the worldly belongings of Rhynwick Williams was pried open, and a suit of clothes, with a light-colored coat and a pair of half-boots, were seized. They resembled the garments worn by the Monster on earlier occasions, but no knife, rapier, or other sharp cutting implement was found.

CHAPTER 6

# RHYNWICK WILLIAMS
# AT BOW STREET

*Now the naughty Monster's fast,*
*Beauty stands no more aghast*
*At the terrifying word,*
*Milk of nature turn'd to curd.*
*Some, as yet, can scarce believe it,*
*Others, as a dream receive it.*
*What, that man of woman born,*
*Woman, fairer than the morn:*
*Woman, nature's choicest flower,*
*Soft as rose-buds in a shower,*
*Sent in pity to mankind,*
*To allay and ease his mind,*
*Could uplift his impious arm. . . .*
—W.H., "The Monster," in the New Lady's Magazine, *July 1790*

ON JUNE 14 and 15, 1790, several newspapers carried the sensational news that the Monster had finally been apprehended: He was Rhynwick Williams, a native of Wales, twenty-three years old, and an artificial flower maker.[1] His odd occupation caused some merriment: That the London Monster, the terror of the capital's female world, made artificial flowers for his living was considered as inappropriate as Attila the Hun being a needlepoint embroiderer or Ivan the Terrible a ladies' hairdresser. The *Times* was alone in not naming the prisoner as Rhynwick Williams; they merely referred to him as "a person whose name with regard to his family we shall at present forbear to mention." The *Times* journalist evidently had some personal knowledge of Rhynwick Williams and his family, and described him as a

young man of genteel appearance, who unfortunately for his family has been in very dissipated habits of life, which have led him into expenses

among women, and a line of conduct extremely injurious to his own character. The misfortune is the greater, as his friends are persons of character
and reputation, who most severely feel for the excesses and wanton behavior of this thoughtless young man, whose person is extremely well
known about town.[2]

Many people were amazed that the Monster was not a rough, coarse
brute, but a young, not unpleasant-looking man of better than average
breeding. Newspaper correspondents soon managed to find out that Rhynwick Williams had received a reasonably good education.[3] At an early
period of his life, Rhynwick's attentive parents put him into the care of
a gentleman friend in London, where he received further education at
a respectable school. This gentleman, apparently a patron of the theater,
found that young Rhynwick was a pleasant-looking lad, with a supple,
graceful body and a talent for music. On his advice, Rhynwick was appren-
ticed to Giovanni Andrea Battista Gallini, the most famous dancing master
in Britain.

A native of Florence, Gallini had made his debut as a ballet dancer at
the Opera House, Haymarket, in 1753, and achieved such a brilliant success
that he was soon the director of the dances, and finally stage manager of the
theater. While on a tour of Italy, Gallini had so delighted the pope with his
dancing that he was made a Knight of the Golden Spur; on his return to
London, he assumed the title "Sir John Gallini," although the papal knight-
hood granted him no such right.[4]

Sir John was a brilliant dancing master, and in his school Rhynwick
Williams could not, as one of his newspaper biographers wrote, "fail to
acquire those personal graces with which all his manners seem to be tinged;
but the trammels of art were too great a confinement to the effervescent
spirit of gaiety and expense which soon marked his conduct."[5] In other
words, young Rhynwick seems to have taken on the habits of a scapegrace
during his period of study at Sir John's establishment. This did not preclude
him from learning both ballet dancing and the violin; he seems to have been
active in the theater orchestra and also to have acted as a dancing master
both in private houses and at least one school. A Mr. Williams is listed
among the second violinists at the Handel Memorial Concerts at Westminster Abbey and the Pantheon in 1784.[6] Not only in ribald eighteenth-century
novels was a private dancing master considered a serious threat to chastity: the dashing *danceur*, while guiding the movements of the limbs of
his pupil, had unique possibilities for seducing the trembling high-born

maidens in his charge. Sir John Gallini had not eschewed these opportunities. When, according to his rather disapproving biographer, he had
been "admitted into the house of the third Earl of Abingdon," he rapidly
won the affections of Lady Elizabeth Peregrine Bertie, the earl's eldest
daughter and a wealthy heiress. Although the earl was aghast that his
daughter wished to elope with a common Italian mountebank, they later
married. Rhynwick Williams, although not as fortunate as Sir John, also
became, or at least aspired to be, quite a ladies' man.

    Some time in the late 1770s or early 1780s, Rhynwick Williams's entire
family came to live in London. His father, Thomas Williams, was a member
of the Society of Apothecaries who had his pharmacy in Broad Street,
Carnaby Market.[7] He was not a mere druggist but an educated man and
an apothecary of some distinction. He died at a relatively young age on
June 9, 1785. In his will, he left one hundred pounds in old South Sea
annuities and the rest of his worldly goods to his wife, Mary Williams.[8]
The apothecary's father, John Williams, who was still living in Beguildy
in the county of Radnor, Wales, had to be content with a bequest of one
guinea per annum for life. In 1785, the apothecary's eldest son, Thomas
Williams, who had also pursued his father's profession, took over his position as member of the Society of Apothecaries by patrimony.[9] There are
hints that, although the old apothecary and his son Thomas were well off,
Rhynwick's mother and sisters soon ran into financial difficulties, having to
fend for themselves in the metropolis after the untimely death of the family
breadwinner.

    In the autumn of 1785, Sir John Gallini became the proprietor of the
King's Theatre, where he wanted to stage his own ballet dancing shows.
Since his finances were stretched to the limit, he had many difficulties in
finding suitable professional dancers, and it is very likely that his apprentice Rhynwick Williams went on the stage. Indeed, one of Williams's newspaper biographers states that he was once "a public dancer on the boards
of the Opera-house."[10] The experience is unlikely to have been a happy one,
however. Not even Sir John's dancing skills could put fire into the bumbling
amateurs he had to employ. The London stage was, as it is now, a highly
competitive arena; but the pitfalls for anyone attempting a second-rate
routine were somewhat more dangerous than today. A review of one of Sir
John's shows in the *World* states that "the dance, if such it can be called,
was like the movements of heavy cavalry. It was hissed very abundantly." On
a later occasion, the dissatisfied audience charged the stage and put the
dancers to flight. Sir John had to fight for his life against a burly assailant,

who tried to throw him into the orchestra pit, but the nimble dancing master dodged his blows and managed to knock his antagonist down. Sir John, along with Rhynwick Williams and the rest of the crew, escaped an audience threatening to murder them. The mob proceeded to sack the entire theater and destroyed everything that could be broken.[11]

Williams's happy, if somewhat perilous, existence at Sir John's dancing academy soon came to an end. There was an incident when Sir John Gallini suspected his scapegrace apprentice of having stolen a watch belonging to him, and Williams was summarily discharged. This, according to his own account, occurred not long after the death of his father, probably in 1785 or 1786.[12] He soon ran into serious financial difficulties, since he continued to visit dancing parlors, restaurants, and assembly rooms. According to the newspaper writer quoted earlier, he was "continually in the company, and probably supported by women to whose gratification he sacrificed all his time and talent." He continued in this way some time, but then apparently made an effort to redeem himself: he managed to obtain a position as clerk to an attorney who aspired to become a member of Parliament. This gentleman was unsuccessful in his bid, although it is recorded that Williams discharged his duty fully satisfactorily, but the young Welshman was again out on the street, without any employment.[13] One of Williams's sisters was employed as an artificial flower maker at Monsieur Aimable Michelle's establishment in Dover Street. She managed to persuade the Frenchman to give her brother a chance in this profession. Rhynwick started learning the artificial flower business in early 1789, and he made rapid progress. In consequence of his superior workmanship, Monsieur Michelle gave him a permanent position on his work force, with a decent salary, from the month of September 1789 onward. For reasons undisclosed, Rhynwick Williams's employment at the artificial flower factory was terminated in early June 1790.[14]

At the time of his arrest, Rhynwick Williams was not only unemployed but also in dire financial straits. He was lodging at a mean-looking public house in Bury Street called the George, where he had been sleeping in the same bed as another man for some time. Some said this arrangement was due to reasons of penury, others made a more sinister interpretation of the Monster's preference for male company in bed and linked this circumstance to his crimes against the female sex.[15] The German chronicler J. W. von Archenholtz, who described Williams as a short man with a dark brown complexion, a long nose, and a wild look in his eyes, was aghast when he found out that Rhynwick slept with men he said he did not know. This was indeed an "inference of horrid propensities, only too consentaneous with his recent practice."[16]

\* \* \*

On June 14, 1790, Rhynwick Williams was taken from Clerkenwell Prison to be examined before the justices Sir Sampson Wright, William Addington, and Nicholas Bond at the Bow Street public office.[17] The rumor that the Monster had been caught had spread like wildfire, and a huge, clamorous mob had gathered outside. Inside the public office was completely crowded with spectators, among them the duke of Cumberland. A cacophony of booing, shouts, and insults from the mob announced that the Monster had arrived, and two sturdy Runners, cordoned by several Bow Street patrols, accompanied the frightened little man in his threadbare blue coat to his seat at the dock.

Anne and Sarah Porter were the first to give evidence. In marked contrast to their earlier, vague descriptions of the culprit, they now declared themselves absolutely certain that Rhynwick Williams was the Monster who had attacked them. They also volunteered the damning evidence that, already before he had assaulted them on the queen's birthday, they had both known him by sight, since he had for some time been in the habit of stalking them in the streets and making indecent proposals.[18] Their younger sisters Rebecca and Martha had also been accosted by him. According to Sarah, his modus operandi was to walk closely behind them, with his head almost leaning over one of the girls' shoulders, all the while talking "the most dreadful language that can be imagined." With as much feeling, Rebecca and Martha Porter respectively described his conversation as "the most horrible language I ever heard in my life" and "the most horrid, dreadful words imaginable"; indeed, they had never heard this foulmouthed man utter a decent sentence.

Anne Porter had first seen the "Wretch," as he was known among the Porter sisters, a year and a half earlier. She was walking back to the bagnio with her sister Sarah when she felt somebody pulling her gown. She turned around and saw a small, big-nosed man. She stopped short, believing he wanted to pass them, but he stood as still as they did, looking at them. They believed that he was drunk, and hurried homeward, but the man followed them all the way to the bagnio door, using language so shocking she could not repeat it. Shortly afterward, as Anne and Sarah walked in Green Park, they saw the mystery stalker standing nearby, grinning at them. They ran home as quickly as they could, but the Wretch pursued them, using his

Figure 19. The Bow Street public office in 1808, plate from Ackermann's *Microcosm of London*. From the author's collection.

usual foul language. In the third incident, Anne Porter was walking in the Haymarket when the Wretch caught up with her and actually put his head over her shoulder and used the same coarse language as on their previous encounters.

In May 1789, Anne was walking in St. Martin's Lane with her sister Martha when she heard someone muttering behind her; she could make out enough of the words to form an opinion as to who was uttering them; sure enough, when she turned around, the Wretch stood grinning at her. Young Martha was very frightened, and they both sought protection with a gentlewoman who was passing along St. Martin's Lane, telling her who they were and that a strange man was following them with evil intent. She let them walk with her, but the stalker was bold enough to stand in front of them and laugh loudly in their faces. Anne Porter then thought they had managed to get rid of the Wretch, but when they got to the pavement of St. James's Street, they saw him racing along the opposite pavement to intercept them. They managed to reach Pero's Bagnio first, however, and immediately told their parents about their harrowing experience. Thomas Porter sent a servant in pursuit of the stalker, but the Wretch easily evaded him.

After this sensational evidence had been presented, John Coleman was called to testify. His account of his pursuit of the Monster was received with some derision, and it was noted that the young fishmonger had shown more caution than was perhaps necessary.[19] Numerous other victims were also called to give evidence, but their testimony varied widely. Miss Reynolds, the companion of Miss Toussaint, who had been cut the same evening as Anne Porter, said that Miss Toussaint's recollection of this incident was too vague for her to identify the culprit, but that she herself had seen him clearly, and he was definitely not Rhynwick Williams. Nor could three other women, whose names we do not know, point out Rhynwick Williams as the Monster. The magistrates must have been somewhat relieved when Mrs. Franklin boldly spoke up and positively identified Williams as the man who had insulted her with foul language on seven or eight different occasions.

Ann Frost, whose clothes has been cut by the Monster in November 1789, did not give the same good impression. There was much laughter in court when she demanded that a round hat be placed on Rhynwick Williams's head. "Whatever for?" asked Sir Sampson Wright. Ann Frost replied that, since he had worn a round hat when he attacked her, she could not swear it was him without it. The magistrate explained that the man's face should be more distinctive than the cut of his hat, and refused her request. Despite the absence of headgear, Miss Frost rather easily identified Rhynwick Williams as the Monster, although the attack had taken place seven months before, on a dark winter night.[20] The next witnesses were more prudent. Miss Elizabeth Baughan thought that Rhynwick Williams resembled the man who had cut her in December 1789, but he was not as tall as she had believed. Her sister Frances was more positive about his identity, and rather hesitantly swore that he was the Monster.[21]

Rhynwick Williams himself spoke only once during this interrogation: he said that he was an artificial flower maker, and that the time Miss Porter was cut, he had been working at Mr. Amabel Mitchell's artificial flower factory in Dover Street, where he had remained until nearly one o'clock in the morning. He thus had a clear alibi for the offense against Anne and Sarah Porter; if he had been allowed to do so, he would have brought Mitchell and his staff into the public office to serve as character witnesses and provide evidence that he had been hard at work at the time the Porters had been attacked in St. James's Street. However, he also volunteered the damning information that he had twice before "been challenged for the Monster, particularly once at the *Play-House*."[22] It does not give credit to the detection ability of the police and magistrates that this lead was, apparently, not followed up. It must have been quite an alarming experience to have been pointed out as the Monster in a crowded assembly room, but fortunately for Williams this incident, which can be traced through Mr. Angerstein's thorough chronology of the Monster's outrages, had happened quite some time before the proper Monster mania. He was identified by Miss Mary Forster, who had been wounded in September 1789.[23] He had been seized by friends of Miss Forster, but released after he had given his address. The other time Williams had been challenged may well have been the one reported in the *Oracle*: A man with an artificial nosegay was arrested after a girl had pricked her finger when she smelled it, but he had been able to show that the girl had in fact pricked her hand with the wire used to bind the artificial flowers together, and he was again discharged.[24]

Rhynwick Williams was extremely frightened when the time came for the prisoner's van to leave the public office. His fears were not unfounded, since the mob surged forward as soon as the carriage appeared. The Bow Street patrols had to form a cordon to keep them at bay, and the prisoner's van was quickly reversed back into the yard. At five o'clock, the patrols made another attempt to leave the public office, with many policemen on each side of the prisoner's van to ward off attacks. The mob charged nevertheless; according to newspaper reports, the immense crowd were so exasperated that they would have torn Rhynwick Williams from the coach and destroyed him if not for the courage and determination of the Bow Street patrolmen.[25] Even these brave constables, however, could not prevent a rotten vegetable from hitting Williams's face.

\* \* \*

On June 16, 1790, Rhynwick Williams was again brought before the magistrates.[26] Quite a crowd of victims were now present. The spectators were as numerous as the day before: among them the duke of Cumberland, the duke of York, Prince William of Gloucester, the earl of Essex, Lord Beauchamp, and many others of rank and fashion. The mob was again very much in evidence: according to the *World*, "Charles James Fox's coalition at the Hastings, and the Monster in Bow Street, were the two attractions of yesterday: and the crowds were immense."[27] According to another newspaper account, the duke of Cumberland was becomingly solicitous on the occasion, but the behavior of some of the others left much to be desired. The levity with which these individuals treated the proceedings, with many loud jokes and guffaws of laughter, was "neither creditable to their humanity or their GALLANTRY. It being the fashion to treat the affair with ridicule, has not been a little instrumental in shedding the blood that has been spilt, and exciting these outrages in a NEST of unnatural banditti that calls aloud for their extermination."[28]

Miss Aride, who had been abused and cut on Jermyn Street, was the first to give evidence. She told the usual story about a man who had stalked her in an attempt at seduction, then abused her with foul language. When asked by Sir Sampson Wright to point out the culprit, she declared that he was not there. Nor could four other of the victims positively identify Rhynwick Williams as the Monster: they either thought he was unlike the man who had wounded them or were unable to identify him due to fright or darkness (many of the attacks had occurred late at night).[29] Miss Toussaint, who had previously said that she could not recall her assailant at all, now appeared in the box, eager for her moment in the limelight. She said Williams much resembled the man who attacked her, and that he was the right height and size, although she could not swear that he was the Monster.[30] Nor could Charlotte Payne, the lady's maid of the countess of Howe, swear positively that Rhynwick Williams had been the man who had assaulted her before Lord Howe's front door. She thought that he very much resembled the culprit, although she was not positive. Here Williams, who was unaided by any counsel, made another damning admission: he "did not deny being in the place mentioned, and said the accident might have happened from something in his pocket."[31]

Next, plain little Elizabeth Davis was brought up. All accounts agree that she identified Rhynwick Williams as the man who had assaulted her, but they differ in important respects with regard to exactly *how* her identification had been staged. According to Williams, he had been standing in the yard, talking to a group of Bow Street patrolmen, about how he was to be saved from the mob, whose behavior was as threatening as the day before. Suddenly he heard from above the words, "Is that him without the hat?" Williams looked up toward a window to observe Elizabeth Davis with some of the Runners, who rewarded her with the words, "Yes, that is him, in blue and buff!" Williams wrote that, since his dress was quite different from that of the Runners, and since he was the only person present not wearing a hat, the identification of him as the prisoner would not have been difficult.[32] According to the *World,* Williams had been standing in the middle of the office with people all around him. Elizabeth Davis was asked to look around to see if anyone present resembled the man who had cut her, and "she immediately and without hesitation fixed upon the prisoner, whom, in the most positive manner, she swore was the man who wounded her."[33] It should be noted that Elizabeth Davis's original description of the Monster was as unlike Rhynwick Williams as it could be, and the query must be raised whether the Runners had decided to coach her beforehand.

Next Miss Mary Forster positively identified Rhynwick Williams as the man who had stabbed her in the thigh. She pointed him out among fifty other men, with the passionate words: "This is the man!—I'll swear to him!—nay more, if I were upon my dying bed, I would take the Sacrament this is the man."[34] Rhynwick Williams objected strongly to her identification of him. He claimed that on the day she claimed to have been attacked he had been in Weymouth, 130 miles from London. Runner Macmanus, who had virtually been Williams's neighbor when the latter had lived in Bow Street, could corroborate this story, since he had actually seen him there. This caused much consternation on the part of Miss Forster and the magistrates; the lady faltered and had to admit that she was by no means certain which day she had been attacked, and that it may well have been a week earlier.[35] She knew for sure it was on a Sunday, however, and that the attack had happened at about eight o'clock in the evening. Sir Sampson Wright then asked her how she could identify the man responsible at such a late hour. "From the bright lights in the shop windows," she replied. There was laughter in the court, since no shops were open Sunday evenings, and Mary Forster again had to retreat. The imprudent Rhynwick Williams did not deny that Mary Forster had later pointed him out as the Monster at the playhouse; indeed, he willingly admitted that this was the case and that, when taken, he had given his address as No. 36 Bow Street, where he had been living at the time.[36]

After Mary Forster had been bound over to give evidence, Miss Kitty Wheeler identified Rhynwick Williams as the man who had several times insulted her with foul language, and from whom she had once been rescued by the intervention of her father.[37] A poor, young servant girl next appeared; she was the one who had been stabbed near the eye with a knife concealed in an artificial nosegay. According to the newspapers, this girl was shockingly disfigured by the cut she had received. She thought Rhynwick Williams looked like the person who had wounded her, but she could not swear positively as to his identity, since three other ruffians had been in the Monster's company at the time.[38]

After this second session, the mob outside the police office was even more threatening than before; many tough-looking ruffians had armed themselves with stones and bludgeons. Runner Macmanus, a veteran of Lord George Gordon's "No Popery" riots in 1780, had a healthy respect for what an enraged London mob was capable of. He was unwilling to let the prisoner's van, containing the terrified Rhynwick Williams, run the gauntlet of the vicious crowd and waited for more than an hour before deciding to move. He ordered some Bow Street patrolmen to open the main doors; as the mob surged forward, Macmanus swiftly had the side gates opened, and the coachman whipped up the horses to pull out the prisoner's van. The mob pursued it, but patrolmen armed with long staffs acted as a rear guard and the van got a good head start. Suddenly, three men dashed out of a public house alerted by the shouts of "The Monster!"; they jumped up onto the running boards, where two Bow Street constables were riding, and tried to push them off. One of them reached inside the prisoner's van and grabbed Williams, who gave a terrified cry. The situation would have been a desperate one had not Macmanus, with admirable presence of mind, kicked the door open with great force. The attacker was forced to release his grasp and was catapulted off the vehicle. The others were also thrown off, and Macmanus shouted "Whip up, man! Whip up!" to alert the coachman of the danger. Driving at breakneck speed, they arrived safely at Clerkenwell Prison, and it was found that Williams had sustained no injury other than a swollen and bloody nose, which had come into contact with the woodwork of the carriage during the fracas. When the other prisoners saw that the Monster was injured, they whooped with delight.[39]

\* \* \*

On June 18, 1790, Rhynwick Williams was brought before Mr. Nicholas Bond, the sitting Bow Street magistrate, for a third and final time.[40] First, Mr. Joshua Williams, a relative of the prisoner who "appeared greatly interested in his favour," spoke as a character witness. His evidence had the diametrically opposite effect, however, since he declared on oath that he had often heard Williams say that he had chased women about town and abused them with obscene language if they refused to take him home and go to bed with him.[41]

As if this imprudent appearance from his kinsman had not been bad enough, Mrs. Sarah Godfrey, described by one journalist as "a Lady of uncommon beauty," was introduced by Mr. Bond to describe how she had been assaulted in May 1789. Williams was standing in a circle of more than thirty men, all wearing their hats, but Mrs. Godfrey pointed him out as the Monster with the words, "If it be any one in this company, this is the man." But when Williams removed his hat, she almost wanted to withdraw her identification of him, and said he looked quite unlike her recollection of the Monster. The magistrates promptly ordered Williams to put his hat back on; Mrs. Godfrey, relieved, now said that she had very little doubt that he was her attacker.

A third, resounding blow to Williams's flagging spirits came when Mr. Bond informed the court of the statutes of law under which he was to be committed for trial. At this time, there was a sharp distinction between felonies and misdemeanors. The former category consisted of "serious" crimes punishable by death or transportation; the latter were relatively milder offenses punishable by prison, the pillory, or a public flogging. Grand larceny, for example, was a felony; minor larceny a misdemeanor. More than two hundred crimes were punishable by death, but the felons often received a pardon. Murderers were of course hanged, as were hardened thieves, highwaymen, and street robbers; other felons were most often transported to a prison colony abroad. Common assault, even with intent to maim or kill, was a misdemeanor, and Williams and his friends had hoped that the Monster's crimes would be categorized as such.[42]

But, on the other hand the authorities were hard pressed to find a legal statute that made the Monster's crime a felony, since they feared a public outrage in London if he was charged with a mere misdemeanor. The Coventry Act, named after Sir John Coventry, whose nose and ears had been slit by the duke of Monmouth and his accomplices, made it a felony to lie in wait to maim and disfigure some person. But it could not be proved that the Monster had actually been lying in wait for his victims, and this Act was thus not applicable. The Black Act made it a felony to go armed while under disguise, and to shoot maliciously, but this was again not applicable to the Monster's crimes.

But the magistrates and judges had discovered an obscure statute from 1721. It had been intended to repress the activities of certain weavers who objected to the importation of Indian fashions that were purchased by the public in preference to the weavers' own goods. The weavers actually poured aquafortis on the clothes of people wearing these foreign fashions. To stop these outrages, it was made a felony, punishable by transportation for seven years, to "assault any person in the public streets, *with intent* to tear, spoil, *cut,* burn, or deface, the garments or cloaths of such person, provided *the act* be done in pursuance of such intention."[43] There had obviously been some debate among the judges as to whether the Monster should be charged under this statute, as the first case ever. Sir Peter King believed the statute was fully applicable to the Monster's crimes; other judges were hesitant, since the Monster had actually cut the clothes to make way to the flesh underneath.[44] Sir Peter quoted a case from the Lent Assizes for Suffolk, in which two men were prosecuted for having cut the nose of another. They were charged with deliberately cutting the nose with intent to maim and disfigure him, which was a capital crime. The men claimed, in order to escape felony convictions for disfiguring him, that they had cut his nose to kill him, the court convicted them nevertheless and they were both executed.

In the newspapers, there was much gloating that the Monster should be tried as a felon. One correspondent proposed that Williams was actually lucky to be considered a felon, since if he were put in the pillory, the mob would probably tear him to pieces.[45] There was no question of Williams being granted bail. Seven ladies (Anne Porter, Sarah Porter, Elizabeth Davis, Mary Forster, Frances Baughan, Sarah Godfrey, and Ann Frost) were bound over to testify against him. It was hoped that, if Rhynwick Williams was found guilty on each of the seven indictments against him, he would have to spend seven times seven years as a convict laborer at the Botany Bay penal colony.[46] When Williams, accused of having cut so many women, was taken back to Clerkenwell Prison, the other felons were disposed to cut *him*: not a single man would speak to the London Monster.[47] The prejudice against him was such that even his local member of Parliament found it necessary to insert the following notice in the *Times*: "The Party denies that the man taken as the Monster voted for Lord John Townshend in the late Westminster Election."[48]

The only newspaper to disagree was the *Morning Chronicle,* where a writer asserted that, although Williams might well be guilty, the descriptions of the Monster lodged by various victims disagreed in many particulars. The ruffian's hair color had been stated to be every shade from black to fair, and the reports of his height varied from the tallest to the most diminutive. Rhynwick Williams was perhaps just one member of a ruthless gang of Monsters, and the journalist urged that plans to establish a special anti-Monster police force should not be abandoned: "Let a proper association be formed: let proper regulations be adopted; and, where is the man of gallantry, humanity, or spirit, who will decline to wear the uniform?"[49]

# CHAPTER 7

# THE FIRST TRIAL

*It is of a Monster I mean for to write,*
*Who in stabing of Ladies took great delight;*
*If he caught them alone in the street after dark,*
*In their Hips, or their Thighs, he'd be sure cut a mark.*
   —*The Monster Represented,* an illustrated set of doggerel
verses published just after the first trial of Rhynwick Williams

ON July 8, 1790, Rhynwick Williams was to stand trial at the Old Bailey.[1] He arrived there in a wretched state, fearful of more rough treatment from the anti-Monster ruffians. As he cowered in one corner of the prisoner's van, he could see angry, red-faced thugs wave their cudgels at him, and hear men, women, and children scream abuse. He became even more frightened and dejected when he heard the boos and insults from the vicious mob standing outside the Old Bailey, baying for his blood. The Bow Street patrols again had to shield the trembling man from the mob as he was led toward the courtroom.

Williams's brother, the respectable apothecary Thomas Williams, had tried to help him arrange his defense, but it had not been easy to find legal counsel willing to represent the man accused of being the Monster. By the offer of a considerable fee, Thomas Williams had been able to recruit Mr. Chatham, a solicitor of renown, to handle Rhynwick's case. The day before the trial, after Chatham had met Rhynwick Williams and heard him speak, this gentleman threw down his brief and left, for undisclosed reasons.[2] Only in the nick of time did Thomas Williams manage to find another solicitor, Mr. Fletcher, and a barrister named Mr. Newman Knowlys, who was to argue the case. Although these two gentlemen were experienced lawyers, they had only one day to learn the case, and to infer from Mr. Chatham's sudden departure if nothing else, they must have suffered considerable prejudice against their notorious client. There was only one indictment: willfully and maliciously cutting Anne Porter's cloak, gown, stays, petticoat, and shift. The somewhat embarrassing fact that the Monster had cut not only the aforementioned articles but also the lady's buttocks was disregarded by

Figure 20. The Old Bailey Sessions House in 1790, engraving by J. Ellis. Reproduced by permission of the Guildhall Library, Corporation of London.

Figure 21. A late eighteenth-century interior from the Old Bailey. Reproduced courtesy of the Wellcome Trust.

the legal luminaries in charge, as was the fact that forty or even fifty women
had been assaulted in a very similar manner. Already before the trial, some
learned judges had been overheard to comment that the law had been
stretched too far to make the Monster a felon, and that this might result in a
backlash as soon as the trial was over.[3]

The judge at Williams's trial was Sir Francis Buller, Bart.[4] He had been
called to the bar in 1772, and in 1778 had become, at the age of thirty-two,
the youngest judge in England. His unfortunate assertion, at a trial in 1782,
that any husband could thrash his wife with impunity provided that the
stick was no thicker than his thumb, had caused some ridicule and inspired
James Gillray's amusing caricature *Judge Thumb*. Judge Buller had also
been accused of helping members of his family line their pockets from
public funds; this scandal had prevented him from being appointed chief
justice, but as a solace he had been made a baronet on January 13, 1790.

The mainstay of the defense Mr. Fletcher and Mr. Knowlys had prepared was that Rhynwick Williams had been at work at the artificial flower
factory when Anne Porter was attacked and well afterward. Rhynwick's
brother Thomas had ascertained that Amabel Mitchell and his colleagues
from the factory were ready to testify that this story was true. He had also
successfully located many acquaintances of Rhynwick Williams who were
ready to testify to his good character. Williams himself later claimed that
several women, namely, Miss Marlow, Miss Fenton and Mrs. Burney, were all
ready to give evidence that he was not the Monster who had wounded them.
Miss Reynolds, the companion of Miss Toussaint who was cut on January 18, was also prepared to testify that Williams was not the culprit.[5]
These ladies, however, were never called as witnesses, nor was any attention given to the fact that at Bow Street many ladies had declared that
Rhynwick was not the man who had cut them. It does not reflect well on
Williams's counsel that none of them was called to give evidence.[6] However,
one victim did volunteer to give evidence in Rhynwick Williams's behalf: the
notorious Lady Wallace came forward of her own accord and declared that
Rhynwick was not the man who had frightened her; she was prepared to
testify about this at any court of law. Thomas Williams thanked her very
much for her kindness and ushered her to her seat in the front row of the
courtroom.[7]

The head counsel for the prosecution was Mr. Arthur Leary Pigot, an
eloquent, highly talented gentleman who had thirteen years of experience
at the bar.[8] After his associate Mr. Cullen had read the indictment against
Williams and Williams pleaded "not guilty," Pigot opened the case against
the prisoner in ringing tones. During his many years at the bar, he said, he

had never seen a case blacker than this: the Monster business was "the most extraordinary case that ever called for the attention of a Court of Justice." Rhynwick Williams's "unnatural, unaccountable, and, until now, unknown offence" was "a scene so new in the annals of mankind; a scene so unaccountable: a scene so unnatural to the honour of human nature that would not have been believed ever to have existed, unless it had been demonstrated by that proof which the senses cannot resist."[9] It was, indeed, a melancholy lesson that no depravity and no unnatural offense, however atrocious, could be considered impossible and contrary to human nature: during this trial, he warned the court, they would have to listen to "enormities without any precedent."

Pigot went on to describe the Monster's assault on Anne and Sarah Porter on the queen's birthday. He treaded lightly when describing Coleman's pursuit of the Monster. When he mentioned that Rhynwick Williams did not lodge at the address given, but that his mother and sister did, many people seemed astonished that the Monster had female relations. Pigot went on to claim that Rhynwick's mother and sister knew very little of him. He described how, when John Coleman had finally managed to persuade Rhynwick Williams to go with him to Pero's Bagnio, Williams had been "unable to refuse it in the state in which he then was"—that is, he had probably been drunk.[10] Either he had been intoxicated already when pursued by Coleman or he had gone to some alehouse to fortify himself immediately after his escape from the fishmonger, only to have the bad luck to run into Coleman just after his drinking bout.

Pigot vowed to prove, without any doubt, that Rhynwick Williams purposely slit and cut the clothes of Anne Porter. He understood that Williams's counsel would attempt to prove an alibi, but he urged the jury to observe closely the testimony of the alibi witnesses and how much they could be relied on (hinting at possible perjury on their part).

Pigot's eloquent opening was the subject of much admiration. The *London Chronicle* found his address "as pathetic as it was humane"; the *Oracle* spoke of his "elegant exordium on the mysterious nature of the charge"; and the *New Lady's Magazine* admired his "very elegant language."[11]

*　*　*

*He met Miss Anne Porter, who chanc'd late to stay,*
*At the Ball at St. James's the Queen's last birthday.*
*Coming home with her sister Miss Sarah we find,*
*He struck Miss Sally's head, and cut Nancy behind.*

Anne Porter was the first witness for the prosecution. She was elegantly dressed in gray muslin and wore a veil as protection from the glances of Rhynwick Williams. Mr. Shepherd, another associate of Pigot, questioned her, and she recounted the details of the attack. When she had turned to see who had struck her, she had observed Rhynwick Williams stooping down. She had seen him three or four times before, when walking with her sisters in the middle of the day: "he insulted me and my sisters with very gross and indelicate language; he walked behind me and muttered." Because her attacker did not run away, but walked up to the top of the steps of the house next to the bagnio, he gave his victim an excellent opportunity to observe his face. Shepherd pointed at Rhynwick Williams and asked her: "Look at him as he stands—there—have you any doubt of that being the person that struck you the blow."

She answered: "No, Sir, I have not the smallest doubt; I could not have been positive, but I saw him three or four times before; I suffered so much from the insults I received, that it is impossible I could be mistaken; I could never forget him."

Anne Porter then brought out the clothes she had worn on the fateful evening of the queen's birthday; they certainly seemed to have been slashed by some very sharp instrument. Finally, she described how she had pointed Rhynwick Williams out to John Coleman, and how the fishmonger had returned to Pero's Bagnio with his prey.[12]

Williams's barrister, Knowlys, rose to cross-examine Anne Porter. He first asked her pardon if any of his questions might confuse her; he assured her that no man in this court could sympathize more with her sufferings and that his duty was the only reason why he questioned her at all. Williams later described how his heart had sunk within him as he heard this remarkable speech; it was now painfully clear to him that even his own legal counsel believed him guilty.[13] Knowlys's questions to Anne Porter were in a similar vein: polite, superficial, and easy to answer. In all her alarm and flutter, did she really have time enough to observe Rhynwick Williams? (She did.) Was there enough light in the street for her to see him clearly? (There was.) Anne Porter's clothes were again produced; when Knowlys suggested that her gown could easily be repaired, the injured lady replied, "No, Sir."

Miss Sarah Porter was sworn in as the second witness for the prosecution. Under Pigot's skillful direction she described how she had at least four times been stalked through the London streets by Rhynwick Williams, who had walked closely behind her "with his head quite leaning over my shoulders, and talking the most dreadful language, that can be imagined." It was easy for her to recognize him since he had impudently stared her in the face before shouting, "Oh ho! Is that you!" and striking her on the head. The street was very much illuminated, and she had also observed him at a closer distance when he ran up to her sister and struck her on the hip with his hand closed around some object.

Sarah Porter also told the court that she had observed Rhynwick Williams just a week before he had been taken into custody.[14] Sitting at work by the front window, she had observed Williams walking down St. James's Street. She called out to her sister: "Good God, Nancy, look over this way!" Anne Porter immediately came to the window and said, "There is the wretch that wounded me." They sent two men after Williams, but they had followed another man by mistake. Like Anne Porter, Sarah was perfectly certain about the identity of Rhynwick Williams as the man who had assaulted them; at Bow Street, she had pointed him out when he was standing indifferently in a crowd of people.

Knowlys again did not distinguish himself in the cross-examining: many of his questions were just echoes of Pigot's. He tried to make Sarah admit that there were many people in the street at the time of the attack, but she resolutely replied that there were very few. Next, Martha and Rebecca Porter testified that Rhynwick Williams had several times stalked them and their sisters in the streets. Knowlys objected as to the relevance of this evidence, but without success.

The fishmonger John Coleman next gave a lengthy, ruminating account of how he had pursued Rhynwick Williams through the London streets. He was certain that the man must have noticed that he was being followed, and that he was well aware for what offense he was being pursued; Rhynwick Williams had clearly seen Anne Porter point him out in St. James's Park, he said. Coleman boasted of his martial attitude during the Monster hunt:

I did every thing that laid in my power to insult him, by walking behind him, walking before him, looking at him very full in the face, making a noise behind him; I used every art I could to insult him, he would not take any insult, he never said a word, I followed him behind, and I behaved in this kind of way, (peeping over his shoulders, and making a clapping with my hands), and I was going to knock him down once or twice.[15]

It is not known how many were taken in by this feeble bravado.

Coleman also claimed that he had at first been prevented from entering Smith's house in South Moulton Street by its owner. Later, when introduced to Williams in the pitch-dark room, Smith had refused to fetch a candle until Coleman had insisted he do so. As soon as the room was lit up, Smith wrote down Coleman's address and also the name and address given by Williams.

To his astonishment, Coleman discovered that the two had actually met before; this was not denied by Williams, who asked if Coleman had not been introduced at a ball in Bond Street to which he belonged. Outside Smith's house, the two men went different ways, but Coleman fortunately changed his mind and managed to overtake Williams. Coleman had to admit that the Monster was a cool customer: when brought before the fainting Porter sisters, he "did not conduct himself in any particular way. I thought he possessed very great resolution in case he was the guilty man."

He had said, "Good God! I hope they do not take me for the person about whom there has been so many Publications," which was considered damning. But Coleman had to admit, at Knowlys's prompting, that Williams had not seemed in the least embarrassed or hesitant when they went to Pero's Bagnio.

Runner Macmanus was sworn in next. He recounted how he had gone to the George public house, which Pigot had described in such derogatory terms, and taken a coat, a hat, and a pair of boots from a box belonging to Rhynwick Williams. Interestingly, Macmanus had a personal knowledge of Williams, since the latter had previously lodged not far from the Bow Street public office, and he had himself seen Rhynwick Williams wear this coat. Knowlys made an effort to rehabilitate the landlord of the George, and suggested that, although these lodgings were not particularly expensive, the public house was a decent one, run by good people. "As good as any that keep a public house," Macmanus answered guardedly.

Knowlys had better luck with Rhynwick Williams's gray coat. It was evident that it was not, as had been previously alleged, a surtout coat; its fit was quite tight, even around Williams's slender frame. This fact threw suspicion on the Porters' identification of this garment as the coat worn over another coat by the Monster, but Knowlys made no attempt to pursue this advantage. Nor did he press the point that Macmanus had found no cutting implements at the lodgings of Rhynwick Williams or those of his mother.

Judge Buller himself asked the Runner a series of important questions. He wanted to rule out the possibility that the address Williams had given—No. 52 Jermyn Street—might apply to the George public house in Bury Street, a cross street to Jermyn Street. Macmanus replied that it did not, but that it might apply to Williams's mother's dwellings in Duke Street, another cross street. He was quite out of his depth to explain the topography of these streets, however:

"What number did the mother live at?"

"I do not know."

"Nor do you know what the number of the house was that you searched?"

"No."[16]

After the Runner had been dismissed somewhat petulantly by Judge Buller, Surgeon Tomkins was sworn in. He testified that Anne Porter's wound was nine or ten inches long, and that its middle part had penetrated the skin to the depth of three or four inches. Knowlys, who was becoming more animated during the course of the trial, asked him "Whether a cut with a sharp instrument, merely to cut the cloaths, would have wounded so deep as that." The surgeon answered in the negative: but for the bow of the stays, the wound might even have penetrated the abdomen. Knowlys turned his attention to Runner Macmanus, who again had to hold forth on the topography of Jermyn Street. He willingly admitted that the dwellings of Rhynwick Williams's mother had been at the corner of Duke Street and Jermyn Street, and that one entered through a door in Jermyn Street. He could not recall if it was No. 52, however.

At this point, there was a defection from the witnesses for the defense. Lady Wallace, who had come into court at her own initiative, offering to testify that Rhynwick Williams was not the Monster who had threatened her, called the counsel for the defense and said that the whole thing had been one of her little jokes. She had never been attacked or insulted by the Monster and was not prepared to give evidence. She would be pleased to retain her front-row seat at this fascinating trial, however, since it would be interesting to see the wretched little man being convicted.[17]

*   *   *

*The wound that he made in this young Lady's hip,*
*was Nine Inches long, and near Four Inches deep;*
*But before that this Monster had made use of force,*
*He insulted their ears with obscene discourse.*

After a brief recess, it was time for Rhynwick Williams to make his defense. One of his biographers wrote that "When it is considered what universal alarm the depredations of the man, denominated *The Monster,* have excited in the metropolis, need we wonder that the moment in which he is about to make his defence, should be considered an interesting one, by a splendid and numerous auditory! silence and attention pervaded every corner."[18] Rhynwick Williams was a disappointment, however. The small, big-nosed

RYNWICK WILLIAMS,
Commonly called
THE MONSTER!

Figure 22. Rhynwick Williams at the dock in the Old Bailey, drawing proposed to be by James Gillray, but "not by Gillray" according to a note at the Department of Prints and Drawings at the British Museum. Reproduced courtesy of the Wellcome Trust.

man in the shabby blue coat, who was the cynosure of all eyes, from those of the duke of Cumberland to those of the lowliest court servant, endeavored to speak from memory, but his shrill, thin voice did not carry; he soon lost recollection and was unable to proceed. He seized a bundle of papers and read the following pathetic speech:

My Lord, and Gentlemen of the Jury, I stand here an object deserving of your most serious attention, from conscious innocence of the very shocking accusations brought against me, I cannot but hope that just and really liberal minds will have reason to commiserate my situation, and must feel me deserving pity and compassion. As my case has been multiplied in horror, though, with submission, I think, in compassion, far beyond even the sufferings of my accusers, I admit in justice that I should have experienced the hardships I have suffered in the process of the law against me, till my innocence could be proved, but while I revere the law of my country, which presumes every man to be innocent till proved guilty, yet I must reprobate the cruelty with which the Public Prints have abounded, in the most scandalous paragraphs, containing malicious exaggerations of the charges preferred so much to my prejudice, that I already lie under premature conviction, by almost an universal voice, I chearfully resign my case into the hands of this tribunal, whose peculiar province and character is to reason on evident motives and circumstances, and which, I trust, will not suffer the fate of a fellow creature to be determined by popular prejudice. . . . I most seriously appeal to the Great Author of Truth, that I have the strongest affection for the happiness and comfort of the superior part of this creation, the fair sex, to whom I have, in every circumstance that occurred in my life, endeavoured to render assistance and protection. I have nothing, my Lord and Gentlemen, further to say, but that, however strange and aggravated this case may appear to you, I solemnly, and with the utmost sincerity, declare to you all, that this prosecution of me is founded in a dreadful mistake, which I hope the evidence I shall bring will prove to your satisfaction.

Williams sat down amid a torrent of hisses from the audience.

Next, the witnesses for the defense were brought in. Pigot and his associates were surprised to find that an entire crowd of people were prepared to give evidence on behalf of Rhynwick Williams. The first was his former employer, the Frenchman Aimable Michelle, proprietor of Mitchell's Artificial Flower Factory at No. 14 Dover Street.[19] Michelle had lived in London for four years, and had decided to anglicize his surname to Mitchell. His Christian name was a more difficult case; in newspaper accounts of the trial, he is variously referred to as "Amabel" or "Amarvel." Mitchell's prolonged residence in London had not induced him to speak proper English, however; he was such a poor linguist that he had to be interrogated through an interpreter.

At the direction of Knowlys, Mitchell testified that Rhynwick Williams had worked at the artificial flower factory for about nine months at the time Anne Porter had been attacked. His normal working hours were from nine in the morning until nine in the evening, but the evening of the queen's birthday, January 18, had been an exception. The factory had many orders for artificial flowers, and Williams had stayed at work until midnight. Mitchell then had the decency to offer his tired employee, who had been making artificial flowers for nearly fourteen hours, some supper; Williams finally left the factory at half past midnight. Mitchell was adamant that Rhynwick Williams had not been absent from his workbench at any time between two in the afternoon and midnight. He credited Williams with "the best character a man could have," and added that he had always treated the female workers with civility and good nature.

It was then Pigot's turn to cross-examine the Frenchman. Pigot expressed amazement at the booming business of the flower factory, which had forced Mitchell to keep Williams and several other employees at work nearly around the clock. Mitchell replied that a large order from Ireland had forced him to keep his entire work force doing extra hours for at least nine days before the queen's birthday. In addition, in the afternoon of January 18 he had received a last-minute order for a lady's gown to be decorated with artificial flowers, after three of his employees had sought, and obtained, permission to go out and enjoy the day's festivities. Mitchell himself, his sister, Reine Michelle, Williams, and two workwomen who lodged in the house had to finish this gown by the following morning. Here Pigot tried to bully the Frenchman into making an admission:

"Upon your oath, had not you and the prisoner at the bar been out that day together?"

"Certainly not."

"You had!"

"I had not."

Pigot then reverted to his former careful probing into the workings of the flower factory and the comings and goings of its staff, and in particular everything Mitchell could remember about what had happened during that evening half a year earlier, which the Frenchman appeared to recall so perfectly, in the hope of being able to shake the inscrutable Amabel's testimony, or at least to demonstrate contradictions in the other alibi witnesses that were to follow. Mitchell patiently told him that during the eight or nine months Rhynwick Williams had been in his employ he had been a model worker: he had never been absent from work, except once or twice when given leave. It was very rare that he was sent out on errands; on a typical day he just sat quietly at his desk, working on the artificial flowers. Pigot asked Mitchell whether he had looked at his watch or clock just when Williams had left the factory, since he was so sure it was exactly half past midnight. When the Frenchman replied that he had not, Pigot quickly challenged him: How could he then swear so positively that it was half past twelve at night when Williams left? Mitchell replied that his maid Molly had, at just that moment, heard the watchman cry out the time; she had remarked to her sister Catherine how well the flower factory clock in Mitchell's parlor kept the time, since it exactly agreed with the watchman's shout. Catherine later repeated this observation to Mitchell's sister Reine, who in turn reported it to her brother two or three weeks later.

Williams had come to work early the following morning and had remained with Mitchell's establishment until the fourth of June. The great order from Ireland for a massive amount of artificial flowers had come from a Mr. Crowe, apparently an artificial flower wholesaler who had come to London in person to bring the order. Mitchell's brother-in-law, Monsieur Jerseaux (alias Jerso), who was taking care of business at the factory while Mitchell was away, had written proof of all this.

Just as Pigot was ending his questioning, Lady Wallace, who was still sitting among the witnesses for the defense, sent a scribbled note to the prosecutor. Its contents were startling: the day before, she had been accosted by a strange, threatening man in Green Park, and later outside Lord William Gordon's house in Piccadilly.[20] She was certain that this man, or rather Monster, was none other than Amabel Mitchell! Pigot immediately went in for the kill. Did the witness know Lord William Gordon's house? Yes, he had been there. Had he happened to pass this house, or pass through Green Park, yesterday evening? The bemused Mitchell replied that he had not.

"And all the rest that you have sworn to-day, is just as true as the last, that you were not in Green Park yesterday evening?"

"Just as true."

"Then, not being in Green Park, I need hardly ask you whether you accosted any ladies in the Green Park yesterday evening."

"No, I did not accost any ladies in the Green Park."

"Or near Lord William Gordon's house?"

"I was not near that way."

Pigot ended his cross-examination by calling out, in a menacing way, "Let that witness not go out of court!" He intended, of course, to call Lady Wallace as a witness, and thus win a brilliant legal victory: he would not only incriminate Mitchell as the possible accomplice of the Monster but also discredit his entire testimony. But when he asked Lady Wallace to testify, she flatly refused: Again, this had been one of her jokes, and she was delighted it had been taken so seriously.

\* \* \*

Mlle. Reine Michelle (alias Miss Raines Mitchell), the flower maker's sister, was sworn in next. Examined by Mr. Knowlys, she confidently testified that, on the evening of the queen's birthday, Rhynwick Williams had been at work from dinner time until twelve o'clock, and that he had not left the factory until half past midnight.[21] His behavior toward her and the other female workers had always been perfectly good-natured. Mr. Shepherd next took over the cross-examination. Raines Mitchell echoed her brother's testimony: the flower factory had had a great deal of work for several weeks, and at six o'clock on the queen's birthday came an order for a gown for the celebrated actress Mrs. Abingdon, who was to wear it the night after the birthday.[22] Mr. Jerso had come to the factory with a pattern of floral decoration that Mrs. Abingdon had given him, and Amabel Mitchell ordered his workers to set about making the flowers and pasting them onto the dress. Of the normal work force of at least eleven people, only Rhynwick Williams, the sisters Mary and Catherine Alman, Frances Beaufils, and Typhone Fournier had been available to finish the work on the gown, and both Amabel and his sister had to help as well. With his own hands, Amabel Mitchell had pasted Rhynwick's artificial flowers onto the gown. Raines Mitchell repeated her brother's story about the maid Molly's comment about the clock. When Rhynwick Williams had been taken as the Monster, the Mitchells had gathered their servants and workers to see what they recalled about the night Anne Porter had been attacked. Molly then told her story about the watchmen and the clock. Probably impressed by Rhynwick Williams's alibi, Judge Buller demanded that Mr. Jerso be called as a witness, and an officer was to accompany Amabel Mitchell back to the flower factory to get his books of trade.

In the meantime, the forewoman Catherine Alman, sister of the maid Molly, was sworn in.[23] Interrogated by Knowlys, she verified Amabel Mitchell's story in every respect: she was absolutely certain that Rhynwick Williams had been at work in the flower factory from two o'clock P.M. until half past twelve on the queen's birthday, and that he had not been absent one moment during this time. Her sister had told her that, at the time she opened the door to let Williams out, it was half past twelve, and she was equally certain about the date. It was her convinced opinion that Williams was a very good-natured man, very sober and attentive in his habits. Under Pigot's cross-examination, she maintained that she could well recollect that her sister had come into the workshop where they had dined, saying that it was half past twelve o'clock, and that she was afraid Williams might be too late to get into his lodgings. At the time, Williams was lodging with Mr. Williams, the china seller, in Duke's Court, not far from the flower factory. Amabel Mitchell, his sister, and the workman Typhone Fournier had been present when Molly told them about the watchman, the clock, and the time being half past twelve. (Pigot here sensed a contradiction, but the witness calmly told him that she had spoken in English, a language the French workers did not normally speak, and they probably did not understand her. Normally, the conversation in the flower factory was in French, but Molly was a bad linguist like her employer, and preferred to speak English whenever possible.) After Molly had shut the door after Williams, she had come straight back into the back shop and made the remark in question. Catherine Alman had not remembered this until Rhynwick Williams had been taken up in the Monster, but then she remembered it perfectly. She also recalled that the following morning Williams had told her that he had managed to get into his lodgings after all, and that the clock had struck one when he finally went to bed.

Molly Alman was the next witness for the defense. Questioned by Knowlys, she repeated her sister's testimony almost verbatim. Shepherd then took over the questioning. The strength of Williams's alibi was surprising, but this witness did not appear to be particularly clever, and he took considerable care in examining her testimony. Molly Alman had been with Mitchell for one or two months at the time. Contradicting her coworkers, she claimed that Rhynwick Williams never stayed late at work, and that the longest she had ever observed him stay was on the day in question. She had been in the workshop all afternoon but did not observe anyone come in to deliver an order. At Judge Buller's prompting, she later corrected herself and said that Jerso had been at the factory at about four in the afternoon, but she had not paid attention to what business he was about. Nor could she recollect Amabel Mitchell leaving the factory for any period of time. She, Rhynwick Williams, Amabel Mitchell, and his sister had worked on a gown all evening: there had been no other people in the room at the time.

Shepherd then moved on to the most important point of all: the time Rhynwick Williams had left the flower factory. Molly Alman declared that just as she had let Mr. Williams out, *he had asked her to look at the clock*.

Shepherd asked her why Williams could not have looked at the clock himself, but she simply replied that he told her to look. Her sister Catherine had
appealed to her about three weeks before to recall the events of the queen's
birthday, at the time when Rhynwick Williams was taken up as the London
Monster. She admitted that she had told her sister that she had looked at
the clock because Williams had asked her to do so, and for no other reason.
She also denied that she had, at any time, said that she was afraid Williams
would be late back to his lodgings.

The workwoman Frances Beaufils was next to give testimony. Questioned by Knowlys, she testified that she had been employed at the flower
factory six weeks before the queen's birthday on January 18. She had been
working there that day until half past eleven, and Rhynwick Williams (a
very good-natured man) had been there the entire time. She knew the time
because she had asked the watchman when she got home in Coventry Court
(off Coventry Street near the Haymarket) and he had told her it was half an
hour past eleven. Cross-examined by Pigot, she said that Amabel Mitchell
had not been out at any time after two o'clock. Neither had, she said, any
order for a dress come in during this period of time; nor could she remember Jerso having made an appearance.

The Frenchman Typhone Fournier, next on the witness stand, agreed
with his coworkers that Williams was a very good-natured man and that he
had been at work at the factory until at least eleven o'clock in the evening.
But Fournier had only worked for Mitchell's flower factory from Christmas
1789 until February 14, 1790, a fact that seemed to imply an unusually high
turnover rate for Mitchell's work force. At about eleven o'clock, Fournier
had left the factory to go to his lodgings off Great Windmill Street; he left
Rhynwick Williams still at work. In a faltering way, the Frenchman swore
that Amabel Mitchell himself had also been at work from two in the afternoon until late at night. Shepherd then cleverly made him swear that he was
just as sure about Amabel Mitchell's whereabouts (which directly contradicted Mitchell's own testimony) as he was about any other circumstance,
and Fournier readily obliged.

Runner Macmanus and Townsend next returned to the court, together
with Amabel Mitchell and his colleague Jerso. Jerso was questioned by
Knowlys, and testified that he had certainly called upon his brother-in-law
Amabel Mitchell on the queen's birthday to give him an order for a gown for
Mrs. Abingdon; he had drawn the pattern for it at Mitchell's house at some
time after seven o'clock that evening. Mitchell himself had been out at
the time, and Jerso was not even sure that he had come home an hour
later, when Jerso had visited the factory to see how the work on the gown

was proceeding. The entry for this gown was in the books, just as Amabel Mitchell had predicted.[24]

\*   \*   \*

*She met with this Monster one day in the Park,*
*As she walk'd with Mr Coleman, who notic'd the spark,*
*She told him how much from this wretch she'd endur'd*
*So he follow'd the Monster, and had him secur'd.*

After the alibi witnesses were done, not less than seventeen character witnesses testified on behalf of Rhynwick Williams. Sarah Brady, a former flower factory employee, had known Williams for six months and pronounced his character to be very good-natured, with no single instance of a spiteful disposition. Sophia Cameron, who had known Rhynwick Williams not less than eight years, and who had later worked five months at the flower factory, also pronounced him "truly good-natured." Pigot, who was apparently mystified by Williams's ways and the company he kept, did what he could to emphasize the prisoner's shady past. He asked Miss Cameron if she had known Rhynwick Williams when he lived with Sir John Gallini, but she gave a noncommittal reply, evidently understanding that this was a somewhat unsavory topic. A Mr. Terry, who worked in the navy office, and in whose house Rhynwick Williams and his family had previously lodged for a year, also gave the prisoner the "most amiable character for good nature, amiable behaviour and politeness." Williams had left Sir John Gallini some time before Terry met him in 1786. Williams had then had no other work except to assist his sister in making artificial flowers, and Terry had often seen him sitting hard at work late in the evenings. The next character witness, Thomas Williams, a respectable china seller in St. James's Street, was quick to point out that the prisoner was no relation. He had known Rhynwick Williams for nearly six years, and the prisoner had lodged in his house at one time. Thomas Williams pronounced Rhynwick a very good-natured young man; his main fault was that he "liked the ladies too well" (an admission that provoked laughter in court). When asked how Rhynwick Williams had earned his bread during the intervening period of time between working for Gallini and Mitchell, Thomas Williams replied, "I know no more than you."[25]

Another character witness, Sarah Seward, of Seven Dials, a plain, inelegantly dressed woman, swore that she had known Rhynwick Williams four years and that he was an honest, young man, for he had once *saved her life*! This statement did not have the desired effect, however. Miss Seward may have appeared ridiculous in her dress or person, or it may be that the idea that the Monster had saved a woman's life appeared exceedingly funny to the audience; it remains a sad fact that there was a great laugh in the courtroom, and Pigot and the other prosecuting counsel heartily joined in. Sarah Seward retreated from the witness box in confusion, amid lewd laughter and insults from the more rowdy members of the audience.

Rhynwick Williams was particularly indignant about the brusque treatment of Sarah Seward. In a later treatise he wrote that, although she did not possess "a silver toned voice, a delicate painted face, nor habited in white muslin, nor declaiming the fashionable cause of the day," she deserved better treatment. He contrasted the laughter at her expense with the great empathy and compassion shown to the Porters and their apparent sufferings: "while telling their tale, did they excite a laugh? Was the audience merry then? No! no! no! certainly not!"[26]

Many other character witnesses followed, and according to the newspaper reports, they often had precious little to say about the elusive Rhynwick Williams. William Baker, in whose house Rhynwick had lodged for four months, had nothing to add except that he believed the prisoner to be an honest young man. According to one of the pamphlets about the trial, a certain Mr. Smith (perhaps the man of mystery from South Moulton Street?) "produced nothing in addition to the character of his old acquaintance, whatever might have been his intention." This was also the case for James Sterling, another character witness.[27]

Many in the audience were shocked that several beautiful women appeared in court to testify to Rhynwick Williams's fondness for women. Their testimony is not contained in any transcript of the case, but one pamphlet writer sneeringly remarked that "*several* young women, whose appearance, however, did not bespeak them of the highest class, but rather of the inferior kind" had appeared in favor of the prisoner.[28] One journalist in the *Oracle,* however, wrote approvingly of these "very beautiful females," and considered that their testimony had proved to everyone's satisfaction that, far from having any aversion to the female sex, Rhynwick Williams was "in habits of fond, constant, and manly intercourse with them."[29]

\*   \*   \*

Judge Buller then addressed the jury.[30] He presumed that every person in the crowded audience knew about the London Monster and his heinous crimes. Considering the prejudice any honest man must feel who entered a court where such issues were discussed, he strongly urged every member of the jury to totally disregard everything they had heard about the Monster before they had entered the Old Bailey: they should disregard all prejudice and consider the case with patience and attention.

Buller reminded the jury that all four Porter sisters were well acquainted with the Monster's appearance: according to their testimony, he had stalked them through the streets on several occasions, and there was little chance they were mistaken as to his identity. The judge ruminated at length about the assailant's uncouth way of making himself known to Sarah Porter: "Oh ho! Is that you!" was a particularly vulgar and distasteful expression, truly befitting a Monster. It surely indicated that the Monster had previously met the Misses, and that the circumstances of their meetings had not been amiable; it thus served to support the Porters' testimony that Rhynwick Williams had previously stalked them. The judge also emphasized the fact that Williams must have known that he was being followed by John Coleman, and that he made several attempts to dodge his pursuer, a circumstance in itself indicative of guilt. He then recapitulated the great fainting scene in the front room of the bagnio—"a more distressful or melancholy scene could hardly be exhibited"—and the fact that Rhynwick Williams was himself the first person to suggest that they took him for the London Monster. When Coleman had affirmed that this was the case, Williams had said nothing and did not attempt to clear his name. These were all circumstances that gave additional credence to the testimony of all four Porter sisters, who had identified him without reservation.

Buller then discussed the testimony in favor of the prisoner. Not less than seven people had appeared to give Rhynwick Williams an alibi for the evening in question. It was evident that Mitchell had gathered his servants and work force in June, after Rhynwick Williams had been arrested as the Monster, to try to recollect what had happened on the queen's birthday and how long Williams had stayed at the factory. The judge considered this not very reliable evidence, with ample opportunity for a mistake with regard to the date, time, and other circumstances. Amabel Mitchell's testimony did not have the same candid appearance as that of the Porters, and there had been some contradictions: in particular, the stories of the sisters Molly and Catherine Alman disagreed in several important particulars.

Buller left it to the jury to decide which side to believe: the artificial flower makers, who swore that Williams had been at the factory at the time Anne and Sarah Porter were attacked (in which case he must be pronounced "innocent") or the positive testimony of the Porter sisters, who identified Williams as the Monster. If they decided to believe the Porters, the next thing to consider was intent. If Williams had intended to cut Anne Porter with intent to murder, he must be innocent, for this was not a felony but a mere misdemeanor. On the other hand, if he had cut her with intent to cut and tear her clothes, then he was a felon according to the 6th Act of George I, and must be punished accordingly. The judge then made the important admission that he himself had some doubts about this indictment, and whether this ancient statute was really the proper one: if Rhynwick Williams was found guilty, he intended to reserve the case for the consideration of the Twelve Judges of England. In the meantime, the jury should consider whether it might indeed have been Rhynwick Williams's intent to cut both the clothes and the flesh: in that case, he must be found guilty as charged. He cunningly pointed out that the instrument used by the Monster was of a particular construction, both very long and very sharp, and that the witnesses had said that their clothes were extremely badly cut. It was of course impossible to strike Miss Porter's person without cutting her clothes, but the damage to the clothes was certainly much worse than could have been expected. He left them with these words: "I can only leave the case, on both points, for your consideration; it is for you alone to discuss, and pronounce the prisoner, GUILTY or INNOCENT; as you shall judge the truth of the case to be."

The jury immediately pronounced Rhynwick Williams guilty as charged. Judge Buller recommended that the sentence was to be respited until the December sessions, for the opinion of the Twelve Judges to be heard in the meantime.

*    *    *

*On the Eighth of July, at the Old Baily try'd*
*After Eight Hours hearing the Jury decide*
*That he was found Guilty, but sentence defer'd*
*Until the Twelve Judges opinion is heard.*

Just at the time Rhynwick Williams had been arrested, John Julius Angerstein finally finished his pamphlet about the Monster. Intended as a complete handbook for the prospective Monster hunter, it contained a detailed summary of all Monster attacks until May 1790; his modus operandi in each case was reviewed, and the description of every victim recorded as to his dress and appearance. The pamphlet, *An Authentic Account of the Barbarities lately practised by the Monsters! Being an unprecedented and unnatural Species of Cruelty, exercised by a set of Men upon defence-less and generally handsome Women,* also contained a brief pen portrait of each of the victims, since Angerstein thought that "a description of the person of each of the fair victims of this novel species of barbarity must be interesting." He would also be certain of a considerable number of subscribers among London's women.[31]

The great clamor over the arrest of Rhynwick Williams made Angerstein's pamphlet obsolete before it was even published. Indeed, although it was advertised in the papers,[32] it is unlikely that any were actually printed, since Angerstein soon saw fit to revise it to include a couple of lengthy chapters about the arrest and trial of Rhynwick Williams. In spite of all the work he put into it, Angerstein did not think it fitting to put his name on the front page. This revised edition was not published until late July, and by that time the market was already saturated with Monster books.

As was the case after the numerous, infamous court trials of our own time, several publishers decided to make money out of the Monster mania and published accounts of the crimes and trial of Rhynwick Williams. The first of these publications, *The Remarkable Trial of Rhynwick Williams,* had been taken down in shorthand by a student in the Temple and quickly printed to be on booksellers' shelves at noon on July 9, the day after Rhynwick Williams had been found guilty. This student was probably dismayed to see that someone else had had the same idea; later that day, another pamphlet entitled *The Trial of Renwick Williams* made its appearance. Its contents had been taken down in shorthand by L. Williams, Esq. and had the advantage not only of low price (one shilling) but also an engraved portrait of Rhynwick Williams "taken on the spot by a capital Artist." It was cleverly advertised all over London with huge posters labeled "The MON-STER" which mimicked Angerstein's posters.[33]

Two more pamphlets appeared shortly afterward: the anonymous *Authentic Trial of Rhynwick Williams* and the *Full Account of the Trial of Renwick Williams,* written by Mr. Nath. Jenkins. Mr. E. Hodgson, the official shorthand writer of the Old Bailey, was completely overwhelmed by his numerous and mercenary competitors. Although he and his publishers did what they could to make haste, his *The Trial at Large of Rhynwick Williams* was not out until July 13. Published newspaper advertisements warned the public that "as there are spurious and Catchpenny trials now publishing, to be particularly careful to order E. Hodgson's *Trial at Large,*" but he lost sales nevertheless. Hodgson's pamphlet is by far the most extensive as well as accurate account of the trial, and the only one that gives the testimony of the alibi witnesses verbatim. It was illustrated with an excellent print of Rhynwick Williams at the bar of the Old Bailey. In spite of its competition, it is, along with the Williams volume, the most common Monster pamphlet one finds today. Hodgson's pamphlet was the only one to carry the Monster mania across the Atlantic: an American edition was printed by Thomas Greenleaf in 1791 and sold by the bookseller Andrew Marschalk in New York.[34]

The trial of Rhynwick Williams also inspired another spate of satirical prints. Already on July 9, two good likenesses of Williams, by Nixon and (possibly) Gillray (see pp. 96, 109), could be purchased in the print shops. *Representation of the Monster,* which was published on July 12 by W. Dent, is a good indicator of the amount of prejudice against Rhynwick Williams. This caricature had several frames: one depicted a villainous-looking Rhynwick Williams on trial at the Old Bailey; another showed him prowling about in one of his disguises; the grand scene of Williams cutting the Porter sisters was in the middle. Its text boldly states that Williams should be hanged, not transported, since the latter punishment would give him an opportunity to exercise his cruelties on the women of another country. In another of Dent's prints, *Spanish Rupture,* the Monster takes a hand in politics as he assumes the form of Prime Minister William Pitt. He dashes his diabolical nosegay into Britannia's face with gusto and stabs her in the behind with his rapier. A violent diarrhea has burst his breeches; the torn parts are inscribed "Sudden—War." The rival politician Charles James Fox stands aghast, calling out to Britannia that, had she trusted to him for protection, he would have "put you on such a BOTTOM that none would have dared to insult you." (Pitt had been unjustly accused of truckling to Spain over the Nootka Sound affair, and this was but one of the several satirical prints lampooning him.)

Angerstein's revised book was quite outmatched in terms of sales by this unexpected competition. His thick pamphlet of 166 pages cost two shillings and had no illustrations. Along with Hodgson's *Trial at Large of Rhynwick Williams,* however, it is by far the best account of the Monster mania and Williams's arrest and trial. Angerstein was *the* expert on the Monster business, and it is particularly interesting to read his opinion of the case. At the time he was writing, he was apparently not entirely convinced that the right man had been convicted. He was very much impressed with the solidity of Williams's alibi, which had, after all, been sworn to by seven different witnesses. The contradictions in their stories could be explained by the fact that the foreign witnesses gave their evidence through an interpreter and were unable to explain or correct any mistakes or mis-

Figure 23. Rhynwick Williams at the dock in the Old Bailey, drawing by Nixon. Reproduced by permission from the British Museum.

Figure 24. *Representation of the Monster*, satirical print by W. Dent that is a good indicator of the amount of prejudice against Rhynwick Williams. Williams is depicted on trial (right) and prowling around in one of his disguises (left), with the grand scene of his cutting the Porter sisters in the middle. It was published in the interval between the two trials, while the Twelve Judges' opinion was awaited. Its anti-Monster author boldly agitates that Williams should be hanged, not transported, since the latter punishment would give him opportunity to exercise his cruelties on the females of another country. From the author's collection.

Figure 25. *Spanish Rupture: The Monster—The Guardian*, print by W. Dent. Prime Minister William Pitt is depicted as the Monster, dashing his diabolical nosegay into Britannia's face with gusto and stabbing her in the hip with his rapier. The rival politician Charles James Fox looks on aghast, calling out that had she trusted to him for protection, he would have her on such BOTTOM that none would have dared to insult her. Pitt had been unjustly accused of truckling to Spain over the Nootka Sound affair, and this was but one of the several caricatures lampooning him. Reproduced by permission from the British Museum.

conceptions that might have occurred. Angerstein also queried why Mrs. Miel, the Porters' chaperone, and their brother John, who opened the door to them, had not been called as witnesses; how could the prisoner's counsel have allowed this to happen, since their testimony was of the utmost importance?[35] The editor of the *Rambler's Magazine* shared Angerstein's doubt about Williams's guilt, claiming that many Londoners who had attended the trial were impressed by his alibi: there were "serious apprehensions entertained by many, that the ladies have mistaken the person of their inhuman assailant."[36]

Angerstein was also convinced, from the dissimilarity of the descriptions of the culprits, that "there are SEVERAL of these *unnatural wretches,* these inhuman MONSTERS, ... or rather *creatures in the shape of men,* a disgrace to society, the outcasts of the creation." Moreover, he was certain that these unnatural men were in league with one another. He particularly noted an article from the *Morning Chronicle* of June 25 which related that a man had been apprehended in Birmingham for deliberately wounding a woman there. It was said that he had been identified as a Londoner, and that he had fled the metropolis because of the measures taken by the authorities to bring to justice the *accomplices* of Rhynwick Williams.[37]

*   *   *

As Rhynwick Williams sat in his cell in Newgate Prison, he is likely to have been the most wretched man in London. Already before he had been arrested as the Monster, his existence had not been enviable. He had been penniless, with hardly any friends; indeed, he had been shunned even by his own relatives and lived under the most dismal circumstances with not even a bed to himself. Now he was the most hated man in London. Had the mob not been restrained, anti-Monster ruffians would literally have torn him to pieces. Newgate served him as a safe haven rather than a prison. There were calls in the newspapers to have him hanged, flogged, pilloried, or at least transported, but most people seemed content to let him rot in prison. Sir Sampson Wright and the other magistrates were much relieved to be rid of the Monster that had put the metropolis into such turmoil.

Angerstein, meanwhile, received congratulations from his many new friends among London's women, satisfied that he had been right all along: there really *had* been a Monster, and Angerstein had been instrumental in his apprehension. The exultant John Coleman could not wait to get his hands on Angerstein's reward money, and the swooning Porter sisters shared a sigh of relief to be saved from their monstrous assailant. Although

RENWICK WILLIAMS
*commonly called*
THE MONSTER.

Figure 26. Rhynwick Williams cutting a lady, print issued just after the first trial.
Reproduced by permission of the Guildhall Library, Corporation of London.

Figure 27. Drawing of the Monster attacking the Porter sisters on the (nonexistent?) steps of the Bagnio, with doggerel verses underneath. A cheap print issued just after the first trial to cash in on the ballyhoo about the Monster. Reproduced by permission from the British Museum.

seven people had sworn, upon oath, that Williams had been elsewhere at the time of the assault on Anne Porter, he had been convicted by a unanimous jury; not even his own legal counsel had believed in his innocence. He had been dragged through the streets to be jeered and pelted by Londoners celebrating the end of the Monster's reign of terror. Had there ever been a man in need of a doughty champion, that man was Rhynwick Williams.

# CHAPTER 8

# THE MONSTER'S CHAMPION

*I loath my own and every wedded wife—*
*I'll drag connubial secrets into day,*
*Stranger myself to all domestic peace,*
*Distracted matrons my revenge shall fear—*
*With phrase obscene I'll wound each delicate ear—*
*Infants with screams my furious threats shall hear,*
*And never shall my efforts cease*
*'Till I have agonized each College dame*
*Blasted her comfort—sneered away her fame—*
*My great revenge shall laugh her griefs to see*
*And RHYNWICK WILLIAMS' self shall be outdone by me!*
*—Theophilus Swift,* Prison Pindarics *(1795)*

IT MUST have come as a surprise to the Londoners when, in September 1790, as Rhynwick Williams was languishing in Newgate, the Irish poet and controversialist Theophilus Swift appeared as his champion. In a startling pamphlet entitled *The Monster at Large,* he advanced the theory that Rhynwick Williams was innocent and that the real Monster was still free and unpunished. He also claimed that the Porter sisters and John Coleman were a gang of imposters who had deliberately planned Williams's arrest and subsequent downfall.

Theophilus Swift was born in 1746, the son of Deane Swift of Dublin, an Irish gentleman of some fortune and a descendant in a collateral line from Jonathan Swift. Theophilus was educated at Oxford, and graduated with a bachelor of arts degree in 1767. He was called to the bar at the Middle Temple in 1774 and practiced law for a couple of years. In 1783, his father died, and Swift inherited his estates in Limerick. A forthright, eccentric character, he spent a good deal of time in Dublin and became involved in much controversy.[1] Nichols's *Literary Anecdotes* tells us that a Captain

Ayscough, a timid military man with literary ambitions, was several times insulted by Theophilus Swift, who treated him as a poltroon.[2]

Swift married an Irish woman, with whom he had many heated quarrels. He himself later wrote that "I am the quietest, best-tempered man, but she was a very termagant." Once, when Swift teased her by reading aloud a lewd and satirical poem he had written about "The Female Parliament"[3]— insane women who imagined themselves equal to men—his wife seized up their son, young Deane Swift, from his cot, and took a swing at her tormentor. Many years later, Theophilus still remembered the resounding knock as his head met that of his son in full swing. After this incident, he decided that he and his wife would do much better living apart.[4]

It took until 1789 for Theophilus Swift to become more widely known. That year, Colonel Charles Lennox challenged the duke of York to a duel after they had a heated argument in the regimental mess room. The two exchanged shots at Wimbledon Common, and Lennox's bullet grazed one of the duke's curls. The duke then fired in the air. Afterward, he refused to say that Lennox was a man of honor and courage, apparently firmly convinced to the contrary. Swift took great exception to this scandalous duel. In a pamphlet entitled *A Letter to the King on the Conduct of Colonel Lennox,* he blackguarded the colonel as "a hot-headed young man, who had conceived his own polluted person insulted by Royalty."[5] He even advanced the audacious theory that Charles Lennox was a secret agent in the employ of Prime Minister William Pitt, on a mission to murder all George III's sons: this attempt on the duke's life was just the first in an intended series of assassinations masked as duels. As a result of this pamphlet, Charles Lennox, son of Lord Charles Lennox and grandson of the duke of Richmond, challenged Swift to a duel.

It took considerable courage for anyone to face up to a man like Charles Lennox, a tough, ruthless character who fancied himself a crack shot. This was something like a Wild West rookie accepting a challenge from Billy the Kid. Swift, from sheer obstinacy if nothing else, nevertheless went through with the duel. His shot missed but Lennox's did not: Swift was hit in the belly, and he was several times thought close to death. According to a contemporary account, both gentlemen had behaved with great coolness and intrepidity during the duel.[6] While recovering from his bullet wound, Swift wrote another venomous pamphlet.[7] In his own words, "When confined with the wound I received from Lenox in the cause of my country, nothing gave me so much pleasure as writing the charming little pamphlet I published on the occasion."[8] He spread the rumor that he had originally wanted to fight with swords, but that Lennox had preferred pistols; had they

Figure 28. *Essay on Duelling*, satirical print by Collings, issued July 10, 1789. Colonel Lennox, brandishing a pair of murderous looking pistols, shoots Theophilus Swift in the stomach with one of them and shoots a curl off the duke of York's head with the other. The startled duke exclaims, "There goes the best part of my poor head!" The prince of Wales stands far right, armed with blunderbusses, rapiers, and pistols, saying, "Never mind your head I am your corps de reserve. George Hanger, in the attitude of a pugilist, says, "Blast my eyes I'll tip him Ward's damper in no time at all!" Reproduced by permission from the British Museum.

fought with swords, Swift would have carved the colonel like a turkey, he boasted. He even hinted that as soon as he recovered from his bullet wound he would challenge Lennox to another duel—with swords—but the *Times* acidly remarked that the colonel would have the choice of weapon if challenged, and "Mr Swift, we believe, has *had enough of that.*"[9] Swift had obviously hoped to gain some preferment by his quixotic adventure, but all he received were the duke of York's compliments and condolences.[10]

In the same year, 1789, Swift made the acquaintance of Rhynwick Williams, whom he later described as "a very ingenious artist and my particular friend." Although Williams's profession was, at the time, that of an artificial flower maker, he was also an excellent engraver and had a remarkably good hand at a frontispiece; Swift claimed that he several times employed him in these capacities.[11] Swift was much surprised when he saw Williams's name in the newspapers after he had been arrested as the London Monster. The exact motivation for him to appear as the Monster's champion, however, is unclear. It may be that he felt inclined to defend his old acquaintance, but this is not particularly likely, since they were by no means close friends. Another possibility is that Williams's respectable brother Thomas had paid Swift to defend him. In his pamphlet, Swift particularly denied that the apothecary had had anything to do with it and stated that he had not been bribed to defend the Monster; if one knows his character, this is in itself an indication that the accusations in question might well be true.

The most likely explanation is that Swift did it all for self-serving motives, or for the sheer fun of it. He wanted to outrage the mealy mouthed, sanctimonious Angerstein and his fellow Monster hunters. A male chauvinist even by the standards of the day, he felt free to attack the characters of the victims, and to enjoy the ribald aspects of the Monster's crimes to the full. He also wanted to keep his own name before the public after his attack on Colonel Lennox the year before; meddling in the Monster business seemed a certain way to achieve this. Swift rather fancied himself as a satirical pamphleteer: "Writing is my Hobby-horse—speaking also I am fond of—Reading is too dull for me. I have always been thought to have remarkable talents for Satire, and thank God I have never hid them in a napkin."[12]

*     *     *

In the beginning of his pamphlet *The Monster at Large,* Swift emphasized that he was not defending the Monster; Swift's only purpose was to prove that this arch-villain, still on the prowl, was not Rhynwick Williams. Well knowing the unpopularity of his cause, he expected that he would soon share Williams's sad fate in being shown with horns and other monstrous attributes in the print shops, but this did not stop him in his quest for the truth. He depicted Williams as a poor, helpless, illiterate criminal whose counsel had been his only hope. Swift was outraged by the way Knowlys had let Williams down through a feeble defense. Knowlys had even apologized to Anne Porter for defending his client, thus indicating his own belief in Williams's guilt, something Theophilus himself would never have done. Swift contrasted Pigot's flowing oratory with Knowlys's faltering efforts; had Pigot's eloquence been employed to defend Williams, instead of most fatally to accuse him, Rhynwick Williams would certainly have been acquitted. Knowlys had committed a serious mistake when he had not called Mrs. Piel and John Parker as witnesses: had he done so, Swift asserted, they would have testified that Williams was not the Monster, and it would not even have been necessary to establish an alibi.

According to Swift, Williams was the victim of another, deadlier monster—the one known as Prejudice. Such was the feeling against him that the Runners had barely been able to shield him from the mob after the examinations at Bow Street: "To what country is our Virtue fled? Where has Humanity taken her flight? Has Reason, has Religion altogether forsaken us? Let us no longer boast the light of the present age, in which a man, *before he has been tried,* with difficulty escapes to Newgate; and finds, in a Land of Freedom, his best asylum in a Jail."[13] The authorities had played along with the popular feeling against Williams, and were glad to punish the first man who had fallen into their hands to end the Monster mania. The law had been stretched beyond its limits to make Williams a felon, and Swift had a field day ridiculing the odd charge made against him: he could just as well have been indicted on the Window Act of William III for peeping up Miss Porter's petticoats, or on the Tobacco Act for smuggling Mrs. Miel.

Swift claimed that Sir Sampson Wright himself was convinced that Rhynwick Williams was not the London Monster; nor had the Bow Street Runners ever suspected Williams in any way. He had had occasion to examine the various accounts of the trial (all partial and badly written, he claimed) as well as the testimony given by the Porters at Bow Street and the complaint lodged by their father just after the assault. It is a great pity that he does not reproduce, or at least properly abstract, this latter document, which is clearly of the greatest interest. In his long and rambling narrative, Swift refers to it from time to time, and claims that Anne Porter had never, at that time, indicated that she knew the Monster or that this individual had been in the habit of stalking her and her sisters. Instead, she said that the assailant was probably a pickpocket who had tried to cut her pocket open but misjudged his strike. Importantly, Swift also claimed that the description of the Monster in Thomas Porter's original complaint did not match Rhynwick Williams at all. The Porters had described him as thirty years old (Williams was twenty-three), six feet tall (Williams was five feet, six inches in height), with fair or very light brown hair (Williams's hair was "as black as Coleman's conscience," according to Swift), very thin (Williams was stoutly built, Swift claimed, although the available portraits do not support this), and with an ugly, prodigiously large nose (not even Swift could explain away Williams's prominent "smeller," but he elegantly added that it was cast in a Grecian mold).[14] Although the Porters had originally sworn to the identity of another man—the real Monster—as the man who had attacked them, Angerstein's reward had tempted them to change their story and implicate Rhynwick Williams.

Swift had also found several contradictions between the Porters' account of the Monster at Bow Street and their testimony at the Old Bailey. First, Anne Porter at Bow Street said that she had seen Rhynwick Williams following them very closely in St. James's Street before he struck her; at the Old Bailey, she swore that she did not see him until after he had cut her. Also, and more strangely, both Anne and Sarah Porter had sworn at Bow Street that Sarah was struck on the head in front of the bagnio itself; at the Old Bailey, as in the original report, they swore that she had been struck at the bottom of St. James's Street. At Bow Street, Swift claimed, Anne Porter had said that she had observed her sister Sarah "change colour" at the Monster's approach. But the time was after eleven o'clock at night, and it was feared, Swift said, that this part of her tale would be "*too high-colored*" for the Old Bailey, and the "cunning minxes" gave "*a new complexion*" to the story, the alteration of color became merely an "agitation." At Bow Street, Anne Porter had also rashly sworn to the identity of Rhynwick Williams's coat as that worn by the Monster, but at the Old Bailey, it was clearly demonstrated that this close-bodied coat bore no resemblance to the greatcoat that fell across the shoulders of the Monster and even covered another coat under it, according to Anne Porter herself.

What were the conditions of light in St. James's Street, and had it been possible for the Porters to identify the Monster on the night of the queen's birthday? To see for himself, Swift went to the "Bagnio of Shame" on the evening of the birthday of the prince of Wales, when the streets were brightly illuminated. With him was his son, the seventeen-year-old Eton student Deane Swift. Swift found that the front of the old bagnio "does not advance itself; it modestly retires; it goes back, as all such houses should." The houses on either side had large bow windows, and however brightly lit the street was, these windows put the entrance in deep shade. Swift asked Deane to stand in the position supposed to have been occupied by Anne Porter, and he himself stood where the Monster had taken his stand after the assault (exactly where this was, he did not state). Deane Swift protested that, had he not known his father's face and figure, he would not have known who stood there. The two changed positions, and the situation was the same, according to Swift, although this was in August, when the streets were much brighter than they had been in January on the queen's birthday.[15]

It had been used as an argument in favor of the guilt of Rhynwick Williams that no women had been assaulted after he had been taken into custody. Swift pointed out that, at the height of the Monster mania, many ladies had falsely declared that they had been assaulted; he went on to claim that "many are *now* wounded, who fear to acknowledge it." The victims, incapable of independent thought, were ashamed to swear to any other man after Williams had been convicted as the Monster: "There may be two *Monsters,* but they know there never can be two *The Monsters.*" Nevertheless, Swift had found two cases of women being attacked in a way rather resembling the Monster's modus operandi, both occurring after Williams had been arrested. One of these concerned Mary Sudbury, a servant of Mr. Holden, a whip manufacturer in St. Sepulchre's Yard. Late in the evening, a man had made a stab at her hip with a sharp instrument, but she was saved by a large cellar key she kept in her pocket. She could not describe this man in any way. A rather more sinister tale was that of Miss Zubery, of Old Palace-Yard. Since the arrest of Williams, this young lady had been attacked by the same man not less than seven times, and wounded during four of these assaults. The first attack had, according to Swift, taken place "four days after the dastard Coleman had received the first wages of his cowardice." According to Miss Zubery, his appearance much resembled the original Monster of Angerstein's posters, both with regard to his build, the color of his hair, and the size of his prominent nose. His behavior, also, had resembled that of the Monster who had attacked the Porters. During one of the attacks, he had shouted, "Oh ho! I know you!" and stooped down to look into Miss Zubery's face as he struck her.[16]

\*   \*   \*

The arguments presented this far are nothing but reasonable; had they been brought up in the Old Bailey, they would have caused consternation among the Porters, and may well have shaken the jury's conviction that Williams was the Monster. Theophilus Swift was not a controversialist for nothing, however; as in the Lennox affair, he saw matters only in black and white, and if Rhynwick Williams was innocent, his accusers must be villains of the blackest hue. Some of the arguments that follow must have seemed almost as ludicrous to Londoners of 1790 as they do to the modern reader; it must be remembered that they were written by a man who had, the previous year, accused the prime minister of Great Britain of a conspiracy to murder the entire royal family.

In his pamphlet, Swift drew a picture of Williams as an honest, innocent, prejudged man, torn from an aged and weeping mother to stand trial for a loathsome series of crimes. He was dragged in irons before a hostile mob that jeered him as "The Monster." Swift claimed that Williams was a manly, forthright, and chivalrous character; after all, he had saved the lives of two women. He recounted the pathetic story of Sarah Seward, who had once been saved from drowning by the valiant Williams and who had been so shamefully treated during the first trial. He added the story of Mrs. Smith, the matron of Magdalen Hospital. Sometime in 1788, Mrs. Smith had been taking a stroll in St. George's Fields. Suddenly, she fell down and sprained her thumb, and was unable to proceed further. (Swift leaves unexplained how such a calamity could have deprived her of the power of locomotion.) The noble Williams found her, picked her up, and carried her a considerable distance to a nearby house. The grateful matron afterward took an interest in Williams and always called him her "son." Swift considered it a physical impossibility that a man capable of such worthy, humane acts as these would be the inhuman, brutal Monster, even if fifty ladies swore to his identity.[17]

Swift went on to admit that Williams had lived a vicious life for the past four or five years. He was obsessed with sex, and his self-indulgence in this respect had "not only hurried him into expenses of which he repents, but into excesses of which he is heartily ashamed."[18] He never saw a beautiful woman without approaching her with his wicked wishes. Sometimes, he was successful; other times, his chase was fruitless. In one of his dreadful puns, Swift commented, alluding to the tale of Mrs. Smith who had been carried to safety by her noble rescuer, that such was Williams's constant attachment to the female sex that when no young women chanced to come his way, he instead *picked up* an old one. But Williams had repented of his wicked ways. To save money, he had moved out of his old lodgings at Bow Street and into the alehouse where he was sharing a bed at the time of his arrest. Exactly how he was employed, if at all, after leaving the artificial flower factory was again unstated; Swift was content with commending Williams for his thrifty way of life.

Mr. Martin, the keeper of a respectable hatter's shop in Chandois Street, informed Swift that Williams, at the time he was apprehended, was in the course of paying him one shilling a week of a debt he owed; a tailor named Barrington had his bill discharged by the same mode of payment. This was made possible only by Williams's finding cheaper lodgings, and that was why he had moved to the George public house. Swift was particularly outraged by the groundless insinuations of some newspapermen that Williams was a homosexual simply because he slept in the same bed as another man. This had just been another of the thrifty young man's money-saving schemes; in fact, all the beds at the George were so occupied by their penniless tenants.

After having spoken to Williams and his brother the apothecary, Swift obtained quite a different version of the events that had led to Williams's arrest.[19] Williams had certainly observed Coleman following him through the streets, but he had taken little notice of him since he had "presumed him to be a catamite." Coleman's various gestures of offense, and his strange way of walking immediately behind Rhynwick Williams, shouting "Buh!" in his ear, and clapping his hands, had been taken as an attempt at seduction. Swift commented that it was quite natural to believe such a person to be one of the "Beasts of Gomorrah." When he himself met with this kind of behavior in the streets of London, he used to lay about him with his stick, so he could not blame Williams for his decision to ignore the buffoon cavorting around him.

Swift then went on to scrutinize Coleman's story of his pursuit of the Monster. Coleman had reported that Williams had looked very steadfastly "up a house"; this was another *untruth* by the fishmonger, however, since Williams had in fact been looking "into a house" through the window, hoping to see his mother and sister there. Such, exclaimed Swift, was Williams's affection for his female relations. Coleman was also very much mistaken to presume that Rhynwick Williams had attempted to enter Mr. Williams's china shop in St. James's Street in order to escape his pursuer: in fact, he had come to speak to Mr. Williams about his prospects of finding employment. Swift also lambasted Coleman for his story of the other fishmonger who had joined in the hunt. Who was he? Why had he not given evidence? The whole story had to be a lie, since it was impossible to find another fishmonger as cowardly as Coleman! Had anyone else been there, he would have arrested the Monster on the spot and dragged him into the bagnio, instead of behaving like a buffoon.

Williams had then repaired to a house in Moulton Street, but not, as Coleman had presumed, in order to escape his pursuers. Williams had in fact visited a "fille-de-joie" of his acquaintance who lived on the first floor. Coleman stated that he had remained there for three or four minutes, and Williams himself maintained that he had stayed there five minutes; the sources thus agree that his rendezvous with the Moulton Street prostitute had not been a lengthy one. Swift does not dwell upon exactly what may have occurred there, but he took the opportunity to praise Williams for his manly love for the opposite sex. The fact that Coleman, when he knocked on the door, received no information about where Williams had gone was airily explained away: Men who visited "nuns" living in the "first floor" were not in the habit of using "visiting cards." (The epithets "nun" and "vestal" were, in these days, euphemisms for "prostitute.")

Swift went on to describe Coleman's valorous conduct at the rails of the house of "Mr. Pearce" in Vere Street. The house, however, was not owned by anyone of that name, but by a respectable merchant named Mr. Pearson. Swift visited Pearson and was informed that Williams had approached Mrs. Pearson with the request that she would offer for sale in their shop a quantity of ornamented "chip hats" manufactured by Williams's own hands. (Such was Williams's devotion to the female sex and its proper adornment.) Swift had also spoken to the mysterious Mr. Smith, who had come to the Old Bailey to testify about how Coleman had entered his house in pursuit of Williams; the muddled Knowlys had not called him, however, and only employed him as a character witness. Smith emphatically denied that he had in any way prevented Coleman from entering; in fact, he had himself invited the timid fishmonger to come in. Coleman had not accused Williams of being the Monster but merely said, with "indications of a mind labouring with Guilt and Cowardice," that Williams had several times insulted some ladies of his acquaintance and that he wanted the satisfaction of a gentleman. Again, Coleman's veracity had been cast into doubt, Swift wrote: "To say that Coleman was a witness as pure, and unexceptionable as Mr Smith . . . would be as absurd as if it should be maintained that the Abortion of Manhood were the Perfection of Human Nature; or that Miss Porter herself were the Flower of Nun's Flesh."[20]

Theophilus Swift wrote that the fact that Williams had come back to Pero's Bagnio with the fishmonger without resistance was another clear indication of his innocence. Williams was, he claimed, an accomplished boxer, and men of superior boxing skill were not apt to take fire at every "gesture of offence" that a street buffoon or something worse may chance to practice. Even at "the Door of Prejudice," the entrance to the bagnio, it was within Williams's ability to make papier-mâché of a better man than Coleman.

Just before they reached the bagnio, Rebecca Porter and one of her sisters crossed St. James's Street with Coleman's brother; they rushed back into the bagnio to report that the fishmonger was returning with his prey. This, Theophilus claimed, would have given the Porters ample time to prepare Williams's reception at the bagnio. So little notion had Williams of where the fishmonger was leading him that he was quite surprised when he saw the inscription over the door they were about to enter. "What here? Why this is Pero's Bagnio!" he said, according to Swift. In other words, he meant, "Is it here you bring me? Sure you don't want me to fight for the Girls of *this* house?" About the fainting scene inside Swift was scarcely less eloquent: the only species of "fits" exhibited by these ladies were of that sort that are known by the name of "counterfeits."[21]

\*   \*   \*

Swift went on to accuse the Porter sisters and John Coleman of having staged an elaborate conspiracy against the innocent Rhynwick Williams. Pigot had treated the court to "a most pathetic and distressing picture of a bleeding lady, attended by a train of sisters, weeping, fainting, terrified!" but in reality, the sisters were nothing but a gang of conniving minxes who had deliberately and wrongfully accused Williams of being the Monster to lay their hands on Angerstein's reward. This philanthropic gentleman's exertions to capture the London Monster, Swift wrote, had only led to Williams's downfall and filled the pockets of the conspirators Anne and Sarah Porter and their dismal accomplice, John Coleman: "Or was it the *Poverty* of Mr Angerstein that bribed the Valor of Coleman, and purified the Veracity of his Mistress?" Even if Angerstein would devote the remainder of his life to philanthropy, this would not repair the injury to society caused by his disastrous meddling in the Monster business. He was not the only one to offer a reward, and Theophilus speculated that Anne Porter and her lover Coleman had earned not less than fourteen hundred pounds. He went on to make the startling claim that the departure of Mr. Chatham, who had been employed as Williams's counsel, had been because Angerstein had applied to Chatham's law partnership and threatened to withdraw his business if Chatham did not abandon his client. Mr. Fletcher had been the only solicitor prepared to disregard Angerstein's threats: "For myself . . . I had rather possess the *Humanity* of Mr Fletcher than the *Gold* of Mr Angerstein. It was Gold that conducted the pious Æneas through a *world of lies*."[22]

What, then, had prompted Anne Porter to set her eyes on poor Rhynwick Williams as the victim of her evil plot? In fact, Theophilus claimed, the two knew each other ten times better than she was willing to admit. He boldly stated that Anne Porter had once had an illicit affair with "Captain" Crowder, "who, though he might not enjoy the rank of Captain, was nevertheless a Soldier of honour, and a distinguished member of the honourable gang of street-robbers that recently infested Westminster." Anne Porter had once eloped from the bagnio and spent several weeks in the arms of this "captain." She was finally dragged back to Pero's Bagnio by her father, in deep disgrace. After Captain Crowder had been arrested, he was sentenced to be "dropt into another world," but the sentence was finally mitigated to transportation. Theophilus Swift claimed that the brazen hussy Anne Porter had visited him several times while he was held in Newgate, before embarking on his one-way journey to the Antipodes.

Like many young men about town, Williams knew about Anne Porter's past indiscretion. In his usual pursuit of cheap sexual thrills—"it was seldom that he saw a beautiful woman, to whom he did not lay siege"—Williams had several times approached the Porter sisters. In particular, he tried to seduce Anne Porter, but she was always disdainful toward him. Finally, he said, "Madam, I do not see that my person is not as good as the Captain's, with whom you went off from the bagnio." This insult highly enraged Miss Porter, and when Williams afterward renewed his attempts, his advances met with nothing but "oppobrious appellations." Anne Porter called him a rascal, a wretch, and a scoundrel. Williams replied by calling her a whore and a bitch. For this insult, Swift claimed the vindictive, malignant woman never forgave him. Driven by "two of the most infernal passions that ever debased the human mind, AVARICE and REVENGE," she had decided, there and then, to denounce him as the Monster when the opportunity arose.[23]

In Swift's pamphlet Anne Porter and her family came in for a torrent of abuse. She was something of a social climber: unwilling to admit her humble background, she had claimed to have been present in the ballroom on the night of the queen's birthday. Swift heavy-handedly reminded her that "the *Ball-room* is appropriated to persons of *one* description; the *Gallery* to persons of *another*. It is sufficient to say, that Miss Porter has not yet been introduced at Court."[24] He went on to claim that it had been inappropriate of Judge Buller to allow the Porters to wear veils during the Old Bailey trial: the reason was not to shield them from the unwelcome stare of Rhynwick Williams, but to "conceal the changes which the emotions of guilt may happen to throw up on the female cheek." He made some ribald comments

128 CHAPTER 8

about the depth of Anne Porter's *décolletage* at the Old Bailey: surely it had influenced the jury in her favor! He was something of a classical scholar, and could well remember the story of how the "Pigot of Athens," the silver-tongued Hyperides, had defended the "Miss Porter of his day": when his arguments failed to impress, he snatched the veil from his client's bosom, and this "well-timed oratory, this silent rhetoric" won over the court. Surely, it had also been a highly inappropriate, not to say indecent, moment when she displayed her damaged petticoat: "has the display of a *Shift* nothing moving or persuasive in it? Does it conceal no *Magnet of attraction*? Have the wounds which it covers no *Center of sympathy*?"[25]

Swift claimed that Pero's Bagnio, the Porters' home, had a very low reputation indeed; it was little better than a common brothel. Both sexes were admitted promiscuously, and the place was a well-known haunt of prostitutes. Swift went on to claim that the Porter sisters, "The Nuns of the Bagnio," were resident prostitutes in this tavern of ill-repute. He ridiculed Anne Porter's fainting fits with the words "Miss Porter is not apt to faint at the approach of a man." Many a classical quotation and many a heavy-handed pun was brought to bear on Pero's Bagnio and its unfortunate inhabitants: "The question has been asked, Whether any man may take a *Fille-de-Joye* into Pero's Bagnio? The answer is this: I do not know whether you may *take* a Fille-de-Joye into the Bagnio, but I know that you will *find* one in it."

Swift made much of Anne Porter's unwise statement (or perhaps rather of her father's evidence given on her behalf at Bow Street) that she had observed Williams from the "steps" of the bagnio's front entrance; in fact, there were no steps to this door:

It is not necessary to *ascend* the Bagnio of Beauty, although the Beauty of the Bagnio has *sworn,* that you approach it by "steps"; and that for a man to enter it, he must "walk up to the top of them!" The reverse turns out to be the *truth:* whoever enters *that* Bagnio, DESCENDS to go into it.[26]

\* \* \*

Theophilus Swift also grossly insulted the fishmonger John Coleman: He was called "a *Dastard*," "a *Frog-blooded Coward*," a "*Despicable Buffoon*," and "*Miss Porter's Puppy*," with an added quotation from "an old poet":

That cow-hearted Coleman,
Pray, is he a half-man, or is he a whole-man?

It was rumored, Swift claimed, that after his successful part in the Monster business, Coleman had risen from his plebeian calling as a fishmonger to become the hackney writer of an attorney. Swift made another tasteless pun about the fishy smell of this "Pimp of the Law." A quotation from *Hamlet,* too, was brought to bear on the luckless Coleman:

POLONIUS. Do you know me, my Lord?
HAMLET. Excellent well: you are a Fishmonger.
POL. Not I, my Lord.
HAM. Then I would you were so honest a man.

The other victims did not escape Swift's abuse: several of them were roundly accused of being harlots bribed by the fiendish Porters to aid in their conspiracy against Williams. Mary Forster, "one of the Greffe-Street Vestals," had lied to Macmanus about the date she had been cut but later conveniently changed her story. Ann Frost, another "daughter of sanctity," had also perjured herself at Bow Street. Kitty Wheeler, who had positively identified Williams as the man who had insulted her, and who had been saved from the Monster's attack by the intervention of her father, was "*another* Tavern-Vestal in St. James's Street." Piling sensation upon sensation in one of his footnotes, Swift went on to claim that "The character of this Vestal is said to be as pure as that of her Sister, who slept in the arms of Molloy, the Highway-man, on the night before he was apprehended." The father of these sisters of ill-repute, "Parsloe" Wheeler, was an arsonist who had burned down his own tavern to get the insurance money; he had then implicated an innocent boy, who was transported for life.[27]

Surgeon Tomkins received his share of Swift's ire due to the excessive sense of propriety in his report on Anne Porter's wound, which led the bold Irishman to question exactly what part of her body was injured. At Bow Street, he had placed her injury at the thigh; at the Old Bailey, at an unspecified region "higher up." Swift speculated at length about the anatomy of Anne Porter's thighs and pelvic region, and found it most likely that she had been cut in the buttocks. With his usual caddishness, he considered it a shame that "the Captain," who must have been in the know, had not been examined to give his opinion of the anatomy of Anne Porter's private parts. From the surgeon's inept description, Williams must be more than a Monster, "whose *Instrument,* through Shift and all, could penetrate *four inches* into a *Virgin!*"[28] More relevantly, he questioned why the surgeon had appeared at all, since Williams was not on trial for assault, but for willfully cutting and tearing Miss Porter's clothes. Surely a tailor should be employed as an expert witness in such a case, not a medical practitioner.

In Theophilus Swift's pamphlet, the low morals and malicious false-hoods of the victims were contrasted with the impeccable, spotless behavior of Rhynwick Williams's alibi witnesses, who had come into court tutored only by Truth and uninfluenced by any hopes of reward. The Porter gang had threatened them, Swift claimed, and sworn that the bread would be taken from their mouths and those of their families; but the loyal, uncom-plaining artificial flower makers still appeared in court to testify. At the Old Bailey, Amabel Mitchell and his staff had come through their ordeal at the hands of Pigot with flying colors, despite the fact that the interpreter was partial and tried to mislead them: "Perjury they leave to the idle, the dis-solute, and the debauched; to *Coal-men* and to *Porters,* whose hearts the music of a *Bribe* alone can soften, and whose consciences acknowledge no Monitor but *Revenge.*"[29]

Swift claimed that it had been the height of fashion among the feather-brained, easily led ladies of all ages and all social classes to claim that they had been wounded by the Monster. The reason for this was, of course, that the Monster was presumed to attack only well-bred, beautiful ladies; in-deed, it was something of a social ostracism *not* to have been given atten-tion by him. Like a flock of sheep, the ladies had followed one another to swear against Williams and enjoy their day in the limelight as among the dreadful Monster's lovely, tearful victims.

Mr. Sybley, the turnkey of Newgate, had told Swift an amusing story. A woman of decent appearance had called on the turnkey to get a view of Wil-liams *before* she went to swear that he was the Monster who had wounded her. The turnkey, a man of ready wit, asked her to sit down, then went to fetch one of the other prisoners, who was to impersonate the Monster. At the sight of this prisoner, she called out "Aye, aye! You are the man: I know you, you villain: it was you who wounded me, and I'll swear it in any Court of Justice!"[30]

*   *   *

Theophilus Swift's pamphlet caused quite a furor. His theories were quoted with respect in the *New Lady's Magazine,* previously a firmly anti-Williams periodical, and it was acknowledged that Williams must be the innocent victim of a conspiracy.[31] One of the London debating societies went so far as to propose the question, "Did the late extraordinary conduct ascribed to Rynwick Williams (commonly called the Monster) originate in an unfortu-nate Insanity—a diabolical inclination to injure the Fair Part of the Crea-tion—or in the groundless apprehensions of some mistaken Females?" Monster hunters, Monster victims, and a leading lawyer with strong opinions on the case (perhaps Swift?) were promised to be in the audience.[32]

There was also a spate of newspaper articles in response to Swift: some claimed that Williams had been falsely accused on the basis of mistaken identity, and that his actions when arrested were certainly not those of a guilty man; others criticized the indictment under which he had been made a felon; still others were outraged by Swift's vile insinuations against the Porter family.[33]

Although the Twelve Judges of England were not scheduled to meet until November 1790, it was becoming increasingly clear that the Monster's offense could not, under any circumstances, be considered as falling within the statute in question. This meant that Williams should not be considered as a felon, but face a retrial for misdemeanor at the sessions of the Peace at Hick's Hall. He was no longer in danger of being transported; the maximum punishment for a misdemeanor was imprisonment.

According to a scurrilous rumor, Williams had decided to celebrate this unexpected victory in a singular manner.[34] He sent fifty cards of invitation to his various relatives, the alibi friends, numerous other prisoners, and "other night hawks of varied trades." At four o'clock one afternoon, this large party sat down to tea at the prison. Afterward, two violins struck up, accompanied by a drum and fifes, and the Monster's Ball began. In the merry dance, the cuts and entrechats of the Monster were much admired. At about eight o'clock in the evening, the company sat down to dine, and a sumptuous meal and a variety of wines and spirits were produced. At nine, the guests departed, since this was the usual hour for locking up the prison. In the newspapers, the Monster's Ball was deplored as brazen and vulgar; it was considered a sign that Williams must have friends (or even accomplices) in high places that this degraded being could revel in such a way while still a prisoner. The *British Mercury* found something mysterious in the Monster's extravagance and dissipation and suspected that some character of opulence, as well as depravity, must be the mastermind behind the entire business.[35] The *Times,* a perhaps more reliable source, commented that "The paragraph inserted in several morning newspapers, of Rhynwick Williams having given a ball and entertainment to several people in Newgate, is without the smallest foundation. His friends are sufficiently unfortunate without having such idle reports to increase their uneasiness."[36]

Swift's comment, as eloquent and punning as ever, was that he rather regretted that Williams's case did not constitute a felony: "An airing to New-Holland, I had considered as preferable to an Airing in New-gate, or preferable perhaps to a more elevated Airing in another place. Poor Williams is at sea again. Madam Prejudice is once more his Pilot." He further recounted Williams's plight: "When the Bloodhound REVENGE snuffs his prey, and FALSEHOOD fastens on the Game which PREJUDICE has started, the Law becomes the snare of Innocence, and Justice is but a gin in the hands of the unlicensed Poacher."[37]

*   *   *

On November 10, 1790, the judges finally met at Serjeant's Inn Hall to discuss whether the indictment against Rhynwick Williams was within the statue regarding the willful cutting of clothes. Nine of the judges present considered that, notwithstanding the verdict of the jury at the Old Bailey, the offense of Rhynwick Williams was not within this statute, and that the indictment was bad in point of form. Williams would thus face a retrial at the Hick's Hall Sessions House for the misdemeanor of willfully and maliciously cutting people with intent to kill and murder them.[38]

On December 8, 1790, Williams was again put to the bar at the Old Bailey. Judge Ashurst ordered him to be discharged of a felony, but detained him to undergo a new trial for a misdemeanor. Williams then produced a manuscript and read a pathetic speech. Theophilus Swift was his only friend in a world full of enemies, he said. In his pamphlet, this learned gentleman had pointed out the weaknesses of the case for the prosecution in no uncertain manner. "Good God! for what am I reserved?" he called out, wringing his hands, "without friends, without money . . . to stand another trial against those who *reward has enriched,* and whose cause has made friends of all men." He went on: "My Lord, I stand an instance of singular misfortune, that while my passion for the sex had nearly ruined me, a sanguinary charge of a nature directly opposite should complete my destruction."[39] According to the *Argus,* a pro-Williams publication, the accused delivered his speech with much energy, and made a lasting impression.[40]

# CHAPTER 9

# THE SECOND TRIAL

*But the Monster now is fast—*
*Thus when surly Winter's past*
*See the primrose deck the vale,*
*Hark, the music of the dale;*
*See, what crouds of nymphs appear;*
*Cheeks, no longer pale with fear;*
*Assignations, long suspended,*
*And by conscious night befriended;*
*Scandal and quadrille renew'd . . .*
*—W.H., "The Monster," in the* New Lady's Magazine, *July 1790*

BEFORE the second trial, the fortunes of Rhynwick Williams seemed at last to have taken a turn for the better. He would be tried for a misdemeanor, not for a felony, and there was no question of his being transported to Botany Bay. At the first trial he had had the useless Mr. Knowlys as his barrister; now he would have the formidable Theophilus Swift. The popular interest in the Monster business had abated, and no mob was standing outside the courtroom baying for his blood. Several papers and magazines, in response to Swift's pamphlet, discussed the probability that Williams was innocent or that there were several Monsters.

The main question was whether Anne Porter would survive an interrogation by Swift, a man well known for his cleverness and audacity. She was reputed to have been greatly put out by his scurrilous pamphlet, which had vilified her entire family and cast a slur on her own good name. Had she been possessed of a gentleman protector, he would, according to the morals of the time, have been perfectly justified in delivering a horsewhipping to Swift or challenging him to a duel. Neither her suitor, John Coleman, nor her brother, John Porter, felt quite prepared for such heroics, however, and neither of them dared to openly challenge a man widely known for his violent and quarrelsome disposition, who had once stood for the fire of Col. Charles Lennox in a duel.

Swift's main strategy, as already outlined in his pamphlet, was to shatter Anne Porter's testimony and to present her and Coleman as a pair of impostors who had "framed" Williams to claim the huge Angerstein reward. Once the evidence of this pair, the star witnesses for the prosecution, had been discredited, Pigot's case would fall like a house of cards, and Swift would have a comparatively easy task to demolish the evidence of the other victims.

*   *   *

At ten o'clock A.M. on Monday, December 13, 1790, Rhynwick Williams was brought down from Newgate to the Hick's Hall Sessions House on Clerkenwell Green by Runner John Macmanus and a Bow Street patrol.[1] Williams was tidily dressed in his blue coat lined with buff. The court was crowded with "a number of very respectable persons," some of whom had come very early to secure a good seat. The judge presiding was William Mainwaring, who had been one of the leaders of the opposition against the police reform bill in 1785. His reputation has later been somewhat tarnished by the fact that he also was a banker, and that he had transferred considerable sums of public money, through accounts controlled by the Middlesex Sessions, into his own bank. He and his friends ran these sessions through a policy of ruthless patronage, bestowing valuable appointments to themselves, their friends, and families.[2]

After Judge Mainwaring had taken the chair, the jury, consisting of twelve respectable men, was called over and sworn. Normally, Pigot would then have opened the case, but Williams, showing much agitation, applied for permission to address the court. Standing at the prisoner's dock, the little man produced a piece of paper from the pocket of his blue coat and read another set of harangues aloud. In despondent tones, he begged the jurors to disregard the immense prejudice against him that had been so evident at the first trial. This prejudice had been such that he had despaired of getting a fair trial, and he had been so despondent that he had informed Swift that he wanted to plead guilty to all charges. Earlier that very morning, he claimed, his relatives had managed to change his mind, and Swift had immediately offered to defend him in court. Williams made a solemn oath before God that he was not "that savage *Monster,* from whom I would this moment, at the risk of my own life, rescue even the very woman who has so barbarously pursued me." His speech ended with bitter words directed at the jury:

My confinement has been long and painful; yet, not content with this, the purse of my prosecutors is still open against my poverty, and against my innocence; but to your candour and impartial justice, which will not suffer Falsehood to triumph over Truth and Innocence, I am sure I may look with confidence.[3]

Just as Williams sat down, Swift stood up. He deplored the prejudice and injustice that had made young Williams a prisoner and pointed out that, since he had only accepted his brief a few hours earlier, he alone would be opposing the four counsel for the prosecution (Pigot was assisted by Mr. Fielding and Mr. Shepherd, and also received occasional advice from Mr. Garrow). He was armed only with his own strong conviction of Williams's innocence. Since the dejected prisoner had intended to plead guilty, no witnesses for the defense were ready. Swift thus asked leave to call all the alibi witnesses from the artificial flower factory "as he understood the case of Miss Porter was to be brought forward."[4]

The prosecution counsel reluctantly agreed to this scheme, although some speculated (probably with good reason) that Swift had planned the whole thing beforehand, and that it was *he* who had written Williams's speech. This suspicion is supported by the fact that the alibi witnesses, and some other individuals, appeared in the courtroom very soon after being summoned by Swift. There were rumors that they had all been waiting at a disreputable public house near Hick's Hall. They poured into court just as Pigot opened the case for the prosecution, with a motley crowd of children, relatives, and interpreters in tow. Swift ushered them to their seats with a contented smile, then returned to his chair and fixed Anne Porter with his basilisk stare.

After a brief pause, Pigot went on with his case. Although Williams's speech and Swift's theatrics must have unnerved him, he delivered his opening address with dignity and restraint. Like everyone else, he saw nothing absurd in the fact that Williams was not charged with the felony of willfully destroying people's clothes but merely with the misdemeanor of cutting human beings with the intent to kill and murder them. Although, he said, some members of the jury might find the construction of the prisoner's offense as a mere misdemeanor inadequate, there was no reason to blame the law of the country, since "the Legislature could not foresee all the depravity of the human heart; this is a crime with which they were un-acquainted—a crime which the Legislature, past or present, could never foresee . . . ; it was a crime baffling all human speculation, confounding all

the chronicles of this court, and all other courts, in all ages of the world."
Pigot lacked words to describe Williams's dreadful barbarity, his shocking
brutality and infernal ferocity as he attacked Anne Porter: the prisoner
must lack all morality and all claims to manhood. Pigot solemnly read the
definition of "monster" from Dr. Johnson's Dictionary: "any thing out of
the ordinary course of human nature." Surely, the crimes committed by the
London Monster fit this description. Even more solemnly, Pigot reminded
Williams that he had just called his Maker to witness his innocence; sadly,
he had thereby added one more vice—namely cant and hypocrisy—to those
he already possessed. His witnesses stood ready to identify Williams as the
Monster: they remembered him well, because he was "a man who talked of
'drowning them in their blood,' who 'blasted their eyes,' [and] it was natural
for them to take particular notice."[5]

Anne Porter was the first witness to be called. As she took her seat in
the witness box, she had her sister Sarah and John Coleman nearby for
support. But before she could even answer Pigot's first question, Swift
called out, "Holt, Madam!" Leering at her, he requested that all the other
witnesses leave the court so they could not influence each other. At a sign
from the judge, the prosecution and defense witnesses rose and left the
courtroom. Anne Porter showed obvious agitation as her sisters left her
alone to face Swift. Again, Pigot began his examination, but again he was
interrupted. This time, it was Rhynwick Williams himself, who agitatedly
pointed out that Coleman was peeping in and listening through a broken
window pane. At first the judge tried to ignore him, but Williams was adamant: his shrill vociferations were met with a cacophony of hisses and
catcalls from the courtroom.[6] Swift joined in, demanding that Coleman be
removed. Judge Mainwaring ordered silence in a stentorian voice, and reproached both Williams and his counsel for their obstreperous conduct.
The audience laughed and jeered. The judge also ordered that Coleman was
not to be allowed to eavesdrop on the trial, and the fishmonger was told to
make himself scarce. Pigot was allowed to proceed with his examination of
Miss Porter's evidence; this time, Judge Mainwaring said, there would be no
interruptions.

As Pigot questioned Anne Porter, she replied in faltering tones, but
gradually gained confidence. The audience took a lively part in the proceedings, and Williams later recounted that he was distressed to observe
that "many persons around me were exclaiming 'Oh, the villain!' 'Oh, the
wretch' and looking towards me with indignant eyes" as she described her
sufferings at the hands of the Monster.[7] Judge Mainwaring wrote in his
notes that the court had been crowded with various rowdy spectators, who

even stood around the prisoner's bar; Williams was almost hidden by them. When Anne Porter was told to identify the man responsible for her attack, she had to approach the bar; as soon as she saw Williams's face peeping at her, she called out with agitation, "Oh! That is the man!"[8] Swift registered several objections to her statements, accusing her of having changed her testimony from that originally delivered at Bow Street. In particular, he pointed out that her original description of the Monster did not match Rhynwick Williams's appearance at all, and she did not deny that she had originally described him as a man twenty-eight or thirty years of age.[9]

When Anne Porter had concluded her evidence, Pigot reluctantly surrendered his witness to cross-examination, and Swift immediately went in for the kill. With a torrent of unpleasant questions about the goings-on at "the Bagnio of Beauty" (is this, Madam, or is it not, the name by which Pero's Bagnio is known among men about town, on account of the *Vestals* to be found within?) and her elopement with Captain Crowder, he had her on the ropes. She apparently swooned, and was unable to give any coherent replies. Pigot and Fielding rushed up with a glass of water and smelling salts, like two seconds trying to restore the flagging spirits of a severely mauled boxer. They objected that Swift's questions were improper and insulting to the witness, and had little to bear on the case itself. The judge agreed and called Swift to order. He had to beg the court's pardon, and requested that they attribute his conduct to his strong conviction that Williams was innocent. He then unabashedly asked her to repeat the foul language that Williams had allegedly whispered in her ear when he had stalked her in the street. She was most reluctant to do so, but Swift persisted, and finally managed to draw her into repeating his words verbatim. "Blast your eyes, you damned bitch, I will murder you, and drown you in your blood!" said the blushing Anne Porter.

Swift soon realized, however, that this line of questioning was not exactly in favor of his client. He decided to torment Miss Porter in another way, and rapidly changed the subject. Now, he tried to make her admit that there was not enough light outside the bagnio for her to recognize Rhynwick Williams as the man who had cut her. He asked her if she had been very frightened at the time. "Yes," said Anne Porter with feeling, "I was almost insensible." Then, being in such a state, Swift continued, how could she know it was Rhynwick Williams? She replied "that however agitated she might be, she should have always known him, as his features were more impressed on her recollection, than those of her most intimate friends."[10] This reply gave Swift another opportunity to dig into her past, and he inquired *exactly in what way* she had previously been acquainted with

Williams. She again became very agitated, and seemed totally deprived of the power of speech. As the audience made threatening noises, Pigot strongly objected to Swift's bullying insults. Instead of apologizing, however, Swift called out, "Your agitation, madam, always seems to occur at the *most convenient time*!"

"Withdraw, Sir!" called out Pigot.

"*I* will not be influenced by stage effects!" replied Swift.

"Shame! Shame!" shouted Reynolds.

"Boo! Boo!" roared the audience, who were getting increasingly rowdy.

At this time, Williams tried to make himself heard, but his shrill voice was almost drowned out by the furious hissing of the audience.

Despite the attentions of Mr. Reynolds, who was holding the smelling salts to her nose, poor Anne Porter seemed almost to have fainted away, and her limp body was held upright in the chair only with Pigot's assistance. Swift was unaffected by the drama, however. In a stentorian voice, he shouted, "A *certain kind* of ladies can faint at any time, as easily as the crocodile sheds tears!" At this time, the opposing counsel loudly appealed to the judge to have Swift called to order, and the court was in an uproar.[11] As Theophilus turned toward the spectators with a satisfied smirk on his face, a young man had to be restrained not to leap over the barriers and assault him.

After the judge had calmed down all the participants, and once more reproached Swift for his clamorous and undignified behavior, the trial continued. Pigot may well have taken this opportunity to brief Anne Porter about Swift's probable next line of attack, since her forthcoming answers were much more clever than her earlier ones. Swift asked her why she was so sure that Rhynwick Williams's appearance exactly matched that of the London Monster; after all, she had described him as having light brown hair, while Williams in fact had very dark brown hair, almost black. Miss Porter calmly replied that the Monster evidently wore his hair powdered on these previous encounters. Swift moved on to Angerstein's reward. Was it not true that she had received a part of this reward herself? Miss Porter denied this emphatically. Well, replied Theophilus Swift, Angerstein himself would be called under oath later, and the court would find out the truth of the matter. Meanwhile, she was forced to admit "some connexion" with the fishmonger John Coleman, to whom closer attention would be given later in the trial. She could not deny, under oath, that this gentleman had received huge sums of money for his part in the capture of the Monster. Anne Porter again showed great agitation, but falteringly denied that she was engaged to marry Coleman. Swift asked that, as he had certainly heard reports to the contrary, could she truly deny that she had, directly or indirectly, received any part of the reward? Anne Porter drew herself up to her full height and replied that this "was the *most infamous falsehood a malicious mind ever dared to advance.*"[12]

Anne Porter stepped down after this heated exchange. Judge Mainwaring wrote in his private notebook that, although the examination had been very long and trying, she had behaved "with great decency and propriety and seemed to give her evidence with much fairness and caution."[13]

Sarah Porter next took her place in the witness box. Questioned by Pigot, she gave the same evidence previously presented at the Old Bailey. She described Rhynwick Williams's vocabulary as "both *threatening, indecent, prophane,* and *inhuman.*" Swift, in his cross-examination, confronted her with the discrepancies between her present description of the Monster and that originally given at Bow Street. She did not deny that in her original description she had described him as thirty years old, but claimed that it was not always easy to discern if a person was twenty-three, twenty-five, or thirty. The Monster's powdered hair, too, could explain the discrepancy between her original description and Rhynwick Williams's present appearance. She had to admit, upon Swift's pressing the point further, that she had never seen the prisoner with such dark hair before, and that this circumstance quite puzzled her. Judge Mainwaring later wrote in his private notebook that Williams had obviously put some dye in his hair for it to appear darker than its natural color.[14]

Sarah Porter also vehemently denied that she had received part of Mr. Angerstein's reward. Only by asking her to repeat some of the words used by Williams while stalking the sisters could Theophilus Swift shake this witness: she absolutely refused to do so, since the words were too dreadful. Pressed further by Theophilus, she reluctantly testified that one of the Monster's threats had been that the next time they met he would drown her in her own blood. Pigot and his associates again objected to this bullying of their witness, and there was an ominous murmuring among the audience. Rebecca and Martha Porter were next to testify, but they escaped the brusque treatment their sisters had suffered. Swift apparently was saving his ammunition for his cross-examination of Mrs. Miel, who was next on the list of witnesses.

But Pigot elegantly outmaneuvered his opponent. At Pigot's prompting, Mrs. Miel described how she had accompanied the Porter sisters to the ballroom. When they were attacked, Sarah Porter called out in fear and pain. Mrs. Miel tried to turn around, but at the same moment the Monster struck her a violent blow to the temple. Instead of witnessing Anne Porter

being cut, poor Mrs. Miel had seen nothing but "flashes before her eyes."
She had managed to remain upright, but it took some time before she was
capable of getting her bearings; by then, the Monster had made his escape.

Swift appears to have been completely taken aback by this unexpected
turn of events, and could resort only to bullying: did she or did she not
consider herself a suitable guardian to "the Nuns of the Bagnio"?

John Porter was next examined. As inflexible as Mrs. Miel, he maintained that, although he had opened the door to his terrified sisters on the
evening of the queen's birthday and observed a man standing outside, he
had not taken particular notice of the man's appearance.[15]

Surgeon Tomkins gave the same evidence as before, and steadfastly
maintained that Anne Porter's wound was nine inches long and four inches
deep in the middle. There had been a considerable effusion of blood, and in
fact the floor of the bagnio was covered with it, because an artery had been
severed. Theophilus did not waste any of his ire on an insignificant person-
age like the surgeon, but saved it for his particular "favorite" John Coleman. The fishmonger was in for many sneering questions, jibes, and jeers,
about his being taken for a catamite after his feeble "gestures of offence" at
the rails. After Runner Macmanus repeated his evidence, John Julius Angerstein was called. He fully corroborated Anne Porter's story that she had
refused his reward money. When, shortly after the Old Bailey trial, he had
gone to Pero's Bagnio and offered her half of the reward, she had told him
that she would not on any account receive even a farthing of it, and her
father had commended her action.[16]

Swift must have realized here that he was losing the fight. As he opened
his defense of Rhynwick Williams, he depicted the prisoner as a poor, helpless, friendless man surrounded by gloating enemies.[17] He went on to claim
that there had been a rumor that he himself, the noble Theophilus Swift,
was an enemy of the female sex, since he had come forward to defend the
London Monster. No man would venture such an *untruth* to his face, he
thundered, since it would be treated as a matter of honor, and he was sure
no woman would. He was not defending the Monster, but a poor, innocent
man hounded by those who profited from his downfall. Angerstein's reward
was now in the hands of John Coleman, and thus his testimony deserved no
credit at all. It was apparent that the conspiring Porter sisters had sworn
Mrs. Miel and their brother into their evil plot to bolster up the evidence. He
ended by quoting the case of poor Miss Zubery, who had seven times been
attacked by a Monster who addressed her just as Sarah Porter's assailant
had; was this circumstance alone not cause to doubt the guilt of Rhynwick
Williams? Rather feebly, he added that he would have called Miss Zubery as

a witness had she not been nursing her elderly father; he himself swore to the truth of this story, however, and if anyone chose to disbelieve him, they were advised to keep this to themselves, since it would otherwise be treated as a matter of honor.

After this martial and threatening remark, Swift called his first witness for the defense: the mysterious Mr. Smith, owner of the house where Rhynwick Williams had given his name and address to Coleman. Smith himself probably appeared in court to scotch rumors that he was the Monster's accomplice. But Swift's purpose was some further "fun" at the expense of John Coleman.[18] Smith was asked about the exact circumstances of "that creature" Coleman's entry into his house. He replied that Coleman had certainly not walked up to his door and demanded entry, as he had previously claimed.

"What?" asked Swift, feigning surprise, "How did the dastard then gain entry?"

Smith replied that Williams had observed an awkward fellow skulking outside by the rails, and Smith had walked out to inquire what he wanted.

"So, Coleman *again* demonstrated his valour at the *rails*!" called out Theophilus. "But what was then Mr Williams's purpose in calling him?"

Smith replied that his friend had thought that the poor fellow was "deranged in his intellects."

"Did you, Mr. Smith, observe anything noteworthy about Coleman as he came into your house and observed the prisoner sitting there?"

"Yes," said Smith, "He was *trembling*."

Having pulled off this further insult to "Miss Porter's Puppy," Swift next called his friend Lady Wallace as a witness. She merrily confessed that she had willfully presented false testimony in the previous trial against Rhynwick Williams and had lied about Amabel Mitchell's actions. Anyone else would have been pulled off to Newgate by Macmanus for flagrant obstruction of justice, but Lady Wallace was let off without even a reprimand, and her actions were thought a good joke.[19]

It was then time for the alibi witnesses to perform. One by one, the artificial flower makers gave their evidence that Rhynwick Williams had been at work at their factory until well after the time Anne and Sarah Porter had been assaulted. The maid Molly, who had contradicted her sister at the Old Bailey, was not present, nor was the workman Typhone Fournier, who had given a muddled impression on his previous examination. Either these individuals had refused to give evidence or Swift may have hoped that selecting only the core witnesses would mean less danger of contradiction. Pigot, however, had heard their testimony once before, and he had decided on a plan of attack for his cross-examination. He first went after Amabel Mitchell. The Frenchman was accused of being the Monster's accomplice, and his replies became confused. He changed his story about Mrs. Abingdon's gown, and stated that he had himself received the order from Jerso. He could not, he said, recollect whether Rhynwick Williams had actually eaten at the factory that evening. No mention was made of the maid Molly and her remarks about the clock and the watchman outside, which had played such a prominent part in the alibi presented at the Old Bailey. Mitchell merely said that he was able, from his long experience in the artificial flower business, to estimate the time from the amount of work done, and that he was certain Williams had not left until after midnight.[20] On this point, he could not be shaken.

Pigot then turned his attention to the female witnesses. Raines Mitchell gave somewhat guarded testimony, and the forewoman Catherine Alman stalwartly repeated her statements from the Old Bailey. She claimed that Williams had been at work almost until midnight, and that he had not left the factory even for a moment. A little before midnight, the cloth was laid for supper, and Williams had dined with Amabel Mitchell before returning home. None of the workers in the artificial flower factory owned a watch or clock, but Catherine Alman claimed, like her employer, that she could estimate the time by the amount of work done, just as precisely as if she had looked at a clock or watch. Pigot vigorously pointed out that to estimate the time of day from the number of artificial flowers made is not particularly accurate. She then told a somewhat revised version of the tale of her sister and the clock: after Rhynwick had left, Molly had told her that she had heard the watchman cry out that it was half past twelve, and that she was afraid Williams would not get into his lodgings that evening. Pigot bullied her as much as he could, but she declared that she was absolutely certain that Williams had been in the house at a quarter past eleven o'clock that evening.

The other workers gave a less solid impression, however. One admitted that a person could actually slip out of the door of the factory without being noticed by the other workers. Another said that Williams had in fact been out of her sight for some period of time during that evening, but she added that he must only have gone out into the yard; it was impossible that he could have gone out through the front door. Why was that, asked Pigot. Because the door had a bell, which rang when it was opened, was the naive reply. Pigot reminded the jury that it was possible to silence such a bell simply by either holding the clapper, or maneuvering the bell out of the door's way, and very politely thanked the workwoman for her valuable evidence. Swift must have ground his teeth when his witness made a complete ass of herself.

The next employee, the aforementioned Frances Beaufils, was as obliging as her colleague when cross-examined by Pigot. Contradicting all her colleagues as to the time, she swore that she had left the factory in the evening, after having supped there, with Rhynwick Williams still present; she arrived at her lodgings at Coventry Court, in the Hay-market, at half past eleven. Pigot was quick to emphasize not only that this witness possessed a clock, which she had consulted as soon as she came home, but that she had also asked a watchman for the time on her way home.

Finally, several character witnesses appeared on behalf of Rhynwick Williams, but not poor Sarah Seward, who had had enough of Monster trials after being so grossly insulted in the Old Bailey. In ringing tones, Swift read out her affidavit that Rhynwick had once saved her life; had any one dared to laugh, Swift would probably have challenged him to a duel.

In his summing-up, Pigot emphasized that Anne Porter's evidence was clearly not contradicted by that of Mrs. Miel and John Porter, and that the Porter sisters had pointed out Williams as their persecutor without any doubt. Whatever one might think of John Coleman's conduct and his "unnecessary stops and turnings," this gentleman was still the person directly responsible for the capture of Williams, and as such worthy of respect. He pointed out the muddled testimony of some of the factory workers: was such a flimsy alibi worthy of any credence at all, he asked the jury, particularly when it had been substantially changed from that at the Old Bailey trial?

The prosecution's summing-up had been lengthy, and more than one juror wished that Swift would keep his summing-up reasonably concise, since it was now ten o'clock in the evening, and they were still hoping to have their evening meal. But this was not to come. For nearly an hour and a half, Swift bludgeoned the court with a rambling summing-up that contained all his pet theories about the Monster. With many a pun and classical quotation, he spoke at length about "Tavern-Vestals," the "Nuns of the Bagnio," the "Amorous Captain," "Miss Porter's Puppy," and the adventures of the "Dastardly Fishmonger turned Catamite at the rails." When at length his soporific audience had been entertained to an entire summary of the case from Swift's perspective, Judge Mainwaring then once more recapitulated the evidence. Well aware of the popular prejudice against Rhynwick Williams, and the amount of hostile newspaper reports about his dark deeds, he addressed the jury:

For God's sake, get rid of all prejudice; let your judgment be biassed by nothing but the evidence before you. One cannot help knowing how much the unnatural attacks on the fair sex have been the subject of conversation; and much I fear, that many there are who came here with a wish to hear the Defendant found Guilty. Guard your own passions; coolly and deliberately consider and weigh every part of the evidence, and then according to your own judgements find him innocent or guilty.[21]

At half past eleven in the evening, the jury finally withdrew to consider their verdict. A quarter of an hour later, they returned and found Rhynwick Williams guilty as charged.

*   *   *

The next day, at eleven o'clock, the trial resumed.[22] Five other victims were waiting to give evidence against Rhynwick Williams. Mr. Fielding opened the case for the prosecution by paying a handsome compliment to the jury for their upright conduct during the long and complicated trial the day before. Rather gloatingly, he made a reference to "a scurrilous and indecent Pamphlet that had made its appearance respecting the prisoner." Theophilus Swift, who had previously been looking gloomy and dejected, leapt up with some warmth when his pamphlet was mentioned, and promised "that another publication, on the subject of the last trial, would make its appearance."

Elizabeth Davis was called first. She again described her perilous encounter with the man with the artificial nosegay. She identified Rhynwick Williams as the man responsible, adding that at Bow Street she had picked him out from among a crowd of people. She also definitely pointed out the prisoner's coat, as shown to her by Macmanus, as that of the man who had assaulted her. It is interesting to note that after she and her landlady had given evidence, the prisoner would have said something, but was stopped by Theophilus Swift, with the words "Not a word, Mr Williams; you was prevented from speaking last night, and you shall not be permitted to speak today!" Davis braced herself for an onslaught from Williams's formidable counsel, but Swift merely said rather airily that "they could prove a clear alibi, but would not attempt it." The prisoner was found guilty.

Elizabeth and Frances Baughan were called next, and they described their meeting with the London Monster on Westminster Bridge. They positively swore that Rhynwick Williams was the culprit. Swift again claimed that he could prove a clear alibi, but that he would not attempt it. The prisoner was once more found guilty, and Mr. Fielding made a gloating speech. He pointed out that there were several other indictments against Williams for the assaults on Sarah Porter, Mary Forster, Ann Frost, and Mrs. Godfrey. The prosecution side had decided, however, that since "the ends of public justice being answered, for which alone these prosecutions were set on foot, he would not go on with them." He made reference to Swift's scandalous pamphlet, and was proud that the Porter family, who had been suffering much agony as a consequence of this vile publication, had now been vindicated.

After the court had considered their final verdict, Judge Mainwaring spoke to the prisoner. For the assaults on Anne Porter, Elizabeth Davis, and Elizabeth Baughan, he was to be confined in Newgate for two years for each offense, each sentence to commence after the expiration of the former one. After spending these six years in Newgate, he was to provide bail for his good behavior for seven years, in the sum of 200 pounds and two sureties in 100 pounds each. After hearing this dismal news, Rhynwick Williams bowed to the court and was led away to prison.

*   *   *

Although the Monster mania of mid-1790 had had time to abate, the newspapers still gave considerable attention to the second trial of Rhynwick Williams.[23] Most were content that the Monster business was finally brought to rest, and that Williams was put away for a considerable period of time. The most lengthy article, from an unnamed newspaper (perhaps the *World*), was openly derisive about Swift's court tactics, particularly his indecent cross-examination of Anne Porter.[24] About Anne Porter's refusal to accept any part of Angerstein's reward, the journalist wrote: "How must that author of a pamphlet, which has lately made its appearance, blush at the above testimony, if he has a blush left; and surely, after the publication of so infamous a composition, we may be allowed to doubt it." Swift's threat to bring out another pamphlet was derided with the trenchant words, "Unless it is a more decent one than the last, we hope that it will never be any where but in the author's closet."

The only newspaper with some sympathy for Rhynwick Williams's plight was the *Argus,* whose brief summary of the second trial had spoken of him as "this unfortunate man."[25] In a lengthy article published just after the trial, Swift was given an ovation for his brilliant defense, which the writer was certain would become part of legal history[26]: "If anything could add to the reputation of Mr Swift, the stand which he made in defence of Rhynwick Williams on Monday last, must have had that effect." Unaided by any counsel, and without even a brief in the case, Swift had battled four formidable opponents for the space of fifteen hours. Swift was favorably compared with the famous lawyer Mr. Erskine, whose defense of Captain Bailey for a supposed libel of Lord Sandwich had attracted much notice. Further, it claimed that "Mr Swift's reply to Mr Pigot, which lasted more than an hour, was perhaps the most animated that had ever been made in any Court of criminal justice." This was probably not the impression of the jury and audience at ten o'clock in the evening, after the trial had gone on for twelve hours. In spite of all the prejudice against Williams, Swift had managed to force Pigot into the situation of having to tell the jury that the alibi story was true, and that Williams had slipped out from the flower factory for a couple of minutes and done the deed in this space of time. The jury was so impressed by his masterly defense that they went out of court for nearly half an hour before returning to find Rhynwick Williams guilty.

Having some knowledge of Swift's character, one is not surprised to find that he contributed signed editorials to the *Argus*. For example, he wrote a leading article about Mr. Hastings and his impeachment just a few days after the trial.[27] It is not at all unlikely that he also wrote the unsigned *Argus* article extolling his masterly defense of Rhynwick Williams. There were also rumors around town at the time that Swift's brilliant defense had so impressed the jury that they had gone out of court for more than half an hour; several jurors had been convinced that Rhynwick Williams was innocent of assaulting Anne Porter, and he had in fact been convicted by a majority of two only. The *World,* however, took exception to this "malicious spreading of untrue rumors about the case," and wanted to "clear the Jury from the slander that it seems the wish of *some Person* to heap on them."[28] The *World* article pointed out that the jury had been out for just fifteen minutes and that they were unanimous on two counts. Only one gentleman objected to finding Rhynwick Williams guilty also of "intent to murder," but he was satisfied after rereading Anne Porter's testimony that Williams had repeatedly said he would drown her in her own blood.

The punishment of Rhynwick Williams was a singular one. At this time, prison sentences were usually very short (six or nine months) and were mainly used to punish petty thieves.[29] Judge Mainwaring was probably influenced by Pigot's arguments about the serious nature of the Monster's crimes and shared his outrage that Rhynwick Williams was not tried as a felon. The judge must also have been aware of the massive prejudice against the Monster at all levels of London society. By inflicting a lengthy prison sentence, he probably wanted to compensate for a punishment thought more suitable for this villain. In that case, it is puzzling that Pigot did not proceed with the other indictments against Williams. After all, four other victims were standing by to give evidence against him. During the first day of the trial, Pigot and Fielding had described Williams as a depraved, brutal fiend who had tried to murder several women; on the second day, they declared that justice had been met when the man had been given a six-year prison sentence.

The conduct of Theophilus Swift is also worthy of attention: during the first day, he made every exertion to save Rhynwick Williams and bullied the prosecution witnesses mercilessly; on the second day, he mostly played the part of spectator. Perhaps he had made a deal with the prosecution and pledged to keep quiet so that another scandalous trial could be avoided; in return, Williams was to be let off after Elizabeth Davis and the Baughans had been called to give evidence. Perhaps Pigot had nevertheless been impressed with Rhynwick Williams's alibi for the Porter assault. It may or not be significant that none of the other women pointed out as "nuns" or "tavern-vestals" by Theophilus Swift were called to give evidence; in particular, one is surprised that Mary Forster was not called. Perhaps Pigot had anticipated trouble since she had actually changed her story at Bow Street.

Just after Rhynwick Williams had been convicted for the second time, posters all over London announced that the SAVAGE MONSTER, a creature of unsurpassed ferocity, was on show for the nobility and gentry near Charing Cross. The creature, however, was not Williams, but a large bear, shaved around the face and breast and dressed in a suit of Indian garments.[30]

CHAPTER 10

# WHAT HAPPENED TO RHYNWICK WILLIAMS?

*And by the heat I once felt glowing*
*At William's Statue's feet—*
*By other Williams' graving tool*
*And by the fame of Eton School*
*The muses dear retreat—*
*By coward Lenox' pistol ball—*
*And by the head of hated Hall—*
*By speech which Deane essay'd to read—*
*By embryo pamphlets in my head—*
*By these and by ought else I swear*
*'Gainst Dublin College lasting war.*
*—Theophilus Swift,* Prison Pindarics *(1795)*

AFTER he had finally been committed to Newgate Prison, there was very little news about Rhynwick Williams. For a time, it was quite fashionable for London society to visit him there, perhaps to give ladies the thrill of seeing the Monster in his cage. The Newgate turnkeys were known to open the prison gates to admit any visitor who gave them a tip for the privilege.[1] Williams himself meekly noted the number of people who had come to see him out of curiosity and to buy his artificial flowers. Apparently he was still busy at his trade in prison, but visitors likely used this merely as a pretext to ogle him. But Williams was something of a disappointment to those who sauntered in expecting to see someone like the lunatics at Bedlam or a crazed street performer; instead they saw a small, big-nosed man in a worn blue coat that still showed traces of gentility, sitting peacefully on a stool making artificial flowers. More than one disgustedly called out, "Is this the man called the *Monster*!?" Williams took this as evidence that they believed in his innocence.[2]

Remarkably, Londoners quickly forgot all about the Monster and his strange crimes. Even after the first trial, which ended the proper Monster mania, people gradually seemed to forget about him. Although Swift's pamphlet and the scandalous second trial did much to keep Williams and his misdeeds in the news, the whole thing was "yesterday's news" as soon as Williams had been permanently jailed. A large part of this was, of course, due to the fact that after the arrest of Williams there had been much fewer attacks on women on the London streets. In 1791, Horace Walpole wrote, in a letter to Miss Mary Berry, that a certain lady acquaintance of theirs "may be sent to Botany Bay, and be as much forgotten here as *the Monster*."[3] The memory of the Monster was perpetuated only by Mrs. Salmon's Waxworks Display in Fleet Street. Along with wax statues of some Cherokee Indians and of Captain Anckarström murdering King Gustaf III of Sweden was a representation of the Monster stabbing Anne and Sarah Porter. A man who saw this display in 1793 could still remember, forty-four years later, how horrified he had been by the bloodstained figures of the king and the Porter sisters and the Monster's bloodthirsty and threatening posture.[4]

There are shades of the Monster in a caricature print issued as late as 1802, entitled *The Little Green Man, or the Bath Bugabo*. Henry Cope was a well-known eccentric who dressed entirely in green, had only green furniture, a green gig, and ate nothing but green vegetables. He was often seen in Brighton and Bath, where he made unsuccessful attempts to get acquainted with various fashionable ladies. In the caricature, Cope is seen in his green apparel, staring intensely at three comely women who flee in terror when they see him, crying, "O Lord the Monster! O dear the Monster! The Monster! The Monster!"[5]

Theophilus Swift's pamphlet *The Monster at Large* was reprinted early in 1791. A reviewer in the *Monthly Review* liked it as a literary performance, but declared himself wholly unconvinced of the innocence of Swift's notorious client. He also complained that the dignity of the work was let down by its "sallies of wanton wit," ill-placed sarcasm and double entendres at the expense of the female witnesses.[6] Swift never kept his promise to write another pamphlet about the second trial. His own explanation was that his mind, always eager to fight injustice, had been caught up by other affairs, mainly those occurring in Ireland. Furious after his defeat at the second trial, he had written some diatribes against the people involved but never made any attempt to publish them. In mid-1791, these papers were turned over to Williams himself.

Williams, still a prisoner in Newgate, felt increasingly uneasy in this rough prison. One would not imagine that the London Monster would have a high standing in the prison hierarchy; already before he was committed to Newgate, the inmates had declared their detestation for this unnatural offender in no uncertain manner.[7] Williams had apparently been impressed with the partial success of Swift's pamphlet, and the only thing he could think of that would expedite his release from Newgate was to publish another pamphlet to draw attention to his plight. Swift had described him as a "poor illiterate man,"[8] but this was as exaggerated as many of his other judgments, since Rhynwick proved perfectly capable of writing a pamphlet on his own. Although his grammar and spelling sometimes failed him, his vocabulary was quite good; Williams appears to have received a decent education. In July 1792, *An Appeal to the Public by Rhynwick Williams, Containing Observations and Reflections on Facts relative to his very Extraordinary and Melancholy Case* was available at the booksellers; the forty-seven-page pamphlet was printed at his own expense.

*       *       *

In his pamphlet, Williams presented a graphic picture of the two trials. Some of this material has already been quoted, particularly the mortification he felt when he was hissed and booed by the mob when he tried to speak. Pigot had mocked and insulted him throughout the two trials and "regarded it a great effrontery of mine to try and set up an *alibi*." Amabel Mitchell had also been grossly insulted as Pigot tried to present him as the Monster's accomplice. Williams's only consolation was that the Porters and John Coleman had received a proper grilling at the hands of Theophilus Swift. John Porter, Mrs. Miel, and even John Julius Angerstein had been hounded by Williams's fearless counsel and retreated from the witness box in confusion. Nowhere does Williams in any way blame Swift for mismanaging his case; indeed, his pamphlet reflects nothing but gratitude toward his eccentric champion.[9] Their defeat at Hick's Hall was blamed on the fact that Swift faced not less than three opposing counsel who took turns obstructing his cross-examination of these "false hussies," the Porter sisters.

Williams declared that he had known the Porter sisters by sight since some years before the Monster mania, "as I believe most young men do, who have frequented the Park, Kensington Gardens, and other places devoted to Gallantry." Williams had been much taken by their pretty looks, and the eldest sister, Anne Porter, was his favorite. He frequently "solicited an acquaintance" but was treated with disdain. Once, when Anne had called him "shop-man, and told to go my way to the shop counter, &c.," Williams retorted that he certainly felt as good as a certain Captain, "with whom you made a short excursion." These words were, he claimed, all of the "gross abuse" attributed to him.[10] He wanted his readers to believe that his uncouth reference to her elopement with Captain Crowder had inspired in Anne Porter's malicious, conniving mind a deadly hatred that had later inspired her to conspire with her sisters and John Coleman to denounce Williams as the Monster. Although Anne Porter had, by the time of the second trial, denied upon oath in front of the fuming Theophilus Swift that she was engaged to marry Coleman, she actually married him shortly afterward, at St. George's, Hanover Square, according to a marriage certificate dated April 28, 1791. This celebrity marriage—although involving rather yesterday's celebrities—was reported in the newspapers, and it was commented that "thus Mr Coleman is rewarded for having brought the *monster* to punishment by the lady whose cause he so gallantly espoused."[11]

In his pamphlet, Williams called Coleman "a cowardly impotently [sic] creature" and claimed that he could have knocked down a dozen like him with the greatest ease.[12] Then, one must ask, why didn't he? He must have realized what was up, but he behaved like an even greater coward than the man pursuing him. If he had slapped Coleman's face with his artificial nosegay during their memorable debate at the rails in front of Mr. Pearson's house, the timid fishmonger would probably have turned and run for his life. As things were now, with Coleman triumphant and himself a wretched convict, Williams could only conclude that "*Mrs Coleman* has had her revenge, and *her Husband* his reward." Coleman had netted fifty guineas from Angerstein and 135 guineas from a private subscription. Williams claimed, perhaps with merit, that these huge sums were the least part of the pecuniary rewards claimed by the avaricious fishmonger.

Much of Rhynwick Williams's pamphlet is devoted to lengthy, maudlin ruminations about his present wretched state and the prejudice against him that had resulted in his conviction. In a feeble attempt to prove that the real Monster was still at large, he quoted a case from Bristol where two women had been cut in the hip, and another instance from Watford, where a serving girl had been cut so viciously that she had to walk on crutches afterward. Finally, a certain Mary Clark had been attacked in Pall Mall, on June 13, 1792, by a tall man in a drab-colored greatcoat, resembling the original description of the Monster. Williams suspected that this man, the proper Monster, had taken to traveling the countryside before finally returning to

Figure 29. Newgate Gaol in 1790, at the time Rhynwick Williams was a prisoner there, print by F. Bourjot. Reproduced by permission of the Guildhall Library, Corporation of London.

his old haunts in the metropolis; the authorities, unwilling to admit that Williams was innocent, were covering up his nefarious activities.[13]

*  *  *

Rhynwick Williams had little success with his pamphlet, as could be expected from its weak arguments and the general lack of interest in the Monster business after a period of more than two years since his reign of terror in the spring of 1790. The pamphlet was neglected by the newspapers and the reading public alike, and is today a very rare book indeed.

The Newgate Prison calendar of September 1792 lists Rhynwick alias Renwick Williams, vulgarly called the Monster, as prisoner No. 31.[14] He had been brought to Newgate on June 14, 1790. He is described as aged 28, 5 feet 6 inches tall, with gray eyes, brown hair (the dye had worn off by then), and a fresh complexion. In the next calendar, dated September 28, 1794, Williams is listed as one of five longtime prisoners. The most famous of them was Lord George Gordon, the instigator of the London riots in 1780, who had been convicted for libeling the queen of France. Gordon, who had converted to Judaism, was an odd-looking figure with his huge beard, wide-brimmed hat, and long cloak. He had bought himself into the more salubrious part of the prison and even held dinner parties and musical concerts for his friends. It is by no means unlikely that Williams met him, since one of Lord George's biographers notes that he liked to walk to the other wards of the huge prison and give concerts to his fellow inmates with his bagpipes or violin, and that he sometimes joined in when some communal ball game was played.[15] Lord George died in Newgate in October 1793. Williams was transferred to the next ledger along with three other long-term inmates: the defrauder John Collins, the child-stealer Mary Wilson, and the thirty-year-old James Carse, who had been spared a death sentence for the "Murder of Sarah Hayes. Cut her head off." The following year, Carse was pardoned to serve in the Royal Navy and hauled on board a man-of-war at the docks; Williams now had the dubious honor of being the veteran prisoner of Newgate.[16]

Friends and family were allowed to visit Newgate daily, and it is to be hoped that the apothecary Thomas Williams and perhaps also Theophilus Swift paid Rhynwick a visit or two. The prisoners had the right to keep animals; although dogs were forbidden in 1792, pigs and poultry were not. There was much gambling and gaming in Newgate at this time, and the keeper's office had a much-frequented taproom from which the prisoners could purchase beer. One might suppose that Williams was a member of the

"Free and Easy Club," a drinking society that prided itself in its ability to procure cheap barrels of beer and kegs of gin from outside the prison. Indeed, the riotous noise from the Newgate taproom was such that the neighbors complained it kept them awake all night. The prisoners freely urinated out the prison windows or deliberately emptied their chamberpots over unsuspecting passersby in the street outside. Even more interesting for Williams, Newgate was at this time a favorite haunt for "lewd women and common strumpets." They paid the turnkeys a shilling to stay with prisoners overnight. If Williams's pocket money could not secure him a rendezvous with one of these accommodating prostitutes, the rates were even cheaper during the daytime; a visiting member of Parliament investigating the conditions at Newgate was outraged when he observed "the grossest scenes in broad daylight."[17]

In spite of these attractions, Newgate was a veritable hellhole. Gaol-fever carried off numerous prisoners every year, and diseases of all kinds ravaged the prison population. Vermin tormented them day and night, and the food was abysmally bad. In September 1793, Rhynwick Williams made a desperate attempt to get free. He had now served three years in prison, half of the original sentence of six years. In a letter dated "Felon's side, Newgate, Sept 17th 1793," he wrote to Home Secretary Henry Dundas to petition for king's mercy and complain about the prejudice he had encountered at Hick's Hall.[18] In particular, he alleged that Judge William Mainwaring had been highly partial, and that he had instructed the Jury to take much notice of the sufferings of the Porter sisters, and to disregard the alibi witnesses from the flower factory. He declared himself willing to again stand trial before any English jury of responsible men, and awaited the Secretary's reply to his letter as to the particulars of this judicial redress.

No answer was forthcoming, however. Henry Dundas, as was the custom in cases where convicted prisoners applied for the king's pardon, sent Williams's letter on to Judge Mainwaring to obtain his comments on the case. Someone, perhaps Dundas, scrawled on the envelope, "If this case has not already, it ought to be particularly investigated"; it is likely he remembered the two sensational trials in 1790 and was not entirely satisfied about the guilt of Rhynwick Williams.

Williams himself had, in a rather imprudent manner, already written to Judge Mainwaring to complain bitterly about how he had been wrongly imprisoned as a result of the false evidence of malicious witnesses. Williams roundly accused the judge of perjury; he claimed that his observations from the bench and his admonitions directed at Williams and his counsel when they tried to cross-examine the Porters had been instrumental in his conviction. It was thus Judge Mainwaring's fault that he had been falsely imprisoned for three and a half years. Williams declared himself ready to stand trial again, before sixteen honest gentlemen. This remarkable letter was signed,

I am Sir, with all due obedience [*respect* written before, but heavily crossed over], and all the respect that is due, the Most injured Man Living R. Williams. P.S. without due attention to this letter thou are not justifiable in giving any unfavourable opinion of me unknown to me and in private.

The standard reply to any petition in favor of a prisoner was that the judge presiding at the trial wrote a letter stating his opinion about the trial, the character of the crime, and whether the individual deserved to be pardoned. Mainwaring's reply was not what Williams had hoped for. Judges' letters giving their opinions of prisoners were usually two or three pages long, but Mainwaring apparently feared that Williams would have some success with his petition: He wrote a thirty-nine-page, closely argued summary of the trial at Hick's Hall.[19] He had been struck by the fact that the Porter sisters, although they positively identified Rhynwick as the Monster, had also observed that his hair looked particularly dark, almost black, in the courtroom. When he had assaulted them, they had described his hair as being fair or light brown in color. Judge Mainwaring strongly suspected that Williams had dyed his hair black before the trial in a futile attempt to disguise himself. He was convinced that the attacks on Anne Porter, Elizabeth Davis, and the Baughan sisters had been committed by the same person, and the five witnesses involved had unanimously pointed out Williams as the culprit. Judge Mainwaring had looked into the transcript of the Old Bailey case and seen that some of the alibi witnesses had changed their stories at the county sessions. He finally declared that he was totally convinced of Williams's guilt and that the entire Bench of Magistrates shared this feeling at the time. Williams was thus not a proper object for a royal pardon, he wrote. The authorities acted accordingly: Williams was to serve his full sentence.

\* \* \*

In 1795, after two more years of imprisonment, Williams got an unexpected companion in Newgate: his old defense counsel Theophilus Swift. After Swift had gone to Ireland, he had started an acrimonious dispute against

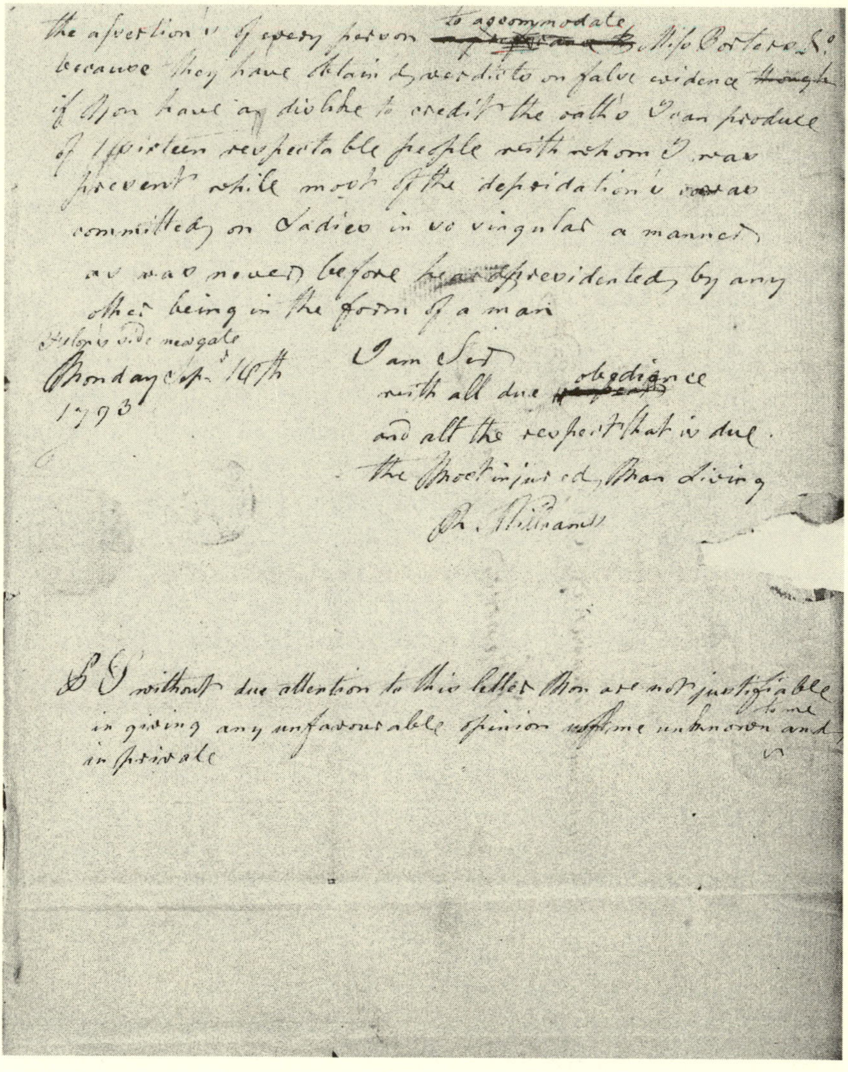

Figure 30. Letter from Rhynwick Williams, "the most injured man living." From the archives of the Public Record Office, Kew (HO 47/17/0), reproduced by permission.

the Fellows of Trinity College, Dublin. His son Deane Swift, "the cleverest lad in all Ireland," had performed badly on his university examinations. He had failed to obtain any prize or distinction; indeed, he was at the bottom of a list of thirteen youths. Deane was a strong, beefy lad, and an expert pugilist (a former pupil of the great bruiser Daniel Mendoza). His actions were hardly those of an intellectual, but Swift claimed that any son of his, and any descendant of the great Jonathan Swift, must be a genius. Swift was present when Deane was questioned by Dr. Hall, an old enemy of his. Of the session, Swift later wrote:

> Skilled in polite, and pugilistic lore,
> Friend to the Muses much, but to Mendoza more.
> Him just arrived from Eton School,
> Ev'n at the Academic Vestibule,
> Cerberus met and bay'd him for a fool.
> The tyrant Hall my modest youth depress'd—
> Twelve were preferr'd to him who must have been the best.

Swift strongly objected to Dr. Hall's questioning, to which Deane Swift had managed few coherent answers. The fearsome Dr. Burrowes then took over the questioning:

> Nor vain my bodings! With his Gorgon look
> He petrified my bashful boy:
> Then threw him Euclid's second book,
> His every prospect to destroy.

In vain, Theophilus objected that, as a result of his kinship with Jonathan Swift, Deane was a "Mathesiphobic" just like the great Dean, and incapable of learning mathematics. Dr. Burrowes and Dr. Elrington, the latter the editor of *Euclid,* soon found this out for themselves; Deane Swift had to leave Trinity College in disgrace. He still had the lease of his college chambers, however, and these were appropriated by his father, who found it convenient to stay there when in Dublin. One day, Elrington wanted to evict this uninvited tenant, claiming that the chambers were vacant after Deane's departure. "Vacant—and I living in them!" replied Theophilus, who immediately sent for Deane and told him about this great insult to the family. Deane armed himself with a stout cane and went out to look for Dr. Elrington. He finally found him and inflicted on the mathematician the chastisement described in another of Swift's stanzas:

> One day Deane met Elrington in the street
> And seeing that he had no stick,
> Deane gave him a kick . . .

This outrage caused the expulsion of both the Swifts from Trinity College, an insult that in Swift's mind cried out for vengeance. He immediately set to work on an even more scurrilous pamphlet than *The Monster at Large,* entitled *Animadversions on the Fellows of Trinity College.*[20] Swift accused certain fellows of being lecherous brutes who had broken the laws that prevented them from marrying. In Dublin College, he wrote, the Muses blushed to be seen, and the only Graces that appeared were *Silence, Stupidity,* and *Sorrow.* He gloated that his strong, manly son had "sent the punctum of his great toe in a rectilineal direction into the sphere of the Mathematician's backside." The Fellows Hall, Elrington, and Burrowes were grossly insulted ("wretched must be the condition of that country whose youths of a high and flaming spirit are enslaved by such a canter as Burrowes, such an oath-monger as Elrington, and such a coxcomb as Magee"), and Swift was prosecuted for libel. The evidence against him was very strong, and a spirited defense could not prevent him from joining his old friend Rhynwick Williams in Newgate for twelve months. His only consolation was that one of his adversaries, the Rev. Dr. Burrowes, was sentenced to six months in prison for libeling *him.*[21]

In December 1795, Swift published a pamphlet while languishing in Newgate: *Prison Pindarics; or a New Year's Gift from Newgate.*[22] It contained scurrilous reflections on the three great episodes of his quarrelsome life: the duel against Lennox, his defense of Rhynwick Williams, and the libel against the Fellows of Trinity College. Colonel Lennox was again blasted as a coward, although "He fought me on it and wounded me severely—but I never retract—anything I say must have been true." Swift boasted that his timely discovery of Mr. Pitt's elaborate plot to murder the entire royal family had prevented this scheme from going any further. He also prided himself on the very eloquent and ingenious defense of Rhynwick Williams, and that his pamphlet "made as many pleasant jeux d'esprits, and double entendres on the ladies who prosecuted him, as I have on the Fellows wives." He complained that the jury at Williams's second trial had deliberately overlooked the discrepancies in the evidence made by the female witnesses: "one lady swore to a man's stooping down, her sister swore to a man rising up, and the jury, in spite of me, would believe that it was the same man who stooped down and then rose up."[23] The Trinity College dons were in for another torrent of abuse:

Curst be your College! Curst its Constitution!
Where Genious never meets regard,
Where access to the Muse is barr'd
Where dullness' leaden sceptre rules
O'er fellow rogues and student fools . . .

\* \* \*

Theophilus Swift was let out of prison in the summer of 1796, but Rhynwick Williams remained in Newgate until December 16, 1796, when he was taken to the Bow Street public office and admitted to bail before the sitting magistrates, his old friend William Addington and Richard Ford. He was bound in the sum of 400 pounds; the people who became bound for him were Mr. Dawson, printer, in Fleet Street, and Mr. Worship, engraver, Union Street, Southwark.[24] One would have expected that a man with Rhynwick Williams's tarnished reputation would either have changed his name or left the country—perhaps both. But this was not the case. It is recorded that on February 22, 1797, Renwich [sic] Williams married Elizabeth Robins in St. Pancras Old Church. It is a fair guess that she was the Elizabeth Robins listed as the daughter of Thomas and Elizabeth Robins, born in November 1774. Remarkably, they at this time had a young son, George Renwick Williams, conceived in Newgate and christened at St. Sepulchre's Church, London, on May 31, 1795.[25]

After his marriage, Rhynwick Williams disappeared entirely. He may have emigrated, but this is unlikely; he may have entered the armed forces against his will; he may have finally decided to change his name. In 1822, Henry Wilson, who apparently had tried to trace what happened to Williams, wrote that "as we cannot find any further notice of this man, we suppose his sentence entirely eradicated those diabolical propensities which so degraded the name of Rhynwick Williams. What time he paid the debt of nature is therefore uncertain."[26] Rhynwick's brother Thomas Williams was listed in *Holden's Triennal Dictionary* of 1808 and 1811 as an apothecary practicing in Vere Street, Cavendish Square. He died in 1829 and left his worldly goods, including valuable shares in the Westminster Gas & Coke Co., to his wife Mary Williams; in his will, there is no mention of Rhynwick or any other relative.[27]

The only lead in the search for what happened to Rhynwick Williams is an inscription on the back of one of the aforementioned Monster caricatures in my collection: "The Monster—Rhenwick alias Henry Williams—an Artificial Flower Maker. † 1831." This inscription indicates that some time after his marriage in 1797, Rhynwick changed his name to Henry. It also suggests that his occupation after his prison sentence was still that of an artificial florist; this, after all, was the only trade he knew. No definite confirmation that a Henry Williams died in 1831 is available, however. Some supporting evidence comes from the 1818 Westminster Poll Book, which lists a Henry Williams, artificial florist, as residing at 9 George Street, Adelphi, Parish of St. Martin.[28] No Henry Williams was in business as an artificial flower maker with his own shop at this or any other time, so this man was probably employed by one of the larger flower factories in London. There were several of these: for example, Amabel Mitchell continued on in his old trade, and his Artificial Flower Emporium in Dover Street was a successful and lucrative establishment for many years. In *Pigot's London and Provincial Dictionary* of 1823–24, Amabel Mitchell is prominently listed as an artificial flower maker and court dressmaker. No Henry (or Rhynwick) Williams is mentioned in *Palmer's Index to the Times* for 1797–1850 as a serious criminal, least of all as an attacker of women; nor does this index give details of any other series of Monster-like crimes from 1798 to 1831.

John Coleman did not pursue a legal career, as presumed by Theophilus Swift. He carried on fishmongering, and was active in his old shop as late as 1818, twenty-eight years after he had brought Rhynwick Williams to justice. He and Anne Porter had at least two children: Ann Coleman was christened in November 1792 and her brother John in August 1796.[29] It is unknown what he did with his Monster rewards. The only sign of wealth was that in 1799 he had two shops, his old one in Gray's Inn Passage and a new one in No. 26 Berkley Square. The long and valuable life of John Julius Angerstein ended in 1824. His business ventures were successful, and he used his considerable wealth to build up a magnificent art collection, which formed the core of the National Portrait Gallery. In his obituary, it was remarked that not the least valuable of his many acts of philanthropy was his part in the detection of the London Monster thirty-four years earlier.[30]

Not surprisingly, Theophilus Swift had a somewhat more exciting and belligerent further career. His old enemy, the Rev. John Barrett D.D., vice-provost of Trinity College, described him in 1811 as a small-statured man of singular appearance, with a pale face, gray hair, and bleared, distorted eyes.[31] He always wore a large cocked hat; he was fond of reading and tolerably well informed, but vain and crochety. In 1811, when Theophilus's estranged wife was still alive, he paid his addresses to a young Irish lady, the daughter of the Rev. Joseph Dobbin D.D. She seems, in a weak moment, to have promised to marry her elderly suitor, but later jilted him, which set

Swift off on his last crusade. In a book entitled *The Touch-Stone of Truth*, he blasted Dr. Dobbin and his daughter as a pair of impostors who had basely betrayed him.[32] As a supplement, he published his collected love letters to Miss Dobbin, whom he called "The Moon of Finglas": they certainly convey the impression that the two were closer friends than the young lady was prepared to admit. John Barrett was of another opinion: only Theophilus's overheated imagination and tremendous self-conceit had made him think he was engaged to Miss Dobbin, and he was certainly not at all the kind of person for a young female to fall in love with.

In his old age, Swift liked to tell stories about the dramatic episodes of his life: how he saved the royal family by dueling against the murderous Colonel Lennox, how his brilliant advocacy had almost wrested the notorious Rhynwick Williams, accused of being London Monster, free from his persecutors; how he had dealt the lecherous Fellows of Trinity College a crushing blow; and how he had taught the hypocritical Dr. Dobbin and his faithless minx of a daughter a hard lesson. After the death of his father, Swift had inherited a number of manuscript papers by his famous ancestor, the dean of St. Patrick's. He also had a great store of stories about Jonathan Swift, which he communicated to the editor of *Swiftiana* and to Sir Walter Scott, who gave them place in their respective publications.[33] The Rev. John Barrett wrote that these stories were inconsistent with the character of that great man, and so full of the vanity and extravagance of the narrator, that any person of learning would perceive that they were Theophilus Swift's own inventions: his ridiculous tales had transformed the great dean into a mountebank or jester.

Theophilus Swift died in September 1815. Several articles appeared in the *Notes and Queries* about him and his family; one stated that not the least of his achievements was that he had "endeavoured with every means in his power, though fortunately with an unsuccessful result, to shelter from punishment the notorious Rhynwick Williams, who by his cowardly and unprovoked assaults upon women had earned him the designation of The Monster."[34]

# CHAPTER 11

# PHANTOM ATTACKS

*Could the law protect the fair,*
*From that Monster fell, Despair,*
*Scandal, still at beauty aiming,*
*And a thousand beyond naming—*
*Woman then might walk secure . . .*
*—W.H., "The Monster," in the* New Lady's Magazine, *July 1790*

THE LONDON authorities of 1790 were particularly outraged by the wanton nature of the Monster's deeds: this epidemic of stabbings was a new chapter in the history of crime, as the prosecutor Mr. Pigot eloquently expressed. Neither in Britain nor abroad had there been a case quite like it. The Monster's only predecessor of importance as a phantom attacker was Whipping Tom, who was active in the 1680s. After dusk, Tom lurked about in the alleys and courts in Fleet Street, Chancery Lane, Fetter Lane, Strand, or Holborn. When chancing upon an unaccompanied woman, he grabbed her, raised her dress, cried out "Spanko!" and repeatedly slapped her buttocks, sometimes with his bare hand, sometimes with a rod. Tom worked with such speed and skill that the popular belief attributed supernatural powers to him. In 1681, he inspired an amusing book entitled *Whipping Tom Brought to Light and Exposed to View*.[1]

Although no case quite captured the mania surrounding the London Monster, the Monster had several heirs. A remarkable series of wanton stabbings that closely resembled the Monster phenomenon occurred in Paris in late 1819.[2] One or more stabbers or *piqueurs* were attacking women in the streets, cutting their thighs or behinds with sharp rapiers fastened to canes or umbrellas. According to M. Froment, a historian of the early nineteenth-century French police, there was widespread popular alarm. Married ladies were advised to be accompanied by their husbands at all times; those without husbands should wear cuirasses or bottom protectors. The prefect of police, M. le Comte Anglès, issued a reward for the arrest of one of the *piqueurs* caught in the act, provided that the victim was thoroughly examined to determine the nature of the crime. Police agents

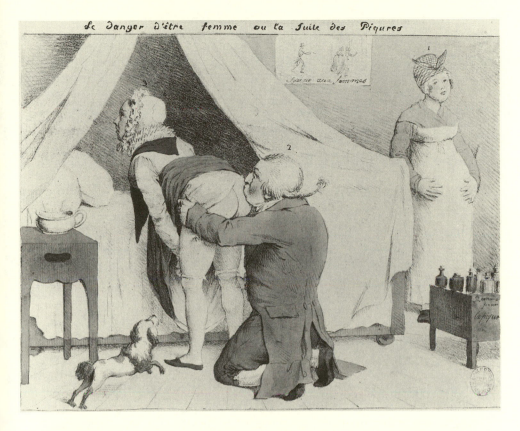

Figure 31. *Le danger d'être femme ou la suite des Piqures,* a satirical print published at the height of the *piqueur* craze in Paris, 1819. Reproduced courtesy of M. Jean-Loup Charmet's picture library, Paris.

and private *piqueur*-hunters were out in force, some of them dressed up as women to tempt the villains to attack, but they had no luck at all.

The enterprising Comte Anglès then thought of a novel idea, which no one had dared to suggest during the Monster mania of 1790. Twenty prostitutes were employed as decoys: they were to walk through the streets of Paris followed by police agents in plain clothes. They were to receive five francs a day, but had to dress respectably and behave decently, walking with lowered eyes and modest demeanor; they were strictly forbidden to ply their trade. Despite these bizarre promenades, no *piqueur* was caught. Not less than 880 francs had been spent on the women and their wine allowance. Later, an officer named Dabasse reported that a tailor, about forty years old, had stabbed a woman. He was taken in by the police while walking to the Hôtel d'Hollande to measure a suit. One of the victims, sitting in a carriage with Dabasse as the man walked by, could not identify him as the *piqueur* who had cut her, however, and he was released. The famous detective chief Eugène François Vidocq finally got his man, however: another tailor was arrested and sentenced to six months in jail as a *piqueur*. After this arrest, the urban panic gradually abated, just as it had done in London after Rhynwick Williams had been taken in as the Monster. But the case against the tailor had not been a strong one, according to M. Froment.

At the same time the French *piqueurs* were terrorizing Paris, the *Mädchenschneider* ("Girl-cutter") of Augsburg, Bavaria, began his long and bloody career.[3] In 1819, several women were cut in the arms, legs or buttocks with some sharp instrument, apparently without motive. A wine-merchant apprentice named Carl Bartle was arrested after the second of these attacks, but no victim could identify him out with certainty, and he was acquitted. Next year, after this phantom attacker had performed several novel outrages, the clamor grew among the citizens of Augsburg, particularly the female ones. A company of vigilantes was set up to help the official police catch the *Mädchenschneider*, and armed men nightly patrolled the streets. In spite of these measures, the Girl-cutter continued his work, and there were new attacks throughout 1820. Many of them were depressingly similar. A servant girl going to fetch beer for her master or for herself would be approached by a well-dressed, pleasant-looking man with a black beard. His manners were much superior to those of the foulmouthed London Monster. He would politely ask her if she was married; if she said she was, he made her a bow and left her; otherwise, he carried on with his well-spoken pleasantries. He asked how old she was, and whether she was not afraid of the *Mädchenschneider*, going out all alone at night. When she said she was not, or made some other defiant reply, he suddenly shouted, "Ich stech' dich!" ("Now I stab you!") and stabbed her with a small dagger.

Finally, late in 1820, a bank clerk named Georg Rügener was arrested after being observed to follow a woman in the street. He was imprisoned and kept in jail for a long time, although he protested his innocence. After the real *Mädchenschneider* had struck again several times while Rügener was in jail, the authorities had to release him; for three more years, he kept the courts busy with lawsuits to recover his job and the small fortune he paid for legal assistance. But no stratagem could capture the Girl-cutter, who was steadily active throughout the 1820s, even though the military was called in and a company of infantry patrolled the streets of Augsburg in search of him. There was persistent speculation that he was a devil or an evil spirit.

The Girl-cutter of Augsburg was finally caught, red-handed, in January 1837, after a reign of terror lasting eighteen years. He turned out to be the thirty-seven-year-old wine merchant Carl Bartle, who had been arrested in 1819 but released due to lack of evidence. According to his own confession, he had injured in all about fifty women. He never cut a man and preferred young, good-looking single women. He was a well-to-do man with the appearance of a prosperous merchant, but had a peculiar and morose temperament. Far from being a ladies' man, he professed aversion, and even disgust, for the female sex. In his house, a formidable collection of knives, daggers, and stilettos was found. Due to the unprecedented nature of this case, a medical/legal examination of Bartle was demanded, and he was handed over to the German alienists, who took pains to determine his motive. Bartle told them that he had always been obsessed with the sight of blood. After the first attack, when he was nineteen, he had seminal emission and experienced intense pleasure. From then on, his sadistic impulses became stronger and stronger until they controlled his life. He was otherwise impotent, and the stabbing of his victims took the place of normal sexual intercourse for him. In July 1839, when Bartle had already been in prison for two and a half years, he was sentenced in Munich to another three and a half years of hard labor. His punishment thus corresponded exactly to that of the man convicted as the London Monster: for cutting fifty women, he had to serve six years in jail.

*   *   *

Less sinister than the formidable Girl-cutter of Augsburg was the *Mädchenstecher* ("Girl-stabber") of Bozen.[4] In 1828 and 1829, a man in the dress of a soldier had cut several women with a penknife. He had previously been active in Innsbruck, and after three women had been cut in Bozen in 1829, a reward of thirty ducats was proposed for his apprehension. Immediately, some soldiers reported that their corporal, a man named Xaver, had been away on the evenings of the latest attacks; the corporal, when questioned, freely confessed his guilt, but without showing any shame or regret for his deeds. The German alienists diagnosed another case of perverted sexuality: in the act of stabbing, Xaver experienced the same kind of satisfaction normally produced by coitus, and this was increased by the sight of the blood dripping from his knife.

In the 1860s, a number of young women were assaulted in the streets of Leipzig by a man wrapped in a cloak who stuck a knife into their arms, just above the elbow, then disappeared. It was a long time before this phantom attacker could be apprehended and put on trial. Psychiatrists again found that the cause was a morbid sexual impulse: the incision with the lancet was often accompanied by seminal emission, and the attacker's entire existence had been absorbed in the alternate excitement and depression that preceded and succeeded his acts.[5]

Another series of attacks took place in Strasbourg in 1880: a man in a dark cloak assaulted respectable women in the streets late in the evening and wounded them in the breasts or genitals with a sharp instrument. After the hue and cry was up for this *Mädchenstecher*, he went to Bremen, where he carried on his campaign; when he was finally arrested, he had clocked up at least thirty-five victims. He turned out to be a twenty-nine-year-old hairdresser named Theophil Mary. No psychiatrist was called in to examine him, and he was considered fully fit to stand trial; his motive was suspected to be sexual perversion coupled with hatred for women. He was sentenced to seven years in prison.[6]

In Mainz, in 1890, a similar series of attacks were made by a sixteen-year-old boy who pressed against women and girls and stabbed them in the legs with a sharp instrument. He was arrested, and appeared to be insane.[7]

In their 1826 article on the London Monster, Andrew Knapp and William Baldwin wrote that Rhynwick Williams did not lack pupils among the young men of London. It was a practice among some of these, whenever they saw a modest, well-dressed, unprotected female, to whisper the most abominable bawdry in her ear and pinch her in the side or behind, so as to put her in both bodily and mental pain.[8] Yet none of these scoundrels came close to the fame of their notorious predecessor. In August 1834, several London women were stabbed in Bloomsbury and Clerkenwell.[9] Charles Fenwick and William Gage, described as ruffian, evil-looking fellows, were taken in the act of stabbing two women in Clerkenwell; in the pocket of the former, a sharp file was found. The two men were imprisoned for two months. In February and March 1885, several women were stabbed by a young man in the streets of Northampton after nightfall.[10] He would stoop, as if to hide his face, then thrust a sharp instrument into their bodies. These attacks caused much alarm, as no motive could be discerned for them; the phantom attacker was still at large in mid-March.

Interestingly, one of the suspects in the Jack the Ripper case was a Monster-type offender. In January and February 1891, a Mr. Colicott was alleged to have attacked six women in the Kennington suburb of London by stabbing them in the behind. He was arrested, but released shortly afterward due to a faulty identification. In early March of the same year, an escaped lunatic named Thomas Hayne Cutbush was arrested for stabbing one woman in the buttocks and attempting to stab another. This time, the identification of the culprit was rock solid, and it was suspected that Cutbush was responsible for the entire series of attacks. The *Sun* went one better: it suggested that Cutbush was none other than Jack the Ripper himself. The writer was able to prove that Cutbush had been working at a tea factory in the East End, in the heart of Ripper country, in 1888, and that his apartment, when searched, had contained a number of extremely lewd drawings of women. The police took this suspicion very seriously, particularly as Cutbush's uncle was Superintendent Charles Henry Cutbush, of Scotland Yard. Sir Melville Macnaghten, assistant chief constable of the CID at Scotland Yard, wrote a memorandum describing the Cutbush case and reasoned that this offender could not be the Ripper. His knife could not have been used in the 1888 killings, and it was unreasonable to believe that the frenzied disemboweler of 1888 could remain dormant for two years after his last awful glut in Miller's Court, then merely stab a few women in the bottom. Cutbush was turned over to the asylum system, and he died in Broadmoor.[11]

In July 1895, a French youth was arrested in Paris for cutting a large number of young girls in the buttocks in broad daylight. He was caught in the act and submitted for a psychiatric examination, which was performed by the leading alienist Dr. Paul Garnier, chief physician of the military psychiatric hospital in Paris. The nineteen-year-old Philippe-Joseph V. was described as a short-statured, pasty-faced, beardless youth, unmanly-looking, and with a timid, embarrassed manner. He apparently hid nothing from his interrogator and described how he had, ever since the age of fifteen, felt a high degree of excitement whenever he saw a woman's buttocks. This craving was soon coupled with an overpowering desire to cut, pinch, or slap this part of the female anatomy. It took an almost superhuman effort for him to master this morbid craving: he continuously trembled, had prolonged feelings of anxiety, and sweated profusely. With time, the impulse to cut became irresistible: he approached an unaccompanied woman in the street, and at the moment his knife stabbed her buttocks, ejaculation took place, and he felt relief. He was otherwise impotent and incapable of normal sexual intercourse. Philippe-Joseph's candor might well be something he later had occasion to regret, since Dr. Garnier's diagnosis was that he was a dangerous criminal lunatic, the victim of mental degeneration and a perverted sexual mind. He was to be locked up in a mental asylum for an indefinite period of time.[12]

Another German *Mädchenstecher* was at large from 1898 until 1901, attacking young women and cutting them in the buttocks or genitals. He was caught in 1901 and turned out to be a twenty-four-year-old railway worker. The attacker was not an imbecile, although not particularly gifted mentally. Unlike the majority of his fellow attackers, he was not impotent; indeed, he was engaged to be married at the time of his arrest and was the father of a child. He was sentenced to nine years of imprisonment.[13] In 1902, another *Mädchenstecher* was arrested and made the subject of a psychiatric inquiry; although he was considered to be an individual of low intellect and perverted mind, he was pronounced fit to stand trial and imprisoned for nine years.[14] Two years later, in Hamburg, a third German offender was jailed for fourteen years for a series of dangerous stabbings.[15]

At the turn of the twentieth century, phantom attackers made their first appearance in the United States. In the 1890s, a maniac was at large in Brooklyn, and specialized in grabbing well-dressed ladies who were walking in the street, and cutting their calves or feet. In Chicago, the manhunt was up for "Jack the Cutter," who had stabbed the shoulders and buttocks of several unwary pedestrians with a sharp knife. In February 1906, it was reported that he had cut seven females in just one day. The Chicago police were flabbergasted: they had no clue whatsoever to his identity, except that he must be a lunatic at large.[16] In the same year, another maniac known as "Jack the Stabber" ran amok in central St. Louis and cut several women's buttocks. He was caught red-handed and proved to be a twenty-two-year-old man named James Lawrence Brady, who worked as a checker in a restaurant. He confessed that he had for some time been in the habit of stabbing women in the streets with a penknife. The wounds were slight, and none of his victims were seriously hurt. Brady seems to have led a dissipated life: he often visited prostitutes and once drank twenty-six glasses of beer just before one of his attacks. His father was a man of a violent temper who had often been in trouble for attacking people with a poker or butcher's knife. He used to thrash Brady with a large bullwhip, and often chased him away from home. There was considerable debate among the American psychiatrists whether Brady was legally insane, and several articles were written on this subject. He was, however, declared fit to stand trial for his crimes.[17]

In 1925, the hunt was on for another American phantom attacker known as the "Connecticut Jabber," of Bridgeport, Connecticut. He worked with almost clockwork regularity: every few months, he stabbed a sharp-pointed instrument into the breast or buttock of a well-dressed woman, then hurried off. There was a widespread hunt for the Jabber, but he was at large

Figure 32. The "Brooklyn Monster" claims another victim. Drawing from an unknown newspaper showing a maniac cutting one of the several women he assaulted. Reproduced courtesy of the Wellcome Trust.

as late as 1928, having by then gained at least twenty-six victims. The attacks took place both night and day, some of them in the streets, others in public places like department stores, churches, and libraries. The descriptions of the Jabber given by the victims varied greatly. The death of one investigator on the case, Superintendent Patrick Flanagan, was blamed on the strain of hunting this elusive Jabber; like Jack the Cutter in Chicago twenty years earlier, the culprit apparently was never caught.[18]

\* \* \*

In 1926 and 1927, there was a series of attacks on women in Halifax, England. In various public places, a man had cut or slashed his female victims' clothes, and on some occasions the skin beneath, with a sharp instrument. Once, he cut the Sunday finery of a woman named Annie Inman, who afterward pointed him out to a policeman; the cutter rapidly made himself scarce, however. On January 28, 1927, two young ladies named Louise Hartley and Mary Whelan were sitting in a theater when a man suddenly thrust his face between them, grinning; they could hear a fabric-ripping sound behind, and their dresses were badly cut up. On February 12, these women led a policeman directly to the man who had cut their clothes: a smart-looking young laborer named James Francis Leonard, of no fixed address. Like Rhynwick Williams, he had a rather peculiarly shaped nose that made him easy to identify; furthermore, several razor blades were found on his person. He was sentenced to two months in prison for each of the three cases found against him.[19] Similar dress-cutters or snippers had operated in Birmingham in 1926, in Portsmouth in 1923, and on the upper decks of London buses in 1910.[20]

The Halifax slasher scare of 1938 had an even more striking resemblance to the Monster mania of 1790. In November and December 1938, there was a baffling series of attacks on both men and women in the same city terrorized by James Leonard eleven years earlier. After three women and a man had been slashed on November 25, the local newspapers were filled with the activities of this mystery assailant. The Slasher was described as a clean-shaven man about thirty years old, wearing a dirty gray mackintosh and shoes with rubber soles that allowed him to sneak up on his victims unnoticed. After a much-publicized series of slashings in late November, the streets of Halifax were deserted after dark; the cinemas and fish and chips shops lost much money, which was instead spent on knuckle-dusters, cudgels, and stout walking sticks for use as protection. Gangs of vigilantes patrolled the streets and sometimes beat up innocent people by mistake. Women took an active part in the vigilante action and carried around pokers wrapped in newspapers or lengths of hose pipe filled with lead shot; others carried bottles of red paint to throw on the Slasher. At the height of the hysteria, the manhunt for the Halifax Slasher was likened to that for Jack the Ripper: at least 122 policemen were working on the case. A troop of 150 scouts were used as an auxiliary anti-Slasher force, but the attacks still spread outside Halifax, and the entire area was in an uproar. The British Legion was mobilized and a considerable part of the adult population of Halifax enrolled in various vigilante societies.

The local police were as baffled by this elusive Slasher as their 1790 counterparts had been by the London Monster. Despite their massive efforts to catch him, their only leads were a few discarded razor blades presumably left behind by the culprit. The local force had to call in the Scotland Yard, and Detective Chief Inspector William Salisbury and Detective Sergeant Harry Stoddard got to work scrutinizing two hundred police reports about the attacks. When these experienced officers re-interrogated some of the Slasher victims, they noticed several contradictions. One woman had two separate cuts on her arm but only one cut in the mackintosh she had been wearing at the time; it did not require the skill of a Sherlock Holmes to figure out that, like the enterprising Miss Barrs in London 148 years earlier, she had faked her injuries to gain compassion. She later admitted that this was the case. One person after the other, when pressed by the police, confessed that they had cut themselves and made up the stories of the attacks to gain sympathy and recognition: a feeble, nervous man, several hysterical women, and a couple of young boys. The police, disgusted with this mixture of "nerves," mischief-making, and plain stupidity, charged and convicted all of them for wasting police time. The police officers in charge considered the Halifax Slasher scare a formidable mass hysteria: There never had been a Slasher, and the whole thing was a typical example of how an urban community could react in an erratic and inexplicable way to an elusive outside threat.[21]

At least according to the newspapers, phantom attackers still walk among us today, although the London Monster, the *piqueurs* of Paris, and the Augsburg Girl-cutter fortunately remain unsurpassed. Although hair fetishists who cut long hair off women and clothes-snippers who remove the backsides of skirts are still common, cases of serial sadists purposely cutting women are rare. In 1977, "Jack the Snipper" or the "Phantom Skirt-slasher of Piccadilly" was active on the London Underground. Before the London Transport Police put an end to his fun in July 1977, he had cut seventeen skirts from behind and exposed their wearers' backsides. He specialized in young, well-dressed women. The culprit turned out to be Graham Carter, a neat, twenty-three-year-old school career officer who had made a meticulous diary of all his offenses. One woman had, to his great satisfaction, walked the entire length of Oxford Street before anyone told her that her backside was exposed.[22]

In Paris, during the same period, another attacker specialized in cornering women in elevators and thrusting fishhooks into their breasts. In 1978, this individual (or individuals) was still at large, using hypodermic needles instead of fishhooks. Another attacker in Malaya in 1978 used the same modus operandi.[23] In 1984, according to the *News of the World,* a very short man had attacked nine women in Birmingham, stabbing them in the buttocks. In 1985, this "pint-sized pervert" was still at large.[24] In China, Wang Jinhou was sentenced to death for slashing twenty-five women on the buttocks and breasts with a fruit knife in 1986.[25] This harsh sentence seems to have brought an end not only to this man, but also to the serial sadistic stabber community at large. At least, no similar case has since been reported, in the newspapers or elsewhere.

*   *   *

Psychiatrists and writers on abnormal sexual behavior in the early twentieth century had no difficulty diagnosing and classifying the *piqueurs* and *Mädchenstecher* as sexual sadists. Today's picture of a sadist is the stereotyped one of middle-aged "consenting adults" applying instruments of torture in their cozy "dungeons" or of a shapely dominatrix flogging a "slave." But as we have seen, there were male sadists in the nineteenth century who often sought unwilling "partners" in the streets. Psychiatrists of this time identified several subtypes of such behavior.[26] The most common were the *frotteurs* and bottom-pinchers that infested the Paris omnibuses. Others stalked women through the streets and slapped their faces or whipped their posteriors when they caught them alone. Some found gratification in throwing dung, urine or other foul substances onto the clothes of well-dressed ladies. Still others were hair fetishists who got satisfaction from cutting strands from women with long and beautiful hair.[27] One hair fetishist, active in the early years of the 1900s, was a student in Hamburg and a leading member of a moral rearmament society. He was impotent, and his major impulse was to cut hair off beautiful women; for this purpose, he traveled extensively within Germany and also visited London and Stockholm. When the police arrested him and searched his apartment, they found 31 long pigtails of female hair, all adorned with colored ribbons and labeled with the date and hour he had cut them off.[28]

Sadistic stabbers are another well-recognized category: they achieved their pleasure from the feeling of the knife entering a woman's warm body, from the sight of her blood, and from her pain and terror. Some authors subdivided this category further: attackers who stabbed or slashed the hand of their victims to see blood flowing from the wound, or who preferred to stab the feet, genitals, or upper arms. The majority, however, were buttock- or thigh-stabbers.[29] There are no known instances of a female serial stabber. There are accounts of a German man who stabbed six young boys in the legs in 1903 before he was arrested.[30]

One scientific review emphasizes that the typical serial sadistic stabber of women is a man whose early experiences have left him with a depraved mind and overactive libido; he is usually impotent and incapable of normal sexual relations. The act of stabbing his object of lust, and the sight of her blood, is often accompanied by ejaculation. This act takes the place of normal sexual intercourse for him.[31] It is interesting that although most writers on the London Monster professed ignorance as to the motive of his "previously unknown" crime, the editor of *Rambler's Magazine,* a publication for libertines and men-about-town, had a theory that was ignored at the time. He ridiculed Mr. Pigot for his talk in court about the Monster's "unaccountable" crime, and asked what "motive impels him who, in his amours, imitates the canine howl, and gnaws the dirty bones rejected by his fair one?" To attack beautiful and innocent women, pour indelicacies into their ear, and stab their buttocks, was that not as likely to provoke a perverted pleasure as the aforementioned practice, which was very common and fashionable among the London debauchees?[32]

As we have seen, serial stabbers of women were by no means rare in the nineteenth century; some German articles around the turn of the century described them as serious threats to decent society. But although other kinds of depraved crimes became more frequent in the twentieth century, sadistic stabbers declined in number. The modern attackers who cut dresses or wound people with needles or fishhooks cannot be compared with their great historical counterparts: the London Monster, the French *piqueurs,* and the Girl-cutter of Augsburg. Nor are there any recent articles in forensic or psychiatric journals about serial sadistic stabbers of women. The subject is only briefly mentioned in recent reviews on paraphilias and sex offenders.[33]

CHAPTER 12

# THE MONSTER, EPIDEMIC HYSTERIA, AND MORAL PANICS

*Out hideous Monster; in thy name*
*Blacknesse and furie dwell:*
*Home to thy Native Hell,*
*Whose foule Complexion is ye same,*

*The same with thee; both Hell & Thee*
*Proud furious DISCONTENT*
*At once begat, & sent*
*DARKNESSE your Monstrous Nurse to bee.*
　　　*—John Beaumont,* Melancholie

CONVERSION hysteria is a psychiatric term for the presentation of symptoms suggestive of organic illness, but for which there is no identifiable physical basis. Mass hysteria, or epidemic hysteria, is also known as mass psychogenic illness; it is defined as the collective occurrence of hysterical conversion symptoms in a more or less well-defined group of people who share beliefs relating to those symptoms. In the Middle Ages, epidemics of dancing, convulsions, and seizures have been described as early examples of mass hysteria; these symptoms are seen as increasingly rare in Western society. Instead, the prevailing form of epidemic hysteria has symptoms of anxiety: abdominal pain, dizziness, nausea, fainting, and hyperventilation. Two typical examples would be an epidemic of fainting pupils in a girls' school or of workers in a canned fish factory complaining of nausea, sore throats and headaches that are blamed on a mysterious gas coming from the cooling system of the plant. These episodes are often triggered by some external stimulus: One of the girls in the school is taken seriously ill just before the fainting fits begin, and the factory workers are told that their jobs will soon be made redundant. One reviewer listed seventy-eight outbreaks of epidemic hysteria from 1872 until 1972.[1] A typical outbreak involved a segregated group of young females; the phenomenon appeared, spread, and subsided rapidly, and was easily controlled when the group was disbanded. The number of people involved was generally around ten to fifteen, but in nineteen cases, more than thirty people were affected. These individuals usually had no history of mental illness. The reaction was brought on by some imagined or real threat to the group, and was supported by deeper, underlying anxieties.[2] A more recent analysis added seventy further outbreaks of epidemic hysteria between 1973 and 1993.[3] There were two major demographic changes: more males were involved, and more people were affected in each episode.

Lately, there have been attempts to redefine epidemic hysteria to encompass much more extensive epidemics of polysymptomatic reactions presumed to be caused by external factors. An example is the "epidemic" of oral galvanism that raged in Scandinavia in the 1970s and 1980s: thousands of people complained of various diffuse symptoms that they believed were caused by the amalgam fillings in their teeth. Some people went so far as to have all their teeth pulled or their amalgam fillings replaced with plastic. The oral galvanism sufferers were supported by a large and vocal patients' union that demanded financial compensation for the victims and the banning of amalgam. As sensationalist journalism played up the amalgam scare, new patients were "recruited" through the media. The reasons for labeling this epidemic psychogenic are strong: there is no solid scientific evidence that amalgam is dangerous; the epidemic had few cases outside Scandinavia, and no cases occurred in Eastern European countries with widespread use of various crude dental filling materials; the scare began in 1970 when amalgam had already been in use for many years; and new cases were more scarce in the 1990s. The explanation has been applied to other outbreaks or diffuse symptoms thought to be caused by the external environment, like the arsenic poisoning scares in Sweden and Germany in the 1910s and 1920s, theories of low-grade carbon monoxide poisoning in the 1940s, and the current spread of an unexplained disorder that has been blamed on computer screens and allergic reactions to electricity.[4] Similar explanations have recently been applied to chronic fatigue syndrome and Gulf War syndrome, but with less impressive evidence.[5]

In most instances, an outbreak of epidemic hysteria is a reaction to an impersonal, unseen threat, and encompasses a definite population. Two exceptions to this rule are two outbreaks of suspected gas poisoning in the United States which both involved mystery stalkers and affected entire communities. The first occurred in Botecourt County, Virginia, from December 1933 until February 1934.[6] On the evening of December 22, 1933, a farmer's wife felt nauseated and smelled a gassy odor. The sheriff was called, but just after he left, the odor returned and all seven family members felt ill. It was suspected that someone had pumped poisonous gas into the house, but no one had been seen near the house and no tracks or footsteps could be detected. The "Mad Gasser," as this mysterious assailant was named by the press, struck twice on December 27: in both instances, people felt ill and detected a strange odor. In January, the attacks became more numerous, and the press coverage more intensive: timorous old ladies stuffed their keyholes to thwart the Gasser, vigilante farmers patrolled the streets with loaded shotguns, and a $500 reward was posted for the arrest of the elusive criminal. In February, the police took pains to investigate the increasing numbers of complaints about mystery gas. One day, they investigated nine calls and found a natural explanation for each: a passing automobile, coal fumes from a stove, or burning rubber. In several cases, only one member of the household was affected by the "gas" while others were perfectly well. In mid-February, the police announced their conviction that the Mad Gasser was a figment of overwrought imaginations, and the local newspaper agreed. There were no more complaints.

A very similar outbreak of alleged gassing took place in September 1944, in Mattoon, Illinois, when a woman reported to the police that someone had opened her bedroom window and sprayed her with a sweet-smelling gas that partially paralyzed her legs and made her feel nauseated. There were many similar attacks, nearly all on younger women, and the press had a field day: The Mad Anesthetist and his "deadly nerve gas" were headline news in the entire district. The Mattoon citizens sat up all night with loaded shotguns, waiting for the Anesthetist to appear or to hear him pumping his spray-gun. Gangs of vigilantes patrolled the area, hoping to take a shot at him. Nevertheless, there were more gassings, and the state police were called in. They discovered that no one had actually seen the Anesthetist, that police patrols responding very quickly to calls of distress found no signs of untoward activity, and that four people taken to hospital after being "gassed" had all been diagnosed as hysterics. Gradually, the epidemic died down, as a psychiatrist worked with the police and with the cooperation of the press. In a later investigation of the Anesthetist of Mattoon, a psychiatrist found that 48 of the total of 52 individuals affected were women, most aged between twenty and twenty-nine, and of a low educational and economic level. They were not mentally ill, but many had a history of minor nervous complaints. The newspapers and the rumor mill of the local community had played a major role in the spread of this epidemic hysteria. The deeper, underlying reason for these two gassing hysterias has been presumed to be anxiety over the use of nerve gases and other chemical weapons in wartime, a topic that was discussed a good deal in America in the 1930s and 1940s.[7]

\*    \*    \*

The definition of "epidemic hysteria" requires that individuals have illness symptoms reminiscent of anxiety and hysterical conversion reactions. There are, however, quite a few reports of community-wide "mass hysterias" that do not involve illness or conversion symptoms. These are categorized as "collective delusions" and follow much the same mechanisms for spreading as epidemic hysteria. Some examples are the bizarre public reaction to the "War of the Worlds" broadcast, an epidemic of windshield pitting near Seattle, Washington, cattle mutilation scares, visions of the Virgin Mary, headhunter panics in Borneo, and the sightings of unidentified flying objects over the state of Illinois in 1897 and in Sweden in the late 1940s.[8] A similar mode of explanation has recently been applied to the American "epidemics" of recovered memories, satanic ritual abuse, and alien abductions.[9] These epidemics of aberrant behavior have spread to parts of Europe, but have not found the same fertile subculture as in their country of origin.

Two other examples in the literature on collective delusions have closer relevance to the London Monster. In early twentieth-century Paris, there were a series of complaints from people claiming that they had been pricked by a long hat pin or a similar instrument. There was a good deal of media interest in the claims, and a suspect was arrested and brought to court but released due to a complete lack of evidence. Psychiatrists explained the whole affair as a collective delusion.[10] In April and May 1956, a remarkable series of alleged razor slashings occurred in the city of Taipei, in Taiwan.[11] A number of people of both sexes, many of them children, had suffered various degrees of injury; most were slight wounds to the hands or head, although one victim, it was alleged, was castrated and killed. There were various theories as to the motive of this phantom slasher: sexual sadism, theft (the attack would draw away the attention of potential victims), or a blood ritual. A local superstition had it that the drawing of blood from a number of small children brought good luck. The police were out in force, and several arrests were made; in one instance, a mob gathered outside the police station and threatened to lynch the woman who had been taken into custody. Vigilantes roamed the streets, and parents kept their children at home in fear of the slasher. Faced with a situation not dissimilar to the Monster mania of 1790, the chief prosecutor of Taiwan ordered an extensive investigation of the slashing episodes. The police could soon report that out of twenty-one recent slashings, twelve were either fakes or complete lies, and the others were still being investigated. In one much-publicized case, a boy had sustained a cut on his elbow from a broken bottle; he had made up a story about being attacked by the slasher rather than face his mother's reproaches for carelessness. The phantom slasher of Taipei did not strike again, and there was no further newspaper interest in the story.

A sociologist found that the slasher "victims" were drawn from those elements in the local society considered to be the most easily suggestible: women and children in families with low income and low education. The vernacular Chinese press played an important part in spreading the slasher delusion with a series of sensational reports, and the local rumor mill was even more instrumental in heightening the suggestibility. As with the Monster mania of 1790 and the Halifax slasher scare in 1938, some individuals deliberately faked their slasher injuries out of various motives, but mainly the desire for personal notoriety. Two deeper, underlying reasons for the phantom slasher delusion were the political unrest in the area (Taipei was the nominal seat of Chiang Kai-shek's government-in-exile) and some pre-existing local Chinese traditions about bloodletting from children and physical mutilation.

After studying the available literature on epidemic hysterias and collective delusions involving phantom gassers and slashers, it is possible to reinterpret some important aspects of the Monster mania. First, however, there is one major difference. While the Mad Gasser of Botecourt, the Halifax Slasher, the Mad Anesthetist of Mattoon and the Phantom Slasher of Taipei were ghostlike figures who did very little actual damage, there was definitely something sinister afoot in London in 1789 and 1790. Quite a few women, perhaps as many as ten or fifteen, were wantonly stabbed by an unknown man who made no attempt to rob them, and who was unlikely to have aimed for their pockets. Many of the attacks took place before the Monster mania began in earnest. There is no question of these attacks being part of the steady undercurrent of crime; before this time, it was quite uncommon for a woman to be stabbed by an unknown person in the street.[12]

These attacks were probably the work of a serial sadistic slasher. Whether this individual remained active throughout the Monster mania in April and May or stood aside to watch the mayhem that ensued is uncertain;

during that period, the descriptions of the Monster varied greatly in almost every particular. The role of the London press in spreading the Monster mania is not negligible, but the newspapers of the 1790s did not reach the lower strata of society, many of whom were either illiterate or unlikely to spend money on reading material. Instead, the role of John Julius Angerstein's campaign cannot be overestimated: his large posters, pasted up on house walls all over London, proclaimed that a bloodthirsty monster was ravaging London's women, and this really started the alarm among women of all social strata. There was no shortage of easily suggestible Monster victims among the nervous, swooning females of 1790, and the number of dubious Monster attacks increased accordingly, just days after Angerstein started his anti-Monster campaign. Some attacks were faked to achieve compassion and publicity, a phenomenon well recognized in the twentieth-century outbreaks. Angerstein's offer of a large reward similarly set the scene for violent vigilante action, which was much more brutal and extensive than in any of the twentieth-century phantom-attacker hysterias, and nearly cost several people their lives.

Was there any deeper, unconscious factor that made Londoners of 1790 susceptible to a collective delusion? In this context, it is impossible to overlook the almost concurrent outbreak of the French Revolution, which changed people's outlook on life to a considerable degree. The fall of the Bastille in 1789 was a momentous event, even more than the sacking of Newgate during the Gordon riots, and there was much unrest regarding what it might portend for Britain's future. The conservative rulers were already conscious of a world changing under the influence of revolutionary ideas, and the reformers were confronted by reaction. There was an increased sense of insecurity, a state of mind conducive to increased suggestibility and collective delusions. But the Monster mania also functioned as a release for hidden social pressures that are less easy to define. The threat of the Monster led to an increase in community spirit: Londoners stood united against this detestable enemy, and the vigilantes and amateur detectives enjoyed posing as the protectors of the Monster's helpless, swooning victims.

Another factor that should be taken into account is the double morals of the time and male-dominated sexual relations. Married women were to obey their husbands, stay indoors, and be industrious with their needlework; young unmarried womsn should be chaste, sensible, and modest. At the sight of a mouse, not to say a man, she was expected to show her delicate, refined nerves. Yet at the same time, predatory male gallants stalked the streets and expected a maidservant or waitress—or for that matter a "Tavern-Vestal in St. James's Street"—to be easy prey. In a way, the Monster mania can be seen as a paradoxical reaction to this situation: an outburst of *show* respectability and sensibility against the sexual threat of the man-monsters surrounding womankind. The Monster phenomenon identified sexual liberty with bloody violence: his sexual deviancy could be linked to political anarchy. In the act of catching a Monster, and putting him away in jail, the authorities demonstrated their ability to control even aberrant sexual urges, thus reestablishing the sentimental definition of human relationships that many people feared was under threat from the French revolutionaries.

*   *   *

A variant form of collective delusion is the so-called moral panic, a concept first defined in a study of adolescent deviance among working-class youth in Britain,[13] which has since been applied to situations of greater social and historical significance.[14] The creation of a moral panic requires an initial deviance of some kind, which can be used as an excuse for focusing the attention of the press and other media on phenomena that may long have been in existence. The media recapitulation of the scare contains elements of distortion and exaggeration, as when a few pickpockets and frightened women became "novel sanguinary outrages." Greater notice is taken of any new instances of the deviance, and there is a reclassification of events: when a woman is pushed over in the street, or frightened by someone who shouts "Buh!" the newspapers report it as the actions of the Monster. These factors result in an overestimation of the deviance, and a "moral entrepreneur" like Angerstein can then impose a "control culture": women are kept indoors, bands of armed men patrol the streets, and the regular police force is criticized in the newspapers by outraged citizens.

It is instructive to compare the Monster mania of 1790 with some other instances of moral panics in London, triggered by crimes that were considered just as new and threatening as the Monster's wanton assaults. In the beginning of 1712, rumors began to circulate in London that the members of a club of wealthy rakes who called themselves the Mohock Club (in emulation of a tribe of violent "savages" in America) roamed the streets of the capital at night, blackguarding, assaulting, and beating innocent passersby. It was said that they slit people's noses, tumbled old women down hills in barrels, and overturned carriages using long weighted poles. They stuck fishhooks through people's cheeks and dragged them about using fishing lines, and tied ropes to women's feet, suspended them upside down, and did them unspeakable mischief. The elderly, defenseless watchmen who patrolled London's streets were favorite victims of the Mohocks. There were many broadsides, pamphlets, and bloodthirsty newspaper accounts about the Mohock outrages, and John Gay's play *The Mohocks* was as successful as the play *The Monster* would become in 1790. People feared to venture out after dark, and women in particular were warned to stay indoors, as many Mohock victims were said to have been women. Just as was the case during the Monster mania of 1790, there were ribald suggestions that the scare had been concocted by jealous married men who wanted to prevent their wives from straying outdoors in the evenings.

In March, the Privy Council met to discuss the disturbances, and it was concluded that although many people had been assaulted and wounded, not a single Mohock had been arrested. A large reward of 100 pounds was offered to any person who brought to justice one of the offenders who had stabbed or wounded people in the streets. It is by no means unlikely that there really was a Mohock club, and it is a fact that six "gentlemen," including Viscount Hinchingbrooke and Sir Mark Cole, were later prosecuted for assaulting a watchman. Lord Hinchingbrooke was acquitted, probably through the good offices of his father, the influential earl of Sandwich; the others were released after paying a fine of just three shillings and four pence each. Yet the number of attacks was exaggerated in number and gravity, and the panic led to more vigorous law enforcement that discovered a fictitious "crime wave" consisting largely of a steady undercurrent of street violence. The Mohock scare died out as quickly it had begun, and the dangerous rakes who had made all London walk in fear were soon forgotten.[15]

The London garrotting scares of 1856 and 1862 also bear more than a passing resemblance to the Monster phenomenon. This time, the victims were almost all male, since no respectable female walked the streets of London after dark in Victorian times. In 1856, there were a number of newspaper reports of a "new" crime that struck Londoners as just as inhuman and disgusting as the Mohock atrocities and the Monster's wanton attacks: several respectable citizens were robbed by gangs of criminals who used a novel technique to subdue their victims. One ruffian would grab the unwary victim from behind and bring his forearm across the Adam's apple to apply a choke hold. His companion in crime could then empty the wretched man's pockets before releasing him. Their semiconscious victim was in no state to raise the alarm or attempt a pursuit. During the winter months of 1856, the *Times* published seven editorials and thirty-one letters on the subject of garrotters and how they should be punished. There were calls for the death penalty, or at least transportation, and two men were actually transported for life after a street assault. The number of reports in the newspapers then diminished, and the panic gradually subsided.

But on July 17, 1862, Mr. Hugh Pilkington, M.P., was garrotted and relieved of his watch by two ruffians as he was walking from the House of Commons to the Reform Club. Such an act against a leading citizen was of course widely publicized, and the panic was reborn with a vengeance. The outcry against the garrotters was taken up by every London paper and diffused into the provincial press. "Garrotter" was an epithet almost as powerful as "Monster" had been in 1790, and the criminals of 1862 were considered a subhuman species. Those who were intrepid enough to venture out after dark armed themselves with cudgels and revolvers; this sometimes led to both dangerous and farcical situations when they mistook each other for garrotters in the dark. For those less belligerent, there was a metal anti-garrotting collar for sale that protected the throat just as the armored petticoats had protected the backsides of women in 1790.

Later research showed that the scare was largely fictional: in the first half of 1862 there were just fifteen robberies with violence, about the same number as in 1860 and 1861, again reflecting the steady undercurrent of street violence. But, just as during the Monster mania of 1790, the number of reported street robberies rose dramatically when the scare was established, and events were given greater notice and reclassified to fit the current mood.

The underlying reason for the garrotting scares was fear of working-class indiscipline, social insubordination and a widespread concern that convicted prisoners were treated too leniently. Transportation had virtually ended in 1852, because the Australian colonies were reluctant to accept any more convicts. The prison overcrowding that resulted, and the liberal prison reforms of the 1830s, led to many convicts receiving a ticket of leave for good behavior when a year or two remained of their prison sentence. During the panic of 1862, there were calls for hanging or transportation of convicted garrotters, or that they should be employed in chain gangs to scour the London streets, or at least be fed a very "low" diet while in custody so that they would not emerge from prison even stronger and ready for new crimes. The lasting results of the garrotter scare, as it gradually died out in 1863, was that the opinion in favor of prison reform had suffered a considerable decline and a number of London criminals caught for offenses that bore any resemblance to garrotting were harshly punished. One of them was imprisoned for life; the judge told him that "he was totally destitute of morality, shame, religion, or any pity, and that if he were let loose he would do what any savage animal would do—namely prey on his fellows." Thus there is good evidence that the judges and magistrates of this time were affected by the scare, and the conservative politicians who wanted to appear as crime fighters and advocates of long prison sentences played along with the scare unashamedly. Indeed, the garrotting panic of 1862–63 played a part in establishing the concept of a "criminal class" of subhuman, amoral brutes: a criminal sewage that polluted the streets of London, that could not be eliminated by hanging or floated out toward the Antipodes on convict ships.[16]

\* \* \*

After these demonstrations of moral panics striking London in 1712, 1790, and 1862, it is tempting to extend the analysis to the sensational events of 1888, when the elusive Jack the Ripper stalked his victims in the streets of Whitechapel. There are several similarities between reactions to the activities of the London Monster in 1790 and those of the Whitechapel Monster (as he was actually called) in 1888.

The mood in Whitechapel was very similar to that in London in 1790. It was hardly possible to see a woman walking alone at the height of the terror, and respectable married women did their shopping in couples before darkness descended. All women, particularly prostitutes, were on guard against male attackers. Posters were pasted up all over Whitechapel not by Ripper hunters, but by the newspaper bill stickers, who wanted to advertise their gory and salacious accounts of the latest murder. A reward of 1200 pounds was posted for the apprehension of the Whitechapel Monster, by private subscription, and vigilantes and amateur detectives were out in force.[17] The police presence also made itself felt; in addition to the uniformed officers patrolling their beats, there were hundreds of plainclothes detectives. Much police time was wasted by people accusing others of being the Ripper, either out of malice or out of genuine belief that they knew the killer,[18] and by drunks and madmen themselves falsely confessing to the crimes.[19] The respectable newspapers were full of letters with suggestions about how to catch the Ripper, and the popular press, headed by the *Illustrated Police News,* had a field day selling illustrated supplements about the Ripper crimes.

A dangerous and excited mob could set on any individual at the slightest excuse, and any man pointed out as Jack the Ripper in the streets was in danger of losing his life. For example, a seaman was rescued by the police from a vicious mob near Ratcliffe Highway; the reason the crowd had singled him out was that his clothes were stained with paint, which was mistaken for blood. When the seaman was taken into a police station for his own protection, the angry mob swelled outside, and it took considerable time before the police deemed it safe to let him go.[20]

Viewed in the terms of a moral panic, the initial deviance was the terrible mutilation of the Ripper's first victim, Polly Nicholls; this was a "new" crime just like the garrottings, and it gave rise to considerable revulsion and fear. This fear led to intense media interest and a reclassification of events. The murders of Emma Smith, in April 1888, and Martha Tabram, in August 1888, were also considered the handiwork of the Whitechapel Monster. But Emma Smith had been robbed by three roughs who had bludgeoned her about the head and thrust a blunt instrument up her genitals. She lived long enough to give a crude description of one of them, who looked like a youth of nineteen. Martha Tabram was stabbed (or probably rather bayoneted) thirty-nine times by two different weapons; it was suspected at the time that two soldiers from the Coldstream Guards might have been involved. Few serious students of the crimes today consider the murders of these two women as crimes committed by the Ripper. The death of Rose Mylett, in December 1888, was also considered to be one of the Ripper's crimes, but she was neither "ripped" nor mutilated in any way, and the authorities at the time were undecided whether she had been murdered at all or had choked to death while drunk. Sir Robert Anderson, the Assistant Commissioner of the Metropolitan Police CID, wrote that, in his opinion, she had died a natural death; had it not been for the Ripper scare, no one would have even considered the possibility of a homicide.[21]

There were also some falsifications: for example, the alleged first Ripper victim, a prostitute called "Fairy Fay," is unlikely to have existed at all. In the evening of November 20, 1888, a prostitute named Annie Farmer was heard to scream; a man raced out of the lodging house to which he had taken her, shouting, "What a—cow!" as he disappeared. Annie Farmer claimed that the man had attacked her, and the police found that her throat was lightly cut by a blunt blade, but in a manner very unlike the Ripper's. They also discovered that she was hiding money in her mouth. Their interpretation was that she had robbed her client and, to protect herself after being discovered, devised the ingenious protection of injuring herself and accusing the man of being Jack the Ripper.[22]

The authorities on the Ripper crimes remain undecided exactly how many victims Jack disposed of: was it five, six, or as many as eleven, and did he remain active into 1889 and 1890? The view of Sir Melville Macnaghten, Sir Robert Anderson, and Chief Inspector Swanson, who all took leading roles in the hunt for the Ripper, was that the Whitechapel serial murderer had five victims only: Polly Nicholls, Annie Chapman, Catherine Eddowes, Elizabeth Stride, and Mary Jane Kelly. This is accepted by the majority of serious researchers,[23] and supported by medical evidence concerning the mutilations, as well as by today's knowledge about serial killers.[24] Already in 1888, it was clear to some American alienists that the killer must have been a sexually insane sadist,[25] and this was accepted also by one of the policemen in charge.[26] But not all Ripperologists agree. It has been suggested, for example, that Elizabeth Stride was murdered by her violent, drunken boyfriend Michael Kidney, who had no motive to perform any of the other murders,[27] and that Mary Jane Kelly was murdered by her jilted, jealous ex-lover Joseph Barnett.[28] It has also been noted that the four trustworthy descriptions of the Ripper are as dissimilar as those of the London Monster at the height of the Monster mania. One witness described the companion of Annie Chapman as a shabby-genteel, foreign-looking, dark-complexioned, short man who was more than forty years old. A policeman and two other witnesses saw Elizabeth Stride with a twenty-eight-year-old, tidy-looking man with a small dark moustache just before she was murdered. Catherine Eddowes was seen with a thirty-year-old rough, shabby character who looked like a sailor, with a fair complexion and moustache. Finally, Mary Jane Kelly was observed with a thirty-five-year-old, Jewish-looking gentleman, with dark hair and an elegantly curled moustache, who was expensively dressed and wore a thick gold watch-chain.[29]

Although it has been suggested that the Ripper was adept at disguises,[30] just as the Monster was supposed to have been in 1790, these descriptions cast further doubt on the presumption that the murders were committed by the same person. Only one author has gone so far as to suggest that there never was a Jack the Ripper and that the crimes were all unrelated, elements of a "murder epidemic" induced by the Ripper scare.[31] The publication of the details of one murder led to "copycat" murders. In the autumn of 1888, not less than seventeen murders took place involving the use of a knife and some degree of mutilation. A copycat Ripper mutilation took place as far away as the outskirts of Newcastle. Detective Chief Inspector Walter Dew, who knew the Ripper business well, wrote in his memoirs that people in 1888 had "what may be described as a Jack the Ripper complex. Immediately a murder and mutilation was reported, whether in Whitechapel or in any other part of the country, they jumped to the conclusion that he was the culprit."[32]

But if the Mohocks, the London Monster, and the phantom garrotters are forgotten today, the Jack the Ripper mass hysteria has never quite died out. The Ripper crimes have inspired a spate of worthless books in which some of the highest in the land, including King Edward VII, the duke of Clarence, Prime Minister William Gladstone, and Lord Randolph Churchill, have been falsely accused of the most loathsome crimes. The groundless denigration of Sir William Gull, a reputable physician, as a Ripper suspect, is a similarly distasteful phenomenon. The elusive Ripper, who quite possibly never existed at all, is also one of the proudest upholders of the pseudo-history presented to London tourists and visitors. The exhibitions in his honor at Madame Tussaud's and the London Dungeon never lack visitors, nor do the Ripper Memorial Walks through the sterile East End landscape, which has changed completely since 1888.

# CHAPTER 13

# WHO WAS THE MONSTER?

*The frightened Ladies tremble, run and shreek;*
*But Ah! in vain they fly! in vain protection seek!*
*For he can run so swift, such diff'rent forms assume;*
*In vain to take him, must the Men presume.*
*This Monster then, who treats you so uncivil,*
*This Cutting Monster, Ladies, is the Devil!*
*—Verses from* The Monster Detected, *a satirical print*
*issued on May 29, 1790*

LONDONERS of 1790 were particularly outraged by the wanton nature of the Monster's dastardly deeds. In the early stages of his career, the Monster was content with insulting his victim with foulmouthed innuendo and cutting her clothes or slightly wounding her. But in 1790, his lust for blood had increased, and a series of more and more violent attacks took place. The Monster was apparently something of an inventor of cutting and stabbing implements, and used quite a variety of diabolical instruments during the attacks. First, there was the "Wangee-cane," the short swordstick with its hidden knife inside; he also had some kind of clasp knife carried in his waistcoat pocket. Then there was the nosegay with its sharp stiletto awaiting the unsuspecting nose, the iron claw with several sharp prongs, and the sharp instruments attached to his knees used to kick women from behind, as in the assault on Mrs. Payne.

London society of 1790 gradually responded to the threat posed by the Monster's actions. The police force, as we have seen, was singularly ill-equipped to cope with a threat of this kind. The parish constables lacked organization, and the watchmen were too feeble, both mentally and physically, to be up to the task of tracking down one or more serial offenders operating under the cover of darkness, particularly since there was no cooperation between parishes. The eighteenth-century watchmen have been ridiculed by criminologists and historians, and they certainly come off very badly in the Monster hunt: once one of them lost the Monster's trail through the most abject stupidity.

The Bow Street Runners were the only detective police in London at the time, and they were continuously kept busy with other cases; furthermore, several of the Runners had private employment as security men or bodyguards. At no time was there a magistrate or police officer in sole charge of coordinating the Monster hunt. Even more seriously, there is no evidence that the Runners tried to liaise with the parish police organization. After John Julius Angerstein had announced his reward, every pretense of cooperation disappeared, and it was every (police)man for himself. The Bow Street magistrates and Runners were overwhelmed by enthusiastic and avaricious Monster hunters who wasted their time with false accusations and even made citizen's arrests of innocent people who were dragged before the magistrates. Indeed, some of the most praiseworthy efforts of the Bow Street police force were to save the lives of several falsely accused persons from the mob threatening to kill them.

In April 1790, Sir Sampson Wright announced that a special "Foot Patrol" consisting of young, able-bodied, armed men had been established at Bow Street; it has been presumed that they were intended to bring the well-organized and tough London footpads to justice, but Sir Sampson may well have had the Monster in mind as well. The Monster hunt must have come as a further reminder to the London judges and magistrates of the woefully insufficient police organization. There were gradual improvements: In 1792, a horse patrol was established to pursue highwaymen and other serious criminals on the main routes into London. Later the same year, the police reform outlined seven years earlier finally became reality. Seven public offices, each with three fully paid magistrates and six full-time constables, with its organization shaped in the image of Bow Street, were built up in various parts of London, thus providing a great increase in the number of full-time, capable police officers in the metropolis. It is unknown exactly what part the Monster phenomenon played in this police rearmament, but it remains a fact that William Mainwaring, the judge in the second trial against Rhynwick Williams, who had been a stern opponent of police reform in 1785, made a complete about-face and strongly supported the new system.[1]

A rather enigmatic figure in the Monster hunt is that of John Julius Angerstein. In no other instance, either before or after the Monster mania of 1790, did this worthy gentleman play the role of a crime fighter. What exactly prompted him to do so in 1790 is unclear, but one would rather suspect that at least initially one of his prime motivators was the opportunity to sympathize with the beautiful victims and obtain a good excuse to visit them repeatedly. Angerstein's actions were directly responsible for the Monster phenomenon's mushrooming from a mere nuisance to a nearly national concern. The pasting up of Monster posters all over London and the offer of an immense reward were recipes for mass hysteria. But Angerstein's actions did not end there. It is clear that by mid-May he, rather than Sir Sampson Wright, was the leader of the official Monster hunt. By this time he had established what was almost a second police office at his house in Pall Mall, where he received callers and sifted through the evidence against various suspects.[2]

The Angerstein reward was justly criticized for opening the door to irresponsible and violent vigilante action, frauds by fake Monster victims, avarice, and even deliberate false arrests by the official police force. But did it also pervert the course of justice? Angerstein had invested a good deal of his own prestige in the Monster hunt, and it was vital for him that a Monster be found and convicted. Had Rhynwick Williams been acquitted, Angerstein would have looked like a complete fool. The newspapers and satirists would have poured scorn on Angerstein's obsession with the Monster, something that had actually begun to happen in late May, just before the arrest of Williams. His great friends the wounded ladies would probably have been depicted in a large caricature print, standing in a row with their skirts above their heads, waiting for their darling Monster to show them some attention again. It is a fact that Rhynwick Williams' original legal counsel left the day before the trial at the Old Bailey; Theophilus Swift's accusation that Angerstein had threatened Mr. Chatham and forced him to withdraw may well have had some foundation.

The use of the term "monster" for a criminal was a novel one in 1790, and thus suited these previously unheard-of crimes. The word itself was used for strange and hideous creatures in its old derivation from the Latin *monstrum natura:* something noteworthy "shown up" by nature. It could be a prodigy or marvel, it could be a misshapen animal or plant or a deformed human being. Chaucer, in *Ariadne,* wrote that "Minus hath a monstre, a wikked beste," and Caxton, in *Eneydos,* described a "monstre fulle terrible, that hath as many eyen in her hede . . . as she hathe fedders upon her." The use of "monster" as a derogatory term applied to human beings starts to appear in early sixteenth-century English; there it signifies an individual with extreme physical ugliness and/or moral perversion. Ben Jonson, in *Every Man out of his Humour,* wrote of a person who would "turne monster of ingratitude, and strike his lawfull hoste." Purchas, in his

*Pilgrimage,* mentions "that Monster of Irreligion, Mahomet." An ungrateful slave trader is spoken of in Raynal's *West Indies* with the bitter words: "They were no sooner landed at Barbadoes, but the monster sold her who had saved his life."

It is interesting that the London Monster appears to have made a small contribution to the etymology of the English language, since the term "monster" for a criminal was, at least for some years after 1790, particularly used for cowardly attackers of women. In 1814, the Hammersmith Monsters assaulted two women in an indecent manner; their trial and conviction was described in a contemporary illustrated pamphlet.[3] Later, "monster" became more commonly used for particularly bloodthirsty criminals, and it still carries this meaning. In 1842, Elizabeth Eccles, the Female Monster, poisoned her three children and ten other people; in 1850, Jane Crosby, another Female Monster, burned her little daughter alive. A famous twentieth-century example is Peter Kürten, the Düsseldorf Monster, one of the most sadistic mass murderers ever.[4]

\*   \*   \*

If one should assume the role of Mr. Pigot and build up a case for the prosecution of Rhynwick Williams, the mainstay of the evidence against him is that he was identified as the London Monster under oath by seven women: Anne and Sarah Porter, Elizabeth and Frances Baughan, Elizabeth Davis, Mary Forster, and Sarah Godfrey. In addition, Martha and Rebecca Porter, Mrs. Franklin, Kitty Wheeler, and Ann Frost, who had been insulted or whose clothes had been cut by the Monster, swore that Rhynwick Williams was the man responsible. Three more Monster victims—Miss Toussaint, Mrs. Payne, and the unnamed servant girl in the Strand—could not swear that Williams was the culprit, although they thought he resembled the man. Looking back into Angerstein's comprehensive account of the Monster's assaults, it is clear that some of the other victims, like Mrs. Chippingdale, Mrs. Drummond, and Jane Hurd, gave descriptions of their assailant that fit Rhynwick Williams reasonably well.[5]

Other circumstantial evidence against Williams is that he himself admitted that previously, on two independent occasions, he had been taken as the Monster by vigilantes but later released. He also voluntarily admitted to being present when Charlotte Payne was assaulted. Another victim, the servant of Mrs. Gordon, was assaulted in exactly the same way as Mrs. Payne. In at least three other instances, the culprit was carrying an artificial nosegay, just as during the stabbing of the servant maid in the Strand

and the assault on Elizabeth Davis, where Williams was again implicated. It was not common for a man, at this time, to carry an artificial nosegay about, and it is certainly a suspicious circumstance that artificial flowers occur in not less than six of the Monster crimes. Williams may well have been proud of his handiwork, and it could have been part of his plan that the woman was to believe that the flowers were genuine for the "surprise" hidden in the nosegay to have the maximal effect. In particular, it should be noted that when Elizabeth Davis resolutely refused to smell his nosegay and said that it looked artificial, the Monster became infuriated and slashed her with one of his other cutting implements. Another argument against him is that after Williams had been arrested, the typical Monster attacks ceased. The two assaults discussed by Theophilus Swift were quite different: one of the women had probably been cut by a pickpocket, and the other probably knew her assailant, since he had cut her more than five times.[6] Still more circumstantial evidence is provided by the discovery that, in early 1797, shortly after Williams had been released from Newgate, there were again reports of women being wantonly stabbed in the streets of London.[7]

In addition, a geographical study of London in 1790 provides some food for thought. If the Monster attacks are plotted, it is seen that a cluster occurs near the flower factory in Dover Street and Rhynwick Williams's lodgings in Duke's Court (and also his later lodgings at the George public house in nearby Bury Street). On January 18, 1790, he could easily have made a dash down Dover Street just after eleven o'clock, cutting Miss Felton on his way down to St. James's Street, where Mrs. Harlow, the Porters, Miss Toussaint, and Mrs. Burney were attacked, before he ran back to his lodgings at Duke's Court. This dismal rookery is not on the London map of today, but perusal of some late eighteenth-century maps shows it to have been some sort of yard accessed from Duke Street, on the block surrounded by the Bury, Jermyn, Great Ryder, and Duke Streets, by a narrow passage.[8] A photograph of the back of some old houses on the west side of Duke Street depicts a warren of dirty, blackened buildings added at different times; it may well be the best likeness of what Duke's Court looked like at the time.[9] Such a place would have been an excellent hideout for the Monster, as would the George public house in Bury Street nearby. At least thirty Monster attacks happened not far from the flower factory and the Bury Street/Duke Street hideouts; and twenty happened in its immediate vicinity.

Rhynwick Williams was desperately poor after Sir John Gallini threw him out, and although he was of better than average breeding, it appears he was not highly regarded by the ladies. Anne Porter was probably not the only supercilious young woman to call this penniless young upstart a "shop-

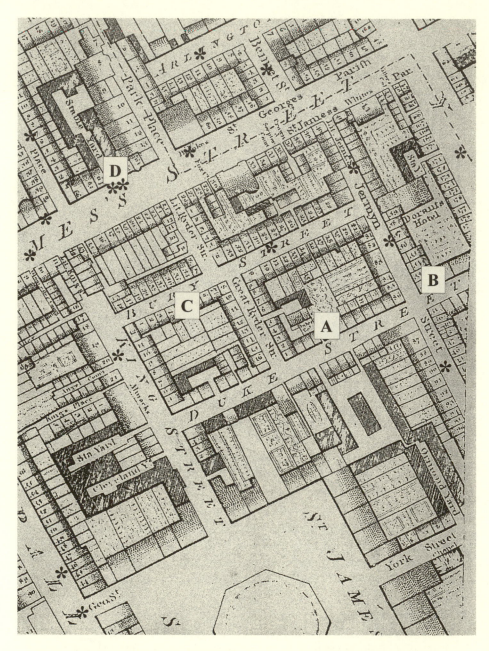

Figure 33. Map of the London Monster's hunting grounds, with Rhynwick Williams's former dwellings in Duke's Court (A), his mother's house in Jermyn Street (B), the George public house where Williams lived (C), and Pero's Bagnio at No. 63 St. James's Street (D). The nearby Monster assaults have also been plotted with a *.

man" and tell him to go back to his shop counter. His odd occupation as an artificial flower maker did not suggest the possession of wealth, social standing, or a superior intellect. According to Theophilus Swift, Williams had for some years been in the habit of pursuing good-looking women through the streets and making them indecent proposals. His kinsman Joshua Williams added that he was in the habit of damning and blasting them if they did not take him to bed. There is no question that he was a well-known harasser who frequently pestered good-looking women, as evidenced by several women who had been abused by his foul language and unwelcome attentions in 1788 and 1789: Mary Forster, Anne Porter, Frances Baughan, Mrs. Franklin, and Kitty Wheeler. It is also clear that Williams's habits were dissolute, and that he often frequented the haunts of prostitutes. Indeed, even the character witnesses who gave such unequivocal evidence concerning Williams's attachment to the female sex were actually women of the streets.

*   *   *

If after this review of the evidence against Rhynwick Williams, one would instead assume the role of his defense counsel, there would be no lack of arguments in his favor. He was clearly not *the* Monster: many victims either said that he was not the man or described culprits of vastly differing appearance. Some attacks are likely to have been the work of bungling pickpockets; others unconnected instances of brutality toward women. There may well have been one or more "copycat" Monsters at work. Finally, quite a few of the alleged attacks in May and June 1790 are likely to have been fakes.

In both trials against Rhynwick Williams, the Porter case was selected as the strongest one by the prosecution, but this does not mean that it was rock solid. It is unfortunate that there is no record of the exact wording of the description of the Monster who attacked Anne Porter, as lodged at Bow Street by her father. According to Theophilus Swift, this description did not resemble Rhynwick Williams: it depicted a tall man of about thirty.[10] Swift is an unreliable source, but it should be noted that, according to Judge Mainwaring's notes, Sarah Porter did not claim that Swift's quotations from the Bow Street deposition were incorrect.[11] Nor did she contest that she had once told Nicholas Bond that she was absolutely unable to describe the Monster. According to Swift, both Anne and Sarah Porter had said they were unable to describe the culprit, although they would recognize him the moment they saw him. It also raises some suspicion that the sisters' early descriptions of the Monster in various newspaper reports are often very brief and that they never mentioned the important fact that the Monster had previously stalked them on many occasions. According to Swift, Anne Porter had instead said that she presumed her attacker to be a clumsy pickpocket who had meant to cut open her pocket.[12]

If one would for a moment assume that Anne and Sarah Porter had been led astray by Angerstein's offer of a reward, what kind of man would they be likely to falsely accuse as the London Monster? Clearly not a respectable tradesman like William Tuffing, or a man of some social standing like Lieutenant Hill. The pathetic Rhynwick Williams, who used to follow them around the streets, would come in very handy, though. He was clearly an individual of low intellect, weird habits, and perverted sexuality; his position in society was a generally despised one, and he would command little sympathy if he were to be taken as the Monster. Anne's stolid, dense boyfriend John Coleman could be relied on as the dupe who "caught" Williams, particularly if Anne herself pointed him out in a dramatic manner, after first having brought up the subject of the Monster hunt in conversation. The presence of several hundred pounds in Coleman's strongbox would definitely make the fishy smell of this persistent suitor much more palatable to a delicate, pretty young lady like Anne Porter.

It was also hinted, by none more strongly than Swift, that neither Anne Porter nor John Coleman was wholly truthful about their relationship, and she may well have perjured herself at Hick's Hall when she denied any relationship with him. It was proven at the second trial that, although the Porter family took no share of the reward, Coleman certainly did; in all probability, the fishmonger managed to lay his hands on both Angerstein's hundred pounds and some other private rewards. And, indeed, John Coleman and Anne Porter were married in April 1791.[13]

Another argument in favor of the innocence of Rhynwick Williams is that his actions when arrested were certainly not those of a guilty man. If, as Anne Porter and Coleman claimed, Williams had seen how she immediately identified him, why, if he was the Monster—the man for whose capture an immense reward had been posted—did he not run away at once? When he was followed by Coleman, he even passed the bagnio twice when walking up and down St. James's Street, although he must have known that this was the home of the Porters. Later, when cornered by Coleman in Mr. Smith's house, he made no attempt to escape and meekly gave the fishmonger his name and address. Nor did he resist when Coleman brought him back to the bagnio. Even considering the "sensitive" female stereotypes of the time, the great fainting scene in the front room seems just a bit exaggerated and theatrical. One of Theophilus Swift's many mistakes during the second trial was that he did not raise the matter of the brown coat, which Anne Porter had identified, with dead certainty, as the garment worn by the Monster on top of another coat when he attacked her. It later turned out that this coat was very close fitting and certainly not the type worn as a surtout. In addition, Williams himself claimed that he could prove that he had bought this coat in April 1790, long after the Porter attack.[14]

Several proponents of the innocence of Rhynwick Williams have pointed out that, at the Old Bailey, his alibi appeared quite impressive: there were seven alibi witnesses, and the contradictions among them were relatively minor. There is every reason to believe that Amabel Mitchell and his work force came forward to give evidence of their own accord, and that they were not influenced by any bribe or threat. After all, Williams was destitute and had no influence whatsoever; he was not even currently employed at the flower factory. In the second trial, the testimony of Amabel Mitchell was still reasonably solid, as was that of the forewoman Catherine Alman. Some of the other alibi witnesses did not shine, however: Mr. Pigot gave them a proper grilling and revealed that they appeared to know less about Williams's whereabouts on the queen's birthday than they had claimed at the Old Bailey. In particular, the fact that none of them had a watch or clock allowed Pigot to demonstrate that their assessment of the passage of time may have been muddled. It should be taken into account, however, that several of the alibi witnesses could not speak English, and that some of them were clearly not particularly clever. Their evidence had to be given through the court interpreter, and they were unable to correct any mistakes or misconceptions; this made it even easier for a skilled prosecuting attorney to make them appear confused and unreliable.

It is clear that in spite of their police informants and the Angerstein campaign, the Bow Street police never suspected Rhynwick Williams in any way before he was taken by Coleman. There are some intriguing hints that, even after the first trial, some of them were still unconvinced of his guilt.[15] Runner Macmanus, who had actually been Williams's neighbor, was as surprised as anyone when he was arrested as the Monster. As evidenced by an article in the *Times*, Rhynwick Williams was well known about town. Many people recognized this odd, rather unsavory little man, who was obsessed with sex and sometimes chased women about the streets, but they had never linked him with the Monster's crimes.[16] Angerstein, at the Bow Street examination of Rhynwick Williams, also heard many people say that they had seen him before, but never suspected him.[17] It should also be remembered that with his reward, Angerstein had created a culture of Monsterism: at any cost, a culprit had to be found. The public hysteria, huge reward, and the great power of suggestion induced by this extraordinary case formulated a potent mix for injustice.

If sufficient doubt is cast on the veracity of the Porter sisters, the other Monster cases fall like a house of cards. The identification made by Ann Frost was ludicrous, and Mary Forster changed her story twice at Bow Street. The Baughans showed some reluctance to identify Williams as the Monster, as did Mrs. Godfrey; a good barrister would have been able to shake the testimony of all these women considerably. Mrs. Godfrey had originally described her assailant as gentlemanly looking and about thirty years old, and her identification of Williams at Bow Street was somewhat faltering. Even more remarkably, Elizabeth Davis, who had originally described the Monster as tall, stout, and very elegantly dressed, later identified scrawny little Williams in his threadbare blue coat as the man who had cut her. There might well some truth in Williams's own story that she had been coached beforehand by the Runners; this possibility raises a whole set of unpleasant questions about how the other witness confrontations had been arranged.

*   *   *

If, finally, one would assume the gown and wig of the judge in the case against Rhynwick Williams, it cannot be denied that several women identified him as the culprit and that there is considerable circumstantial evidence against him. It is certain that he abused and insulted several women, and probable that he cut the clothes and sometimes the flesh of some early Monster victims. It is by no means unlikely that his actions set off the Monster hysteria, which then mushroomed out of proportion. But was there really sufficient evidence to convict Williams in a court of law? We will never know, since both trials were deeply flawed by the massive prejudice against Williams; in both trials, his defense was seriously mismanaged.

In the Old Bailey trial, the feeble exertions of Knowlys on Williams's behalf left the field open for Pigot to show off the injured, veiled Porter sisters as witnesses for the prosecution; from the transcripts of the trial, it almost appears as if Knowlys himself was convinced of Williams's guilt. Knowlys did not take full advantage of the alibi witnesses, and it appears to have been a surprise to him as well as to the rest of the court that the alibi was as strong as it really was. Judge Buller exaggerated the contradictions from the alibi witnesses in his summing-up, and contrasted the candor of the fair sufferers with Amabel Mitchell's unprepossessing countenance. Even more remarkably, he directly challenged the jury to choose whom to believe: the flower makers whose testimony he had just discredited or the heroines who had been so barbarously treated by the Monster. The outcome could only be one. It would have been more natural for a judge to emphasize that seven people had sworn that Rhynwick Williams was elsewhere when the Porters were cut, to ask the jury to consider whether this cast any reasonable doubt on the identification of him as the Monster who had cut Anne Porter; in that case, they should acquit him. It is questionable, however, in view of the reigning hysteria in London, whether even this measure would have altered the outcome; it was not a man the jury convicted, it was a Monster, and London had to be cleansed of this abomination.

At the time of the second trial, the anti-Monster hysteria had had time to abate, and there was less prejudice against Williams. What the wretched man would now have needed was a clever, experienced lawyer, who could expose the flaws in the case against him and knock the Porters down from the pedestal onto which Angerstein and the popular sentiment had put them. But if he had hoped for a doughty knight errant to defend him, poor Williams instead got a champion resembling the ridiculous knights in Monty Python's *Holy Grail*: Theophilus Swift was egocentric, vain, and irresponsible, and he mishandled William's defense in an almost incredible manner. Swift was certainly right in calling Coleman a coward, but the fishmonger's testimony was rock solid, and Swift's only recourse was to resort to insults.

Swift's main argument—that the Porters were ladies of low morality— cannot be given any credence. It is clear, from the contemporary sources, that the Porter family was a respectable one, and although Swift may well have been correct about Anne Porter's previous elopement with "Captain" Crowder, this did not make her and her sisters prostitutes or have any bearing on the Monster business. At this time, a male chauvinist like Swift defined every young unmarried woman who was not a virgin as a "whore."[18] Swift's ribald jokes about the "Nuns of the Bagnio" and their way of entertaining young men about town are worthy only of contempt. Although the word "bagnio" was, at this time, almost synonymous with "brothel," certain London bagnios, like the Royal Bagnio in Bath Street, the Duke's Bagnio in Long Acre, and Pero's Bagnio itself, were respectable and legitimate enterprises (whereas the bagnios near Covent Garden were indeed little more than concealed brothels).[19] Swift, who may well have frequented this latter form of bagnio, probably believed Pero's Bagnio was an establishment of a similar kind.

Swift's scandalous behavior in court was counterproductive, damaging rather than aiding the case for Williams's innocence. It appears that Theophilus must have been enjoying himself when he harried the female witnesses and ridiculed the wretched Coleman, who bore the brunt of his heavyhanded jibes and jeers. To see the rude, unattractive Theophilus Swift, the Monster's champion, blast and bully the beautiful Porter sisters must have given rise to powerful protective feelings in the breasts of Judge Mainwaring and the jurors; this cannot have predisposed them in favor of the Irishman and his already notorious client.

An innocent man would not dye his hair to confuse witnesses as to his appearance, as Rhynwick Williams did in the second trial. Judge Mainwaring, who saw through this ruse, thought this was further evidence of Williams's guilt. Theophilus Swift was clearly not a sincere and upright person, and it appears that he may have been a party to his client's deception, since he described Williams's hair as being "as black as Coleman's conscience." It is likely that the hair dyeing was in fact Swift's idea, since he had the effrontery to write in his pamphlet that "Black takes no dye; we cannot alter nature; we cannot change into a light brown those locks which nature had formed as dark as the Raven's wing."[20] Swift was a supporter of lost causes and desperate actions, but he was also an unmitigated liar and scoundrel. He probably appeared as Williams's champion for self-seeking motives, to get into the public eye, just as he had when he challenged Colonel Lennox the year before. For someone capable of accusing the prime minister of planning to assassinate the royal family, it is a mere trifle to act as the defense counsel for some wretch just for the fun of it, and to besmirch the honor of the Monster's female victims.

Had a fictitious third trial of Rhynwick Williams taken place today, the outcome might well have been a different one. Perhaps, unlike the situation in 1790, the court would have assessed the evidence calmly and with circumspection, without the emotional overtones of Monster mania. It would have spoken in Rhynwick Williams's favor that he had stubbornly denied any guilt and made every effort to get his case retried. There was no forensic evidence whatsoever against him: no bloodstains on his clothes, no signs that a sharp knife had been carried in his pocket, no cutting implement found in his possession. When his artificial flower making tools were produced at Bow Street, the magistrates were convinced that they could not have been used for cutting or stabbing people. The histrionics of the Porter sisters would have been to little avail if Williams's barrister had raised the subject of the discrepancy between their original description of the Monster and the appearance of his client: Clearly, there was quite a difference between a six-foot-tall, thirty-year-old Monster and a twenty-three-year-old man of just five feet, six inches. These swooning, irrational creatures would no longer have been regarded as defective males (the prevailing female ideal): Once knocked down from their pedestal they would have some hard questions to answer. No one could deny that the heightened tensions in London at the time promoted falsehood and perjury, and that Angerstein's immense reward had led to many false accusations. The Porters' statements that they could not describe the Monster, but that they certainly would recognize him if they saw him, might have meant that they were plotting to accuse someone. Their readiness to (falsely) identify Williams's brown coat as the one worn by the Monster over another coat might also have been viewed with suspicion.

The evidence given by Mrs. Miel and John Porter at the second trial appears solid at first sight; at least, it seems to have completely surprised Swift, who made no attempt to cross-examine them. It should be pointed out, however, that none of the accounts of the attack on the Porters, some of them very detailed indeed, mentions a blow to the head of Mrs. Miel. John Porter's assertion that he could recall nothing about the Monster is similarly suspect; would it not have been natural for him to take particular notice of a man whom he had clearly observed, and who moments later turned out to have wounded his sister? Rhynwick Williams's barrister could have done nothing to improve the linguistic and intellectual level of the alibi witnesses, but unlike Theophilus Swift, he could at least have seen to it that they all appeared in court and were relatively well aware of what was expected of them. Had the alibi been anything as solid as at the Old Bailey, and the arguments throwing doubt on the Porters been taken into account, it is quite possible that Rhynwick Williams would have been acquitted.

If the Porter case had resulted in an acquittal, the others are likely to have ended the same way. None of the other ladies had identified Williams with the same certainty. For two of the cases (Baughan and Davis), Williams claimed to have an alibi.[21] Both Ann Frost and Mary Forster had behaved somewhat oddly at the confrontation, and a clever barrister could have made much of their errors and histrionic behavior. Similarly, Mrs. Godfrey and Elizabeth Davis had previously given descriptions of the Monster that did not fit Rhynwick Williams.

As remarked earlier, the Monster mania was a typical moral panic, in which people in an urban community reacted to an elusive outside threat in a neurotic way. Had no Monster been caught, the Monster mania from April until June 1790 would have been regarded as a textbook example of a collective delusion. It would have been claimed that there never had been a Monster, and that the attacks had been either invented or exaggerated.

Monster mania would have been compared with the escapades of the Mad Gasser of Botecourt, the Halifax Slasher, and the Phantom Slasher of Taipei. But as we know, there were at least ten or fifteen bona fide stabbings of women, some of them in 1788 and 1789, before the onset of the mania. These attacks, and probably a proportion of those occurring in 1790, are likely to have been the work of a sadistic serial stabber of women. It is rather questionable whether Rhynwick Williams fits the psychological profile of such a sadistic stabber. There is some evidence that he used to stalk good-looking women through the streets, making indecent proposals. The step from stalking unaccompanied women and abusing them verbally to actually cutting and assaulting them would not have been a great one for him. It is typical for a sadist not to run away after an assault, but to remain to gloat over the sight of the blood, and the terror and confusion of his victim, just as the Monster did on several occasions. On the other hand, early psychiatrists that specialized in this area agree that the typical sadistic stabber is impotent, and incapable of normal sexual relations. This was clearly not the case with Rhynwick Williams, who appears to have been a young man of very active sexual desires. He had no girlfriend or steady female companion but was a regular client of various low-class prostitutes, some of whom even testified in court about his sexual prowess.

In 1790, many considered the punishment of Rhynwick Williams to be ridiculously lenient, at least compared with the wholesale hanging of petty thieves and bandits. It was clearly out of touch with the prevailing mood in London at the time, which demanded pillory, transportation, or even hanging. As we know, it was at this time a capital offense to steal a sheep or to pickpocket more than a shilling. In 1777, a destitute woman with starving children took a piece of raw linen from a shop counter, but put it back when the shopkeeper observed her. She was arrested, tried, and executed.[22] Even many years later, the biographer of John Julius Angerstein marveled at what he called the benignity and mercy of the English laws, which had sentenced the degraded Monster to only six years in prison for crimes that in many other countries would have been punishable with death.[23] Had Rhynwick Williams been found guilty in a court of law today, he might well have been committed to a mental hospital rather than sent to prison.

*   *   *

London has changed very much since 1790, but the broad outline of the streets is basically the same, and it is still possible to identify some of

Rhynwick Williams's old haunts. The old rookery in Duke's Court is no more. Not even the court itself exists today, but at the site is a modern house with an underground garage. I managed to gain entry to the inner court of this building, but there was no trace of Williams's old hideout; nor are there any alehouses, disreputable or otherwise, in Bury Street. Although the Dover Street flower factory is no more, the house next to it, a fashionable shop for antiques and gentleman's effects, looks Georgian in character. The shop has been there since 1812, when Amabel Mitchell, and perhaps Rhynwick alias Henry Williams, were still active next door.

It is also possible today to reenact the "Monster Memorial Walk," the exact route by which Rhynwick Williams was pursued by John Coleman on June 13, 1790. St. James's Park is as busy as it was on the afternoon the Porters took their afternoon stroll with Coleman, but there are no longer any narrow passages near the admiralty leading to Spring Gardens. In Pall Mall, where Williams was closely pursued by Coleman, there are a few older houses that must have been there in 1790, and St. James's Palace at the bottom of St. James's Street is of course unchanged. At the corner of Pall Mall and St. James's Street, formerly the site of the china shop where Williams tried to gain entry, are the offices of the Dunhill tobacco company. Some of the houses on the east side of St. James's Street, like Berry Bros. wine merchants in No. 3 and Lock & Co. Hatters in No. 6, must also have been there in 1790. It is of particular interest that No. 62 St. James's Street, near whose bay windows Anne and Sarah Porter faced the Monster, is still in existence. That it is the same house seen in the engravings of St. James's Street from 1750 and 1800 is apparent from its characteristic windows and tall five-funneled chimney. Pero's Bagnio at No. 63 was purchased by Francis Fenton in 1800; he had the old building pulled down in 1824 and a new hotel erected in its place. The elegant office building that today is at No. 63 was constructed in 1886–88, after Fenton's second hotel had been pulled down, and bears no resemblance to the old bagnio formerly occupying this site. The "Stable Yard" through which the Porter sisters once escaped their stalker to gain entrance through the bagnio's back door is today Blue Ball Lane, in which there is a restaurant and a mews development.

Although there are some remaining older houses in Bolton Street, its character must have changed beyond recognition since 1790. If Rhynwick Williams were to search this sterile area of forbidding-looking office buildings for a *fille-de-joie* willing to give him a five-minute rendezvous, he would have been unsuccessful. There are some older houses on Old Bond Street, but it is difficult to find one with rails, since these have mostly been

Figure 34  Contemporary map of London, with all possible Monster assaults plotted.

taken away to make room for pedestrians. New Bond Street has changed even more and John Coleman and Rhynwick Williams would not have found any familiar landmarks in South Moulton Street.

As we know, there are some indications that Rhynwick alias Henry Williams lived in London in 1818, and perhaps even until his presumed death in 1831. He had at least one child: a son, George Renwick Williams, born in 1795. It is unknown whether George Renwick had any little monsters of his own, and indeed whether any descendants of Rhynwick Williams are today walking the streets of the metropolis. If one of them would set his mind to carry on the work of his infamous ancestor, the Underground would provide a perfect setting. It is true that the policing of the London Underground is far more efficient than the London night watchmen's patrol of 1790, but it is not impossible to evade capture in these warrenlike underground structures. After all, the notorious "Jack the Snipper," the young man who cut young women's skirts and exposed their backsides, managed to dodge the London Transport Police for five months in 1977. He turned out to be a school career officer, not a profession known to attract criminal masterminds. The presence of closed-circuit television equipment in the Underground and railway stations, and indeed in many other buildings, would certainly impede the career of a Millennium Monster; he would have to become even more adept at disguise than the Monster of 1790 and carry not only a cloak ready to be discarded, but also several jackets and baseball caps in different colors, and a false beard and moustache. Another, more formidable threat is that his victims would be unlikely to scream and swoon like the females of 1790; martial arts experts among the women could provide him with some unpleasant surprises, as could the presence of tear gas and pepper spray in their handbags.

Once the attacks got under way, it would not take much media hype to build up the figure of an insane, bloodthirsty attacker prowling the streets of London, attacking unaccompanied women, and specializing in seeking out his victims late at night in the Underground. As clearly demonstrated by the Halifax Slasher hysteria in 1938, a serial attacker of this kind has a particular fascination. The popular newspapers have advanced very little since 1790 with regard to their credulity and sensationalism, and they would seize with gusto upon the prospect of an elusive maniac slashing women in the Underground. The articles in these dismal tabloids would probably be much less amusing than the 1790 newspaper debate concerning the Monster's existence; the ribald eighteenth-century caricatures would probably be replaced with a pair of exposed buttocks, decorated with a tastefully inserted artificial nosegay, on page 3. If the attacks would persist, there would be increasing fear and criticism of the police, and maybe vigilante action, with volunteers patrolling the Underground and arresting innocent people. If there were no attacks for some time, the previous outrages would be blamed on a "phantom" and the whole thing considered a hoax or mass hysteria. It would thus, even today, not be difficult to make a sad, pathetic little man with an unfortunate sexual perversion into a formidable Monster with a syringe and needle, perhaps containing HIV-contaminated blood, hidden in his artificial nosegay. Perhaps he is waiting for you?

# APPENDIX:

# ALLEGED VICTIMS OF

# THE LONDON MONSTER

| Name | Location | Date | Nature of assault |
|---|---|---|---|
| Unnamed woman | | March 1788 | Cut |
| Mrs. Wright | Bow Lane | March 1788 | Cut |
| Mrs. Maria Smyth, wife of Dr. Smyth | Johnson's Court | May 1788 | Abused and cut |
| Mrs. Chippingdale | St. James's Place | May 1788 | Abused and cut |
| Servant of Mr. Collins | Jermyn Street | May 1788 | Abused and beaten |
| Mrs. Sarah Godfrey | Leicester Street | May 1789 | Abused and cut |
| Miss Kitty Wheeler | Bennet Street | Summer 1789 | Insulted |
| Servant girl | New Boswell Court | Summer 1789 | Cut in thigh |
| Miss Mary Forster | Dean Street | September 1789 | Abused and cut |
| Miss Ann Frost | Jermyn Street | November 9, 1789 | Abused and cut |
| Miss Ann Morley | Whitehall | October 1789 | Thrice cut |
| Miss Eleanor Dodson | St. Martin's Lane | November 1789 | Abused and cut |
| Frances and Elizabeth Baughan | Bridge Street | December 7, 1789 | Abused and cut |
| Anne Porter | St. James's Street | January 18, 1790 | Abused and cut |
| Sarah Porter | St. James's Street | January 18, 1790 | Knocked on the head |
| Miss Felton | Dover Street | January 18, 1790 | Clothes cut |
| Miss Toussaint | St. James's Street | January 18, 1790 | Clothes cut |
| Mrs. Burney | St. James's Street | January 18, 1790 | Clothes cut |
| Mrs. Harlow | St. James's Street | January 18, 1790 | Clothes cut |
| Mrs. Allan | Piccadilly | late January 1790 | Clothes cut |
| Maidservant of Mrs. Gordon | | late January 1790 | Kicked and cut |
| Mrs. Drummond | Theater | early February 1790 | Clothes cut |
| Mrs. Charlotte Payne | Grafton Street | mid-March 1790 | Kicked and cut |

| Name | Location | Date | Nature of assault |
|---|---|---|---|
| Mrs. Blaney | Bury Street | March 28, 1790 | Stabbed |
| Unnamed maidservant | Holborn | late March 1790 | Clothes cut |
| Unnamed servant girl | Holborn | early April 1790 | Stabbed in the nose |
| Mrs. Harlow | Pall Mall | early April 1790 | Pushed and clothes cut |
| Servant girl | Strand | April 1790 | Stabbed in the face |
| Mrs. Susannah Thompson | Princess Street | April 1790 | Abused and cut |
| Rebecca Lohr | St. Martin's Lane | April 19, 1790 | Arms scratched |
| Jane Hurd | Edgeware Row | April 26, 1790 | Cut across breast |
| Servant girl | Greville Street | late April 1790 | Clothes cut |
| Servant girl | Holborn | late April 1790 | Clothes cut |
| Mrs. Green | Coventry Street | April 27, 1790 | Knocked down |
| Two unnamed women | Bishopsgate Street | April 29, 1790 | One pushed, one cut |
| Unnamed woman | Leadenhall Street | April 29, 1790 | Shoulder cut |
| Unnamed woman | Vigo Lane | April 30, 1790 | Abused and cut |
| Unnamed woman | Salisbury Square | April 30, 1790 | Face cut |
| Mary Carter | Conduit Street | May 1, 1790 | Abused and cut |
| Miss Barrs | Marylebone Street | May 2, 1790 | Twice cut? |
| Servant of Mr. Sullivan | Arlington Street | May 4, 1790 | Abused and threatened |
| Unnamed woman | Marybone Street | May 4, 1790 | Wounded |
| Mrs. Elizabeth Davis | Holborn | May 5, 1790 | Cut and beaten |
| Jane Read | Glanville Street | May 5, 1790 | Threatened? |
| Servant to Mr. Vickery | Cheapside | May 6, 1790 | Arm scratched |
| Jane Hooper | Vigo Lane | early May 1790 | Clothes cut |
| Miss Aride | Jermyn Street | early May 1790 | Wounded |
| Servant to Mr. Pettit | Fleet Street | May 10, 1790 | Clothes cut |
| Unnamed woman | Bank | May 11, 1790 | Clothes cut |
| Mary Fisher | Charing Cross | mid-May 1790 | Knocked down |
| Mrs. Smyth | King Street | May 15, 1790 | Face injured |
| Unnamed woman | Johnson's Court | mid-May 1790 | Threatened |
| Unnamed woman | Pall Mall | May 18, 1790 | Cut several times |
| Two unnamed women | Edgware Road | late May 1790 | Wounded |
| Lady Wallace | Green Park | May 27, 1790 | Frightened? |
| Unnamed woman | Westminster | June 10, 1790 | Threatened with nosegay |

# NOTES

Dates of newspapers are 1790 unless otherwise stated. References are given with the newspaper's name, then the date, then the page and column. "*Times* May 2 3b" thus refers to the second column on the third page of the *Times* of May 2, 1790.

Newspaper clippings from Miss Banks's Monster scrapbook are referred to by newspaper name and the page number on which it is pasted, except in the case of those newspaper clippings pasted directly onto folio 53. Other material from this scrapbook is referred to by folio number.

Four recurring key titles: John Julius Angerstein, *An Authentic Account of the Barbarities lately practised by the Monsters* (London 1790), E. Hodgson, *The Trial at Large of Rhynwick Williams* (London 1790), Theophilus Swift, *The Monster at Large; or, the Innocence of Rhynwick Williams Vindicated* (London 1790), and Rhynwick Williams, *An Appeal to the Public by Rhynwick Williams, Containing Observations and Reflections on Facts relative to his very Extraordinary and Melancholy Case* (London 1792) are referred to by short title after they are first mentioned in a note. The notes of Judge William Mainwaring, in the Public Record Office, are also referred to by short title.

## INTRODUCTION. THE COMING OF THE MONSTER

1. J. M. Bulloch, "The Monster," *Notes & Queries* 173 (1937): 44–45.
2. P. D. James and T. A. Critchley, *The Maul and the Pear Tree* (London 1987).
3. Donald Rumbelow, *The Complete Jack the Ripper* (London 1987); Martin Fido, *The Crimes, Detection and Death of Jack the Ripper* (London 1987); Colin Wilson and Robin Odell, *Jack the Ripper* (London 1991); Paul Begg, *Jack the Ripper: The Uncensored Facts* (London 1988); Melvin Harris, *The True Face of Jack the Ripper* (London 1994); Philip Sugden, *The Complete History of Jack the Ripper* (London 1994); and Paul Begg et al., *The Jack the Ripper A-Z* (London 1996) are some of the superior books on this mystery.
4. Henry Wilson and James Caulfield, *The Book of Wonderful Characters* (London 1869), pp. 265–66.

5. Andrew Knapp and William Baldwin, *The New Newgate Calendar* (London 1826), vol. 3, pp. 511–18.

6. This and other instances are discussed by Michael Goss, *The Halifax Slasher,* Fortean Times occ. paper 3 (London 1987).

7. Ronald Holmes, *The Legend of Sawney Bean* (London 1975) is the only longer account of this elusive bogeyman.

8. On Spring-heeled Jack, see Peter Haining, *The Legend and Strange Crimes of Spring-heeled Jack* (London 1977); for a recent and particularly well-researched account, see the article by Mike Dash, "Spring Healed Jack: To Victorian Bugaboo from Suburban Ghost," *Fortean Studies* 3 (1996): 7–125.

9. On Sweeney Todd, see Peter Haining, *Sweeney Todd: The Real Story of the Demon Barber of Fleet Street* (London 1993).

10. British Library shelfmark L.R. 301.h.3–11. Sarah Sophia Banks's Monster scrapbook was bound into vol. h3 when the volumes were restored. Under the heading "The Monster" are five folios, numbered 44–48, of handbills and letters, followed by mounted pages from the original scrapbook containing clippings from newspapers, numbered 1–20. There follows a mounted copy of L. Williams's pamphlet on the Monster trial, an extract from the *New Lady's Magazine* on the same subject, and, finally, five more folios numbered 52–57.

11. Both are bound into a volume labeled "Account of Rynwick Williams," donated to the Library by Mr. John Ashhurst 3rd (Librarian, 1916–32).

12. The author wishes to thank the British Library, the Wellcome Institute Library, the Guildhall Library, the Westminster Library Archives, the Public Record Office, the Department of Prints and Drawings, British Museum, and the Library of the Royal Society of Medicine, all in London; also the Historical Library of the National Library of Medicine, Washington, D.C., the Free Library of Philadelphia, Philadelphia, and the Boston Athenæum Library, Boston.

## CHAPTER 1. A MELANCHOLY OCCURRENCE IN ST. JAMES'S STREET

1. On Charles Burney, see the *Dictionary of National Biography*; on his newspaper collection, see Arundell Esdaile, *The British Museum Library* (London 1946), pp. 208–10.

2. For an account of the eighteenth-century newspaper press and its methods, see Pat Rogers, *Grub Street: Studies in a Subculture* (London 1972).

3. *World* May 17 3b.

4. *Public Advertiser* April 15 3a.

5. *Public Advertiser* Feb 5 3c.

6. *World* March 15 3a.

7. On the Gordon riots, see John Paul De Castro, *The Gordon Riots* (London 1926), and Christopher Hibbert, *King Mob* (New York 1989).

8. Frank McLynn, *Crime & Punishment in Eighteenth-Century England* (Oxford 1991), pp. 232–39.

9. For general accounts of crime and punishment in the eighteenth century, see Peter Linebaugh, *The London Hanged* (London 1991); J. M. Beattie, *Crime and the*

*Courts of England 1660-1800* (Oxford 1986), pp. 582–637; Donald A. Low, *Thieves' Kitchen: The Regency Underworld* (London 1982), pp. 13–62; McLynn, *Crime & Punishment*; and David Taylor, *Crime, Policing and Punishment in England, 1750-1918* (New York 1998).

10. Beattie, *Crime and the Courts of England,* pp. 582–93.

11. McLynn, *Crime & Punishment,* p. 6.

12. McLynn, *Crime & Punishment,* and Beattie, *Crime and the Courts of England,* pp. 582–93.

13. Beattie, *Crime and the Courts of England,* p. 599.

14. *Times* December 11 1789 4a.

15. On women as victims of crime in the late eighteenth century, see Anna Clark, *Women's Silence, Men's Violence* (London 1987), and McLynn, *Crime & Punishment,* pp. 96–115.

16. Skitch's plight is detailed in the *Times* of April 14 1789 3d, and the hangings in the *Times* of May 12 1789 3b.

17. This anonymous article was in the *Gentleman's Magazine* 60 (1790): 1185.

18. McLynn, *Crime & Punishment,* pp. 282–85.

19. *British Mercury* 14 (1790): 336–37.

20. On eighteenth-century London debating societies in general, see Donna T. Andrew: *London Debating Societies, 1776-1799* (London 1994). The debate whether women had souls was announced in the *Times* of November 18 1789 1b.

21. *Times* Oct 29 1789.

22. *Times* March 26 1789 3c.

23. On eighteenth-century female "sensibility," see G. J. Barker-Benfield, *The Culture of Sensibility* (Chicago 1992).

24. See the article by Jennie Gray, "Hags and Heroines of the 1790s," *The Goth* 8 (1992): 3–6.

25. On the role of women in late eighteenth-century London society, see Roy Porter, *English Society in the Eighteenth Century* (London 1991), pp. 22–34.

26. On late eighteenth-century sexual mores, see Roy Porter, "Mixed Feelings: The Enlightenment and Sexuality in Eighteenth-Century Britain," in *Sexuality in Eighteenth-Century Britain,* ed. P. G. Boucé (Manchester 1982), pp. 1–27, and Porter, *English Society in the Eighteenth Century* (London 1991), pp. 260–65.

27. Anthony E. Sampson, "Vulnerability and the Age of Female Consent," in *Sexual Underworlds of the Enlightenment,* ed. G. S. Rousseau and Roy Porter (Manchester 1987), pp. 181–205.

28. McLynn, *Crime & Punishment,* p. 99. It is not known what the proportion would be today.

29. *British Mercury* 14 (1790): 282.

30. For contemporary accounts of the sport of "ratting," see an anonymous article in the *Annals of Sporting* 2 (1822): 265, and Henry Mayhew, *Mayhew's London,* ed. Peter Quennell (London n.d.), pp. 401–14. A later analysis is that by E. S. Turner, *All Heaven in a Rage* (London 1964), pp. 151–56.

31. Probably from intestinal obstruction; see *World* March 11 3c.

32. *World* Jan 9; quoted from Lysons' *Collecteana* (C 103 K.11.), f. 159, in the British Library.

33. *Public Advertiser* Feb 3 4b.

34. *World* Jan 13 3c.

35. On the festivities on the queen's birthday, see the *World* Jan 19 2a–b; *Public Advertiser* Jan 19 2b.

36. About Pero's Bagnio, see F. H. W. Sheppard, *Survey of London* (London 1960), vol. 30, pp. 459–60; Edward Walford, *Old and New London* (London 1873), vol. 4, pp. 167–69; Edwin Beresford Chancellor, *Pleasure Haunts of London During Four Centuries* (London 1925), pp. 181–85; Bryant Lillywhite, *London Coffee-Houses* (London 1963), p. 407; and E. J. Burford, *Royal St. James's.* The first of these sources places Pero's Bagnio at No. 19, the others at No. 63 St. James's Street. The *Survey of London* states, on what authority is not known, that there were two bagnios in St. James's Street: one at No. 63 and one at No. 19, on the other side of the street; the latter, active in the early eighteenth century, was Pero's Bagnio. What definitely settles this question is that Anne Porter said she had once escaped from the Monster who stalked her, through the "stable yard" leading to the rear of the bagnio; there was such a yard next to No. 63, but not in the vicinity of No. 19. Pero's Bagnio had originally been based in the northernmost of three narrow houses built on the site of No. 63 in 1699, but in 1733 the bagnio took over the middle house and also used a substantial building behind the street houses. In 1748, a man named Will. Stevens was listed as keeper, and his wife kept the bagnio until 1757, when it was taken over by Edward Wilson, who kept it until 1780; it is not unlikely that Mr. Porter purchased Pero's Bagnio in that year.

37. See Ben Weinreb and Christopher Hibbert, eds., *The London Encyclopædia* (London 1992), pp. 742–73 and Roy Porter, *London: A Social History* (Cambridge, Mass. 1998), pp. 171–72; also E. J. Burford, *Royal St. James's.* There was only one regular brothel in St. James's Street at this time, Miss Fawkland's Temple of Love, an elegant upper-class establishment that boasted that it never lacked "fresh goods."

38. The assault on the Porters was reported by John Julius Angerstein, *An Authentic Account of the Barbarities lately practised by the Monsters* (London 1790), pp. 37–41; the *World* June 15 3a–b and July 9 3b–c; the *Oracle* July 9 (from Banks p. 12); the *London Chronicle* 68 (1790): 33–34; the *New Lady's Magazine* 5 (1790): 372–77; and E. Hodgson, *The Trial at Large of Rhynwick Williams* (London 1790), pp. 9–17.

39. Theophilus Swift, *The Monster at Large; or, the Innocence of Rhynwick Williams Vindicated* (London 1790), pp. 98–100; also referred to by Judge Mainwaring in his handwritten notes (Public Record Office, HO 47/17), ff. 9–10.

40. Judge Mainwaring's notes (Public Record Office, HO 47/17), ff. 13–14.

41. *Diary* May 1, from Banks p. 5.

42. The London police of the 1790s has been described by Gilbert Armitage, *The History of the Bow Street Runners 1729–1829* (London 1932), pp. 101–43; Anthony Babington, *A House in Bow Street* (London 1969), pp. 164–209; and McLynn, *Crime & Punishment,* pp. 17–35.

43. For an account of the mid-eighteenth-century night watchmen, see Beattie, *Crime and the Courts of England,* pp. 67–72. For an acrid criticism of the watch of 1797, see Patrick Colquhoun, *A Treatise on the Police of the Metropolis* (London 1797). For a not less critical account of the Watch in 1811, see P. D. James and T. A. Critchley, *The Maul and the Pear Tree* (London 1987), pp. 18–24.

44. David Philips, " 'A New Engine of Power and Authority': The Institutionaliza-tion of Law-Enforcement in England, 1780–1830" in *Crime and the Law,* ed. V. A. C. Gatrell et al. (London 1980), pp. 155–89.

45. The role of the Bow Street public office has been described by Percy Fitz-gerald, *Chronicles of the Bow Street Police Office* 1–2 (London 1888); Armitage, *The History of the Bow Street Runners,* pp. 101–43; Joan Lock, *Tales from Bow Street* (London 1982), pp. 43–58; and particularly Babington, *A House in Bow Street,* pp. 164–96.

46. These three assaults were described by Angerstein, pp. 34–37; see also the second edition of Angerstein's *Authentic Account of the Barbarities lately prac-tised by the Monsters,* which contains a supplement of additional Monster attacks, including that on Mrs. Harlow, which is detailed on p. 169. The author thanks Mr. Stephen Z. Nonack, head of reference at the Boston Athenæum Library, which owns what is probably the only extant copy of Angerstein's second edition, for sending relevant copies and information.

47. *World* April 28 (from Banks, p. 5).

## CHAPTER 2. A MONSTER ON THE PROWL

1. For the assault on Mrs. Smyth, see Angerstein, pp. 9–13, and the *Diary* of May 1 1790 (Banks p. 5). Angerstein adds that, since this cruel assault was so inexplicable (he made no attempt whatsoever to rob her), Mrs. Smyth's friends advised her not to report it to the Bow Street magistrates unless she heard of simi-lar attempts made upon others. There are actually two even earlier examples of a Monster-type assault. One was very briefly described in the *Times* of March 7 1788 3d. The other, concerning a certain Mrs. Wright who was stabbed in Bow Lane, Cheapside, by a man "of a shabby appearance, much like a hair-dresser" in March 1788, is described in the second edition of Angerstein's *Authentic Account of the Barbarities lately practised by the Monsters,* pp. 167–69.

2. Angerstein, pp. 17–21.

3. Angerstein, pp. 17–19; *Morning Herald* April 12 1790 (Banks p. 1).

4. Angerstein, pp. 22–25; *Public Advertiser* June 17 3d–4a.

5. Angerstein, pp. 25–26.

6. The Morley and Dodson assaults are described by Angerstein, pp. 26–31.

7. The Baughan case was discussed by Angerstein, pp. 31–33, in the *Lawyer's and Magistrate's Magazine* 2 (1790–91): 345–60, and by Judge Mainwaring (Public Record Office HO 47/17).

8. Angerstein, pp. 42–45.

9. Angerstein, pp. 41–42.

10. Angerstein, pp. 45–48; *Public Advertiser* May 1 4b; *Public Advertiser* June 17 3d–4a; *British Mercury* 13 (1790): 272.

11. Angerstein, pp. 48–50.

12. Notice from unstated newspaper, Banks p. 4; Angerstein, pp. 51–52.

13. See Banks p. 1 for several examples of imaginative newspaper articles. Andrew Franklin may have been the poet and playwright by that name, with eleven works to his name in the British Library. His letter was published in the *Morning*

*Herald* April 20 (from Banks p. 4), and it gives reference to earlier letters from him about the Monster business.

14. *Morning Herald* April 8 (from Banks p. 1); *World* April 14 3b.

15. *Morning Chronicle* April 3 1790, quoted by Angerstein, pp. 72–75.

16. *World* April 20 3d; *Morning Herald* April 20 (Banks p. 3); *Diary* May 1 (Banks p. 5); Angerstein, pp. 82–89.

17. *Times* April 20 3b; Angerstein, p. 87.

18. This critical account was in the *Oracle* April 20 (Banks p. 3).

19. *British Mercury* 13 (1790): 216–17.


## CHAPTER 3. THE ANGERSTEIN REWARD

1. John Julius Angerstein's biography was told in the collection *Public Characters* 6 (1804): 385–404, in the *Annual Biography and Obituary* 8 (1824): 275–98, by William Jerdan in vol. 1 of the *National Portrait Gallery* (London 1835), and later by Charles Wright and Charles Ernest Fayle, *A History of Lloyds* (London 1928), pp. 114–15 et seq.

2. Cyril Fry, "The Angersteins of Woodlands," in *John Julius Angerstein and Woodlands 1774-1974* (Woodlands Art Gallery, London 1974), pp. 1–9.

3. Angerstein apparently had many paintings of females in various states of undress. His descriptions of the Monster victims are often very detailed and sometimes have ribald elements; those of Miss Toussaint and the Porter sisters are to be found on pp. 35 and 38 in his pamphlet.

4. Angerstein, p. 33.

5. See Miss Banks's Monster scrapbook, pp. 2–3 and 6 for many press cuttings of Angerstein's advertisement, which appear to have been published in almost every newspaper.

6. The actual Angerstein handbills are today quite rare: The only examples I know of are in Miss Banks's Monster scrapbook, ff. 44–45.

7. *Gazetteer* May 17 3a; *Times* May 15 3a.

8. *Times* 21 April 3c–d.

9. Angerstein, pp. 52–53.

10. The second attack on Mrs. Harlow is described in the second edition of Angerstein's *Authentic Account of the Barbarities lately practised by the Monsters,* pp. 169–70.

11. Angerstein, pp. 53–54.

12. Angerstein, pp. 54–56 and the *World* April 29 3b.

13. *Times* May 4 3c.

14. Angerstein, pp. 56–58.

15. *Public Advertiser* May 1 4b.

16. *Gazetteer* 6 May 3b.

17. The assault on Elizabeth Davis was described by Angerstein, pp. 59–61; further details were added by the *World* of May 8 3b and June 17 3d, the *Gazetteer* of May 8 3c, and the *Oracle* of May 11, quoted from Banks p. 6. Still more details appear in the *Lawyer's and Magistrate's Magazine* 2 (1790–91): 345–60.

18. *World* May 8 3b, and *Court Chronicle* of May 15, quoted from Banks (p. 7).

19. *Oracle* May 12, from Banks p. 7.

20. *Gazetteer* May 10 2d; *World* May 10 3a; *Times* May 10 2d. Walter Hill, alias Walter Hill Coyney, had become a lieutenant in 1785 but resigned his commission in 1795, according to *The Commissioned Sea Officers of the Royal Navy 1660-1815*, ed. David Syrett and R. L. DiNardo (Aldershot 1994).

21. *World* May 10 3a.

22. *Morning Herald* May 10, from Banks p. 6.

23. *World* May 14 3a.

24. Angerstein, pp. 13–16, 28–31.

25. Angerstein, pp. 61–64.

26. Angerstein, p. 65.

27. From Mr. Angerstein's poster of May 7 in the Banks scrapbook, f. 45.

28. Angerstein, pp. 58–59.

29. *Times* May 8 3a.

30. From Mr. Angerstein's poster of May 7 in the Banks scrapbook, f. 45.

31. This poster, and even the handwritten protocol of the meeting, are in the Banks scrapbook at the British Library, ff. 46–47.

## CHAPTER 4. MONSTER MANIA

1. *Oracle* May 15, quoted from Banks (p. 7). Anna Clark, *Women's Silence, Men's Violence* (London, 1987), pp. 110–27, mentions the Monster briefly in a discussion of whether the streets of London were safe for women in the eighteenth century, but misdates the Monster mania by one year, placing it in 1791.

2. Angerstein, pp. 98–99.

3. Georg Forster, *Werke,* vol. 12 (*Tagebücher*) (Berlin 1973), pp. 297–98. (Author's translation.)

4. *British Mercury* 13 (1790): 212.

5. Ibid.

6. *British Mercury* 13 (1790): 371–72.

7. M. Dorothy George, *Catalogue of Political and Personal Satires* (London 1938), vol. 6, pp. 725–26; *Times* May 19 3a.

8. M. Dorothy George, *Catalogue of Political and Personal Satires* (London 1935), vol. 5, p. 242, mentions that cork rumps, a support that extended the dress at the back, were all the rage among fashionable women in the 1770s and 1780s.

9. *Times* May 4 3b and *Gazetteer* May 4 1790, quoted from Banks p. 6.

10. *World* May 11 3b.

11. *Diary* May 14, quoted from Banks p. 7; *World* May 14 3b and *Gazetteer* May 14 3a.

12. *Oracle* May 17, quoted from Banks p. 8.

13. *St. James's Gazette* May 15–18, 2b.

14. On Astley's popular play, see *World* May 15 1c; *Public Advertiser* May 12 3c; *St. James's Gazette* May 6–8 3a; *Times* April 30 3c; *Morning Herald* April 27 (from Banks p. 4). The Coventry Act, named after Sir John Coventry, whose nose and ears had been slit by the duke of Monmouth and his accomplices, made it a felony to lie in wait to maim and disfigure someone.

15. *British Mercury* 13 (1790): 320.

16. Charles Beecher Hogan, ed., *The London Stage* (Carbondale, Ill. 1968), vol. 5, pp. 1252–53.

17. *World* May 5 2d; *British Mercury* 13 (1790): 270.

18. *World* May 14 3b; *Times* May 15 3a and May 19 3c.

19. *World* May 14 3b.

20. *Times* May 15 3a.

21. *Times* May 21 3d.

22. *St. James's Gazette* May 13–15 4d.

23. Extract from unnamed newspaper, Banks p. 5.

24. Angerstein, pp. 66–67.

25. Angerstein, pp. 67–69.

26. *British Mercury* 13 (1790): 240–41.

27. Angerstein, p. 106.

28. *St. James's Gazette* May 13–15 4d.

29. Quoted from Angerstein, p. 100–102.

30. Georg Forster, *Werke,* vol. 12 (*Tagebücher*), pp. 297–98. (Author's translation.)

31. Angerstein, pp. 102–5.

32. *Gazetteer* May 17 3a.

33. See Hester Lynch Piozzi: *Thraliana: Diary of Mrs Hester Lynch Thrale, later Mrs Piozzi, 1776-1809,* ed. Katherine C. Balderson, (Oxford 1942), vol. 2, p. 770. Like some others, Mrs. Thrale was of the opinion that the Monster was a member of an unnatural society of homosexuals, who held women in abhorrence. See also the article by Darryl Jones, "Frekes, Monsters and the Ladies: Attitudes to Female Sexuality in the 1790s," *Literature & History* 4, 2 (1995): 1–24, although this author wrongly accuses the Monster of "vaginal mutilation" and compares his ferocious assaults with those of the Yorkshire Ripper.

34. Angerstein, pp. 105–6.

35. *Times* May 31 3a.

36. *British Mercury* 13 (1790): 307.

37. *Oracle* June 10 (Banks p. 8).

38. *Diary* May 31 (Banks p. 18).

39. On Lady Wallace, see the *Dictionary of National Biography.* Her supposed encounter with the Monster was detailed in the *Times* of May 27, 2d.

40. The story of "Fat Phillis" and his perilous encounter with the two timid young gentlemen is in the *British Mercury* 13 (1790): 343–44, under the heading "A Shocking Charge!"

41. On eighteenth-century caricatures in general, see volumes 5–8 of George's *Catalogue of Political and Personal Satires,* and Mark Hallett, *The Spectacle of Difference: Graphic Satire in the Age of Hogarth* (New Haven, Conn. 1999). J. A. Sharpe, *Crime and the Law in English Satirical Prints 1600-1832* (Cambridge 1986), is a valuable source on crime and criminals in eighteenth-century satire, and mentions the Monster briefly on pp. 184–85.

42. J. M. Bulloch, "The Monster," *Notes & Queries* 173 (1937): 44–45, and Anon., "The Monster," *Notes & Queries* 173 (1937): 106.

43. On Philip Thicknesse, see Philip Gosse, *Dr. Viper* (London 1952), in particu-

lar pp. 273–76, for his quarrel with Captain Crookshanks. For some of Thicknesse's own comments, see the *World* June 15 2c. The poster is in the Banks scrapbook f. 48, and the caricature is f. 57.

44. George, *Catalogue of Political and Personal Satires,* vol. 6, p. 729, discusses this caricature, but is unable to identify the person pilloried. Nor does B. M. Benedict, "Making a Monster," in *Defects,* ed. H. Deutsch and F. Nussbaum (Ann Arbor, Mich. 2000), pp. 127–53, have a correct perception of the campaign against Captain Thicknesse. The same author also misinterprets Gillray's *Swearing to the Cutting Monster* as a caricature of Rhynwick Williams at Bow Street.

## CHAPTER 5. THE ARREST OF RHYNWICK WILLIAMS

1. Accounts of these dramatic events are in the *World* June 15, 3 a–b and July 9, 3b–c; *Oracle* July 9 (Banks p. 12); *London Chronicle* 68 (1790): 33–34; E. Hodgson, *The Trial at Large of Rhynwick Williams* (London 1790), pp. 19–22.
2. L. Williams, *The Trial of Renwick Williams* (London 1790), p. 8.
3. Theophilus Swift, *The Monster at Large* (London 1790), pp. 168–70.

## CHAPTER 6. RHYNWICK WILLIAMS AT BOW STREET

1. *Diary* June 15 (Banks p. 8); *Morning Herald* June 15 (Banks p. 8); *World* June 15 3a–b.
2. *Times* June 15 3c.
3. *World* July 17 (Banks p. 16); *World* July 12 2d.
4. Sir John Gallini is in the *Dictionary of National Biography,* but a better account of his life and career in London is in Philip H. Highfill Jr. et al., eds., *Biographical Dictionary of Actors &c. in London, 1660-1800* (Carbondale, Ill. 1978), vol. 5, pp. 444–49.
5. *World* July 17 (Banks p. 16).
6. See Highfill et al., eds., *Biographical Dictionary of Actors,* vol. 16, p. 113.
7. Angerstein, p. 125.
8. Public Record Office; will of Thomas Williams dated June 9, 1785, PROB 11/1131/346.
9. List of Members of the Society of Apothecaries, Guildhall Library Archives, Ms. 8206/2-3.
10. *World* July 17 (Banks p. 16).
11. Highfill et al., eds., *Biographical Dictionary of Actors,* vol. 5, pp. 447–48.
12. Rhynwick Williams, *An Appeal to the Public by Rhynwick Williams, Containing Observations and Reflections on Facts relative to his very Extraordinary and Melancholy Case* (London 1792), p. 13.
13. *World* July 17 (Banks p. 16).
14. On June 4, the king's birthday, according to Amabel himself, giving evidence at the Old Bailey; see Hodgson, p. 30.
15. *World* June 15 3a–b; *The General Magazine* 4 (1790): 282–83.
16. *British Mercury* 14 (1790): 49–50.

17. The first examination of Rhynwick Williams is described in the *World* June 15 3a–b and the *St. James's Gazette* June 12–5 4d.

18. Although these alleged previous observations of the Monster were alluded to by Angerstein, pp. 38, 41, and Hodgson, pp. 10–11, 14–15, by far the most complete account is that by Judge Mainwaring in his handwritten notes (Public Record Office, HO 47/17), ff. 4–7.

19. *World* June 15 3a–b.

20. Swift, *Monster at Large,* p. 204.

21. Angerstein, pp. 112–13.

22. *World* June 15 3a–b.

23. Angerstein, pp. 24–25.

24. *Oracle* June 10 (Banks p. 8).

25. *World* June 15 3a–b; Swift, *Monster at Large,* p. 212.

26. The second examination of Rhynwick Williams at Bow Street is covered by the *Morning Herald* June 17 (Banks pp. 9–10); *World* June 17 3d; *Public Advertiser* June 17 3d–4a; *Diary* June 18 (Banks p. 10).

27. *World* June 18 3c.

28. *Morning Herald* June 17 (Banks pp. 9–10).

29. *The General Magazine* 4 (1790): 282–83; *Public Advertiser* June 17 3d–4a.

30. *The General Magazine* 4 (1790): 282–83.

31. *Morning Herald* June 17 (Banks pp. 9–10).

32. Williams, *Appeal to the Public,* p. 41.

33. *World* June 18 3c.

34. *The General Magazine* 4 (1790): 282–83.

35. Williams, *Appeal to the Public,* pp. 40–41; Swift, *Monster at Large,* pp. 154–55, 203.

36. *Morning Herald* June 17 (Banks pp. 9–10); *World* June 17 3d.

37. *Public Advertiser* June 17 3d–4a;

38. *Morning Herald* June 17 (Banks pp. 9–10).

39. Extract from an unnamed newspaper, Banks f. 54.

40. The third and final examination of Rhynwick Williams at Bow Street was covered by the *World* June 19 3c and the *Diary* of June 21 (Banks p. 12).

41. *The General Magazine* 4 (1790): 282–83; *World* June 19 3c. The identity of this unwise and imprudent Joshua Williams remains obscure; it is unlikely that he was Rhynwick's brother. There was a tea broker in London by that name.

42. For a discussion of the difference between a felony and a misdemeanor in the eighteenth century, see McLynn, *Crime & Punishment in Eighteenth-Century England,* pp. x–xi.

43. *World* July 8 3d.

44. *Gazetteer* June 19 3b; *Times* July 6 2c; *World* July 3 3c; *Diary* June 23 (Banks p. 12).

45. *British Mercury* 14 (1790): 105–6.

46. *Morning Herald* June 19 (Banks p. 11).

47. *World* June 22 3c.

48. *Times* June 17 3a.

49. Quoted from Angerstein, pp. 127–29.

## CHAPTER 7. THE FIRST TRIAL

1. The trial of Rhynwick Williams was headline news all over Britain. It was reported in many newspapers, among them the *World* July 9 3b–c; *Times* July 9 3a–c; *London Chronicle* 68, 33–34, 1790; *Oracle* July 9 (Banks 12–14). It was also reported in the magazines, among them the *New Lady's Magazine* 5 (1790): 372–77, the *Lady's Magazine* 21 (1790): 369–73, the *Annual Register* 32 (1790): 264–67, and the *Gentleman's Magazine* 60(2) (1790): 660–62. It even penetrated to the European continent, most particularly in the *Annalen der Brittischen Geschichte* 5 (1791): 175–83.

2. See Swift, *Monster at Large,* pp. 128–29.

3. *World* July 3 3c; *Diary* July 27 (Banks pp. 16–17).

4. On Judge Buller, see the *Dictionary of National Biography,* and in particular William Charles Townsend, *Lives of Twelve Eminent Judges* (London 1846), vol. 1, pp. 1–32.

5. Williams, *Appeal to the Public,* pp. 36–37.

6. Neither Hodgson nor any of the other transcripts of the trial mentions any witnesses of this description.

7. Swift, *Monster at Large,* pp. 192–94.

8. On Mr. Pigot and his distinguished later career, see the *Dictionary of National Biography.*

9. Hodgson, p. 6.

10. Hodgson, p. 8.

11. See the *London Chronicle* 68 (1790): 33–34; *Oracle* July 9 (Banks pp. 12–14); *New Lady's Magazine* 5 (1790): 372–77.

12. Hodgson, pp. 9–12.

13. Williams, *Appeal to the Public,* pp. 16–17.

14. Hodgson, p. 16.

15. Coleman's evidence is in Hodgson, pp. 19–22.

16. Hodgson, pp. 22–23. From contemporary maps, there is evidence that No. 52 Jermyn Street was really at the corner of Duke Street and Jermyn Street.

17. Swift, *Monster at Large,* pp. 192–94.

18. L. Williams, *Trial,* p. 10. Williams's speech is in Hodgson, pp. 25–26.

19. Mitchell's evidence is in Hodgson, pp. 26–32.

20. The questions and answers are from Hodgson, pp. 31–32; the explanation from Swift, *Monster at Large,* pp. 192–94.

21. Her evidence is in Hodgson, pp. 32–35.

22. She was quite a famous Irish actress, active in London at this time; see Anon., *The Life of Mrs. Abington* (London 1888).

23. The testimony of the Alman sisters, Frances Beaufils, and Typhone Fournier is in Hodgson, pp. 35–47.

24. Hodgson, pp. 47–48.

25. Hodgson, pp. 48–49.

26. Williams, *Appeal to the Public,* pp. 19–21.

27. L. Williams, *Trial,* p. 15; Nathaniel Jenkins, *A Full Account of the Trial of Renwick Williams* (London 1790), pp. 26–27.

28. L. Williams, *Trial,* p. 15.

29. *Oracle* July 9 (Banks pp. 12–14).

30. Judge Buller's summing-up is in Hodgson, pp. 49–55. It is not known whether the conservative judge's distaste for the uncouth phrase "Oh ho! Is that you?" was justified; one might imagine that a man-about-town or an easygoing lady might use such a greeting.

31. Angerstein, p. 8.

32. *World* July 9 (Banks p. 15); this advertisement did not mention the trial of Rhynwick Williams.

33. An example of these posters is in the Banks scrapbook, f. 52; the scrapbook also contains several advertisements for this pamphlet, one of them marked *World* July 13, on p. 16.

34. See the NUC catalogue under R. Williams; it also lists a U.S. edition of Hodgson's pamphlet published in 1791, held by the Library of the Historical Society of Pennsylvania.

35. Angerstein, pp. 159–60.

36. *Rambler's Magazine* 8 (1790): 285–86.

37. Angerstein, p. 129.

## CHAPTER 8. THE MONSTER'S CHAMPION

1. *Dictionary of National Biography,* article on Theophilus Swift.

2. John Nichols, *Literary Anecdotes* (London 1812), vol. 3, p. 181.

3. Theophilus Swift, *The Female Parliament* (London 1789).

4. Theophilus Swift, *Prison Pindarics; or a New Year's Gift from Newgate* (Dublin 1795), p. 8.

5. Theophilus Swift, *A Letter to the King; In which the Conduct of Mr Lenox, and the Minister, in the Affair with his Royal Highness the Duke of York is fully considered* (London 1789).

6. *Annual Register* 31 (1789): 215–16.

7. Theophilus Swift, *A Letter to Sir William Augustus Brown, Bart., on a Late Affair of Honor with Mr Lennox* (London 1789).

8. Swift, *Prison Pindarics,* p. 22.

9. *Times* July 7 1789 2c, July 14 1789 1c, August 3 1789 3a.

10. Anon., "The Late Edmund Lenthall Swifte, Esq.," *Notes & Queries* 5s. 5 (1876): 60.

11. Swift, *Prison Pindarics,* p. 9. But Swift himself asserts, in his *Monster at Large,* p. 194, that he did not know Williams or any member of his family at the time of his arrest as the Monster! Swift was such an accomplished liar that one does not know which version to believe.

12. Swift, *Prison Pindarics,* p. 7.

13. Swift, *Monster at Large,* p. 212.

14. Swift, *Monster at Large,* pp. 98, 143.

15. Swift, *Monster at Large,* pp. 81–83. It is quite true that No. 62 St. James's Street, on one side of the bagnio, had (and still has) a large bow window. On the other

side of the bagnio was a stable yard, however, and no contemporary map or illustration shows a house with a bow window even on the other side of this yard.

16. Swift, *Monster at Large,* pp. 95–97.

17. Swift, *Monster at Large,* pp. 37–39.

18. Swift, *Monster at Large,* p. 104.

19. The pursuit of Rhynwick Williams is detailed in Swift, *Monster at Large,* pp. 119–32.

20. Swift, *Monster at Large,* pp. 112–14.

21. Swift, *Monster at Large,* pp. 140, 142.

22. Swift, *Monster at Large,* pp. 128–29.

23. Swift, *Monster at Large,* pp. 65–66, 103–5.

24. Swift, *Monster at Large,* p. 51.

25. Swift, *Monster at Large,* pp. 49–50.

26. These pleasant jokes are in Swift, *Monster at Large,* p. 150 and p. 66.

27. Swift, *Monster at Large,* p. 156.

28. Swift, *Monster at Large,* p. 158.

29. Swift, *Monster at Large,* p. 184.

30. Swift, *Monster at Large,* pp. 43–44.

31. *New Lady's Magazine* 5 (1790): 438.

32. *Times* July 12 1b.

33. *Diary* July 27; *Oracle* Aug 9; *Morning Herald* Nov 12; *Diary* Nov 13, all from Banks, pp. 17–18; also *World* Oct 17 3d.

34. On the Monster's Ball, see R. Thuston Hopkins, *Life and Death at the Old Bailey* (London 1935), pp. 82–83, and a contemporary account in the *Oracle* of Aug 20, quoted from Banks (p. 18).

35. *British Mercury* 14 (1790): 398–99.

36. *Times* Aug 23 2b.

37. These two quotations are from Swift, *Monster at Large,* p. 200 and p. 89.

38. The meeting of the judges is described in the *Oracle* Nov 12, *Morning Herald* Nov 12, *Court Chronicle* Nov 20, Banks pp. 18–19.

39. The proceedings at the Old Bailey were described, and Williams's speech quoted, in the *Diary* of Dec 9, from Banks pp. 19–20.

40. *Argus* Dec 9 3c.


## CHAPTER 9. THE SECOND TRIAL

1. The first day of the second trial of Rhynwick Williams was extensively covered by the *Lawyer's and Magistrate's Magazine* 2 (1790–91): 345–60, by a large extract from an unnamed newspaper in the Banks scrapbook f. 53, and by the notes of Judge Mainwaring, PRO (HO 47/17).

2. Anthony Babington, *A House in Bow Street* (London 1969), pp. 170–71.

3. *Lawyer's and Magistrate's Magazine* 2 (1790–91): 345–60.

4. Banks f. 53.

5. *Lawyer's and Magistrate's Magazine* 2 (1790–91): 345–60; Banks f. 53.

6. Williams, *Appeal to the Public,* p. 21.

7. Williams, *Appeal to the Public,* p. 21.

8. Mainwaring ff. 3–4.

9. Banks f. 53; Mainwaring f. 10.

10. Banks f. 53.

11. Williams, *Appeal to the Public,* pp. 20–22, graphically describes these dramatic moments.

12. Banks f. 53.

13. Mainwaring f. 10.

14. Mainwaring f. 17.

15. Banks f. 53; Mainwaring ff. 17–18.

16. Mainwaring f. 23.

17. *Lawyer's and Magistrate's Magazine* 2 (1790–91): 345–60.

18. Williams, *Appeal to the Public,* p. 31.

19. Lady Wallace's part in the trial was described in the *Times* of Dec 22 3b.

20. The evidence of the artificial flower makers is in Mainwaring ff. 26–27, with a few additions in Banks f. 53.

21. *Lawyer's and Magistrate's Magazine* 2 (1790–91): 345–60.

22. The second day of the trial was covered by the *Lawyer's and Magistrate's Magazine* 2 (1790–91): 345–60, by Miss Banks's scrapbook f. 53, and by the notes of Judge Mainwaring, PRO (HO 47/17).

23. See, for example, the *World* Dec 14 3d; *Public Advertiser* Dec 16 4c; *Argus* Dec 15 3d.

24. Banks f. 53.

25. *Argus* Dec 14 4d.

26. *Argus* Dec 15 3d.

27. *Argus* Dec 21 3c.

28. *World* Dec 17 3d.

29. See J. M. Beattie, *Crime and the Courts of England 1600-1800* (Oxford 1986), pp. 582–93 and Frank McLynn, *Crime and Punishment in Eighteenth-Century England* (Oxford 1991), pp. 294–98.

30. *British Mercury* 15 (1790): 400.


## CHAPTER 10. WHAT HAPPENED TO RHYNWICK WILLIAMS?


1. See Arthur Griffiths, *Chronicles of Newgate* (London 1987), pp. 186–87 and elsewhere for instances of various notorious prisoners being put on show by the warders; for example, the turnkeys earned not less than two hundred pounds by exhibiting Jack Sheppard.

2. Williams, *Appeal to the Public,* p. 29.

3. Paget Toynbee, ed., *The Letters of Horace Walpole* (Oxford 1905), vol. 14, p. 381.

4. Richard D. Altick, *The Shows of London* (Cambridge, Mass. 1978), p. 53.

5. See George, *Catalogue of Political and Personal Satires,* vol. 8, pp. 116–17. Cope committed suicide in 1806 by jumping from a precipice in Brighton, according to the *Annual Register* 48 (1806): 451–52.

6. Anon., *Monthly Review* N.S. 4 (1791): 81–82.

7. See *World* June 22 3c. According to the *British Mercury* 14 (1790): 281, even the felons in Newgate shunned the Monster's company.

8. Swift, *Monster at Large,* p. 12 and elsewhere.

9. Williams, *Appeal to the Public,* p. 16, 17, 28 et seq.

10. Quotations are from Williams, *Appeal to the Public,* pp. 16–18, 26–27.

11. From an unknown newspaper, quoted by Anon., "Mr John Coleman," *Notes & Queries* 2s. 8 (1859): 229.

12. Williams, *Appeal to the Public,* p. 30.

13. Williams, *Appeal to the Public,* pp. 43–46.

14. This prison calendar (HO 26/56) and those for 1793–96 (HO 26/3–5) are at the Public Record Office.

15. See Robert Watson, *The Life of Lord George Gordon* (London 1795), pp. 107–9 and Christopher Hibbert, *King Mob* (New York 1989), pp. 167–72.

16. Public Record Office (HO 26/3).

17. W. J. Sheenan, "Finding Solace in 18th Century Newgate," in *Crime in England,* ed. J. S. Cockburn (London 1977), pp. 229–45.

18. This letter (and its envelope) is kept at the Public Record Office (HO 47/17).

19. This report, as well as the letters of Rhynwick Williams, are at the Public Record Office (HO 47/17).

20. Theophilus Swift, *Animadversions on the Fellows of Trinity College* (Dublin 1794), pp. 10 et seq.

21. *Dictionary of National Biography,* article on Theophilus Swift.

22. Theophilus Swift, *Prison Pindarics; or a New Year's Gift from Newgate* (Dublin 1795).

23. Swift, *Prison Pindarics,* pp. 9, 18.

24. See the *Oracle* of Dec 16 1796 3d.

25. Both the marriage and the christening are verified in the International Genealogical Index (on CD-ROM).

26. Henry Wilson, *Wonderful Characters,* (London 1822) vol. 3, pp. 42–52. Nor did a well-informed writer of an article entitled "An Old Story retold: Renwick Williams, The Monster" in the *All the Year Round* magazine NS 26 (1881):324–29) have any success in tracing what happened to Williams.

27. See the Quarterage Book of the Society of Apothecaries, vols. 4–5, Guildhall Library Archives, Ms. 8208/4–5. His will is at the Public Record Office (Thomas Williams, July 1829, PROB 11/1759/460).

28. *Westminster Poll Book of 1818* (Reprinted Exeter 1996), p. 131.

29. All according to the International Genealogical Index (CD-ROM).

30. *Annual Biography and Obituary* 8 (1824): 275–98.

31. John Barrett, manuscript annotations to Theophilus Swift, *The Touch-Stone of Truth* (Dublin 1811), in the British Library.

32. Swift, *The Touch-Stone of Truth.* Miss Emma Dobbin married her father's curate, Thomas Philip Le Fanu, and became the mother of J. Sheridan Le Fanu, the celebrated novelist. The Le Fanu family have of course had little good to say about Theophilus Swift. See W. J. McCormack, *Sheridan Le Fanu and Victorian Ireland* (Dublin 1991), p. 4.

33. John Nichols, *Illustrations of the Literary History of the Eighteenth Century* (London 1828), vol. 5, pp. 374–97. On Swift's eccentric actions as his great

ancestor's literary executor, see the article by George Mayhew, "Swift's 'On the Day of Judgment' and Theophilus Swift," *Philological Quarterly* 54 (1975): 213–21.

34. Anon., "Theophilus Swift," *Notes & Queries* 5s. 5 (1876): 60, 153, and also the articles by E. Solly, "Theophilus Swift," *Notes & Queries* 5s. 5 (1876): 434–35, and W. F. Prideaux, "Miss Trefusis," *Notes & Queries* 9s. 6 (1900): 281–83.

## CHAPTER 11. PHANTOM ATTACKS

1. Whipping Tom is described by Magnus Hirschfeld, *Sexual Anomalies and Perversions* (London 1939), pp. 393–94. Several contemporary pamphlets and poems celebrated his bizarre exploits; some of them are still kept at the British Library.

2. M. Froment, *La police dévoilée depuis la revolution,* vol. 1 (Paris 1829), pp. 236–40; Francis Wharton, *A Treatise on Mental Unsoundness* (Philadelphia 1873), §573; and Dr. Cormier, "Le 'Piqueur' de Londres," *Aesculape* 37 (1955): 20–23.

3. Wilhelm Ludwig Demme, *Das Buch der Verbrechen* (Leipzig 1852), vol. 1, pp. 281–329; Wharton, *A Treatise on Mental Unsoundness,* §573; Richard von Krafft-Ebing, *Psychopathia Sexualis* (London 1906), pp. 109–10; Hirschfeld, *Sexual Anomalies and Perversions,* pp. 392–93.

4. Wilhelm Ludwig Demme, *Das Buch der Verbrechen* (Leipzig 1851), vol. 2, pp. 341–54; Krafft-Ebing, *Psychopathia Sexualis,* pp. 108–9; Hirschfeld, *Sexual Anomalies and Perversions,* p. 392.

5. Wharton, *A Treatise on Mental Unsoundness* (Philadelphia 1873), §621.

6. D. Travers, "Mädchenstecher," *Archiv für Kriminal-Anthropologie und Kriminalistik* 15 (1904): 396–97.

7. Krafft-Ebing, *Psychopathia Sexualis,* p. 109.

8. Andrew Knapp and William Baldwin, *The New Newgate Calendar* (London 1826), vol. 3, pp. 511–18.

9. *Times* 28 August 1834 4d.

10. *Times* 13 March 1885 8d.

11. Paul Begg et al., *The Jack the Ripper A–Z* (London 1996), pp. 85, 96–97.

12. Paul Garnier, "Le Sadi-fétichisme," *Annales d'Hygiène Publique et de Médecine Légale* ser. 3 43 (1900): 97–121, 210–47.

13. Dr. Doerr, "Mädchenstecher," *Archiv für Kriminal-Anthropologie und Kriminalistik* 15 (1904): 280–81.

14. Dr. Paffrath, "Ein sogenannter Mädchenstecher (Piqueur) und die Begutachtung seines Geisteszustandes vor Gericht," *Aerzliche Sachverständigen-Zeitung* 9 (1903): 301–8.

15. D. Travers, "Mädchenstecher," 396–97. Erich Wulffen, *Encyclopädie der modernen Kriminalistik VIII: Der Sexualverbrecher* (Berlin 1910), pp. 334–36, also briefly discusses cases from Metz (23 victims), Berlin, and Copenhagen.

16. Charles Fort, *Complete Books* (New York 1974), pp. 896–97; Paul Sieveking, ed., *Man Bites Man* (London 1980), p. 23; Michael Goss, *The Halifax Slasher,* Fortean Times occ. paper 3 (London 1987), pp. 42–43.

17. Sidney I. Schwab, "A Critical Analysis of the Expert Testimony in the Jack

the Stabber' Case," *Interstate Medical Journal* 13 (1906): 927–38, and D. S. Booth, "A Critical Analysis of the Expert Testimony in the 'Jack the Stabber' Case: A Retort Courteous." *Medical Forthnightly* 31 (1907): 75–79.

18. Goss, *The Halifax Slasher,* p. 43.

19. Goss, *The Halifax Slasher,* pp. 6–7.

20. Anon., "Compulsions," *Fortean Times* 28 (1979): 12.

21. Goss, *The Halifax Slasher,* is the great authority on this business. He later added some further material in his article, "The Halifax Slasher and Other 'Urban Maniac' Tales," in *A Nest of Vipers,* ed. Gillian Bennett and Paul Smith (Sheffield 1990), pp. 89–111.

22. Goss, *The Halifax Slasher,* p. 36; Anon., *Fortean Times* 28 (1979):12.

23. Bob Rickard, "Compulsions," *Fortean Times* 39 (1983): 19–21.

24. Anon., "A Festival of Fetichism," *Fortean Times* 46 (1986): 12–14.

25. Ibid.

26. Léon Henri Thoinot, *Attentats aux mœurs et perversions du sens génital* (Paris 1898), pp. 449–54, and Garnier, "Le Sadi-fétichisme."

27. On hair despoilers, see an anonymous case report in the *Revue de l'Hypnotisme et de la Psychologie Physiologique* 4 (1889–90): 247–50, Krafft-Ebing, *Psychopathia Sexualis,* pp. 241–45, and Erich Wulffen, *Encyclopädie der modernen Kriminalistik VIII: Der Sexualverbrecher* (Berlin 1910), pp. 535–42.

28. Hirschfeld, *Sexual Anomalies and Perversions,* pp. 543–49.

29. Garnier, "Le Sadi-fétichisme." Garnier's work on sadism is discussed by Vernon A. Rosario, *The Erotic Imagination: French Histories of Perversity* (Oxford 1997), pp. 145–51, but without any new insights about the serial stabbers.

30. Hirschfeld, *Sexual Anomalies and Perversions,* p. 393.

31. Krafft-Ebing, *Psychopathia Sexualis,* pp. 105–11, and Wulffen, *Encyclopädie,* pp. 334–36.

32. *Rambler's Magazine* 8 (1790): 285–86.

33. See M. J. MacCulloch et al., "Sadistic Fantasy, Sadistic Behaviour and Offending," *British Journal of Psychiatry* 143 (1983): 20–29; P. E. Dietz et al., "The Sexually Sadistic Criminal and His Offenses," *Bulletin of the American Academy of Psychiatry and the Law* 18 (1990): 163–78; T. Gratzer and J. M. W. Bradford, "Offender and Offense Characteristics of Sexual Sadists," *Journal of Forensic Sciences* 40 (1995): 450–55; A. Rose, "Verhaltenstherapie bei Frotteurismus—ein Fallbericht," *Verhaltenstherapie* 5 (1995): 154–60.

## CHAPTER 12. THE MONSTER, EPIDEMIC HYSTERIA, AND MORAL PANICS

1. François Sirois, "Epidemic Hysteria," *Acta Psychiatrica Scandinavica* suppl. 252, 1974.

2. See the papers by Sidney M. Stahl and Morty Lebedun, "Mystery Gas: An Analysis of Mass Hysteria," *Journal of Health and Social Behavior* 15 (1974): 44–50; Simon Wessely, "Mass Hysteria: Two Syndromes?" *Psychological Medicine* 17 (1987): 109–20; Robert E. Bartholomew, "Ethnocentricity and the Social Construction of Mass Hysteria," *Culture, Medicine and Psychiatry* 14 (1990): 455–94; and

"Tarantism, Dancing Mania and Demonopathy: The Anthropological Aspects of 'Mass Psychogenic Illness,'" *Psychological Medicine* 24 (1994): 281–306. The book *Mass Psychogenic Illness: A Social Psychological Analysis,* ed. Michael J. Colligan et al. (Hillsdale, N.J. 1982) gives an extensive overview of the field; the chapter by Alan C. Kerckhoff, "A Social Psychological View of Mass Psychogenic Illness," pp. 199–236 was particularly pertinent to this study.

3. Leslie P. Boss, "Epidemic Hysteria: A Review of the Published Literature," *Epidemiologic Reviews* 19 (1997): 233–43.

4. See the paper by C. J. Göthe et al., "The Environmental Somatization Syndrome," *Psychosomatics* 36 (1995): 1–11.

5. Elaine Showalter, *Hystories: Hysterical Epidemics and Modern Culture* (London 1998), pp. 144–58.

6. Robert Bartholomew and Simon Wessely, "Epidemic Hysteria in Virginia," *Southern Medical Journal* 92 (1999): 762–69.

7. Donald M. Johnson, "The 'Phantom Anesthetist' of Mattoon: A Field Study of Mass Hysteria," *Journal of Abnormal Social Psychology* 40 (1945): 175–86.

8. See the papers by David L. Miller et al., "A Critical Examination of the Social Contagion Image of Collective Behavior," *Sociological Quarterly* 19 (1978): 129–40; Robert E. Bartholomew, "Redefining Epidemic Hysteria: An Example from Sweden," *Acta Psychiatrica Scandinavica* 88 (1993): 178–82; and "Collective Delusions: A Skeptic's Guide," *Skeptical Inquirer* 21(3) (1997): 29–33.

9. Elaine Showalter, *Hystories: Hysterical Epidemics and Modern Culture,* pp. 171–201.

10. Robert Bartholomew and Simon Wessely, "Epidemic Hysteria in Virginia," 762–69, giving reference to W. H. Burnham, *The Normal Mind* (New York 1925), pp. 337–38.

11. Norman Jacobs, "The Phantom Slasher of Taipei: Mass Hysteria in a Non-Western Society," *Social Problems* 12 (1965): 318–28.

12. A survey of reports of non-Monster stabbings of women in the *Times* newspaper in 1785–89 turns up eight instances. A man cut his wife (Aug 11 1786 3d), a journeyman comb-maker cut his wife's throat (Nov 24 1787 3d), a hairdresser cut a prostitute's arm after a quarrel at an alehouse (Nov 28 1788 2d), an old woman was stabbed with a bayonet after being mistaken for a thief (April 29 1789 2d), a man stabbed his wife to death (July 13 1789 3b), a shipbuilder stabbed his wife and then himself (Nov 25 1789 3c), and a butcher cut a woman's throat and married her after she had recovered (Nov 27 1789 2d). The only odd one out is the "Uncommon and melancholy circumstance" reported on October 12, 1789 (3d). A young servant girl was familiarly addressed by a young man on the steps of Old Boswell Court. She replied that "she was not the person he wanted," i.e., that she was not a prostitute. The man then laid hold of her and stabbed her in the body. The woman was taken to the hospital "without hope of recovery," and the man was arrested.

13. Stanley Cohen, *Folk Devils and Moral Panics: The Creation of the Mods and Rockers* (London 1972).

14. An overview is given by Erich Goode and Nachman Ben-Yehuda, *Moral Panics: The Social Construction of Deviance* (Oxford 1994).

15. See the articles by Daniel Statt, "The Case of the Mohocks: Rake Violence in Augustan London," *Victorian Studies* 20 (1995): 179–99, and Neil Guthrie, "'No

Truth or Very Little in the Whole Story'?—A Reassessment of the Mohock Scare of 1712," *Eighteenth-Century Life* ns 20(2) (1996): 33–56.

16. On the London garrotting panics, see Rob Sindall, *Street Violence in the Nineteenth Century* (Leicester 1990); the articles by Jennifer Davis, "The London Garotting Panic of 1862," in *Crime and the Law,* ed. V. A. C. Gatrell et al. (London 1980), pp. 190–213; and Rob Sindall, "The London Garotting Panics of 1856 and 1862," *Social History* 12 (1987): 351–58. Boston had a garrotting scare in 1865, which was described by Jeffrey S. Adler in "The Making of a Moral Panic in Nineteenth-Century America: The Boston Garroting Hysteria of 1865," *Deviant Behavior* 17 (1996): 259–78.

17. Peter Turnbull, *The Killer Who Never Was* (Hull 1996), p. 252, and Paul Begg et al., *The Jack the Ripper A-Z* (London 1996), pp. 464–65.

18. A number of letters denouncing various people as the Ripper have been reproduced by Stephen Knight: *Jack the Ripper: The Final Solution* (London 1977), pp. 225–35.

19. Turnbull, *The Killer Who Never Was,* pp. 244, 256.

20. Turnbull, *The Killer Who Never Was,* pp. 249–50.

21. Begg et al., *The Jack the Ripper A-Z,* pp. 309–11.

22. Begg et al., *The Jack the Ripper A-Z,* p. 131.

23. For example, those by Donald Rumbelow, *The Complete Jack the Ripper* (London 1987); Martin Fido, *The Crimes, Detection and Death of Jack the Ripper* (London 1987); Colin Wilson and Robin Odell, *Jack the Ripper* (London 1991); Paul Begg, *Jack the Ripper: The Uncensored Facts* (London 1988); Melvin Harris, *The True Face of Jack the Ripper* (London 1994); and Philip Sugden, *The Complete History of Jack the Ripper* (London 1994).

24. See the articles by William G. Eckert, "The Whitechapel Murders," *American Journal of Forensic Medicine and Pathology* 2 (1981): 53–60, and "The Ripper Project: Modern Science Solving Mysteries of History," *American Journal of Forensic Medicine and Pathology* 10 (1989): 164–71.

25. See the articles by Jas. G. Kiernan, "Sexual Perversion and the Whitechapel Murders," *Medical Standard* 4 (1888): 129–30, 170–72, and E. C. Spitzka, "The Whitechapel Murders: Their Medico-Legal and Historical Aspects," *Journal of Nervous and Mental Disease* 13 (1888): 765–78.

26. Stewart Evans and Paul Ganey, *The Lodger* (London 1995), pp. 180–81. See also Martin Fido, *The Crimes, Detection and Death of Jack the Ripper* (London 1987), pp. 177–84.

27. A. P. Wolf, *Jack the Myth: A New Look at the Ripper* (London 1993), pp. 33–46; Begg et al., *The Jack the Ripper A-Z,* pp. 192, 222–23.

28. Bruce Paley, *Jack the Ripper: The Simple Truth* (London 1996); Begg et al., *The Jack the Ripper A-Z,* pp. 35–36.

29. An analysis of these descriptions can be found in Sugden, *The Complete History of Jack the Ripper,* pp. 95–96, 113–17, 200–208, 220–24, 333–38, and in Begg et al., *The Jack the Ripper A-Z,* pp. 195–96.

30. William G. Eckert, "The Ripper Project," 164–71, and Sugden, *The Complete History of Jack the Ripper,* pp. 366–67.

31. Turnbull, *The Killer Who Never Was.*

32. Walter Dew, *I Caught Crippen: Memoirs* (London 1938), p. 156.

## CHAPTER 13. WHO WAS THE MONSTER?

1. Anthony Babington, *A House in Bow Street* (London 1969), pp. 169–75. Mainwaring's involvement is described by David Philips, "'A New Engine of Power and Authority': The Institutionalization of Law-Enforcement in England 1780–1830," in *Crime and the Law,* ed. V.A.C. Gatrell et al. (London 1980), pp. 155–89.

2. Angerstein's posters and advertisements (see Banks ff. 44–45 and pp. 2–3) told the Monster victims and witnesses to report what they knew directly to his house in Pall Mall or to the Bow Street public office.

3. Anon., *The Trial of the Hammersmith Monsters* (London 1814).

4. On the Düsseldorf Monster, see Theodor Lessing and Karl Berg, *The Monsters of Weimar* (London 1993), pp. 161–289.

5. Angerstein, pp. 9–15, 44–45, and 54–56, respectively.

6. Swift, *Monster at Large,* pp. 95–96.

7. *True Briton* February 22 1797 3d.

8. "Horwood's Plan of London, Westminster, Southwark, & Parts Adjoining, 1792–99," London Topographical Society publ. 109 (London 1966). Duke's Court was called Grey's Yard in 1746; it still existed in 1818, according to a later edition of Horwood's map book, but was gone in 1894, according to the Ordnance Survey Map of that year.

9. Reproduced in F. H. W. Sheppard, *Survey of London* (London 1960), vol. 29, p. 309.

10. Swift, *Monster at Large,* pp. 98–100.

11. Mainwaring, f. 10, 17.

12. Swift, *Monster at Large,* p. 143.

13. Their marriage certificate is in the Guildhall Library Archives.

14. Williams, *Appeal to the Public,* p. x.

15. See Swift, *Monster at Large,* p. 162.

16. *Times* June 15 3c.

17. Angerstein, p. 125. It should be noted here that a short essay on the Monster came to my knowledge when this book was in press: B. M. Benedict, "Making a Monster" in *Defects,* ed. H. Deutsch and F. Nussbaum (Ann Arbor, Mich. 2000), pp. 127–53. This author is wrong in claiming that Rhynwick Williams was charged under the Coventry Act, and also erroneously states that the arrest of Williams was a result of his again approaching Anne Porter with a shout of "Oh ho!" and his usual gross and improper language when she was walking with Coleman in Green Park, but otherwise has a correct perception of the Monster mania. Benedict expresses doubt concerning the guilt of Rhynwick Williams, and questions the motives of the individuals who received parts of the Monster rewards, although it is going a bit too far to claim that Williams's arrest as the Monster was a direct result of his "sociability and innocuousness," and his gentleness and conformity to the sentimental social rules of the time. His weird habit of pursuing women through the streets, and damning and blasting them if they rejected his advances, was in fact considered wholly aberrant by both men and women at the time, and there is little doubt that already before his arrest as the Monster, he was well known for pestering women in the streets.

18. Anna Clark, "Whores and Gossips: Sexual Reputations in London 1770–

1825," in *Current Issues in Women's History,* ed. Arina Angerman et al. (London 1989), pp. 231–48.

19. Edwin Beresford Chancellor, *Pleasure Haunts of London During Four Centuries* (London 1925), pp. 181–85. For an amusing account of the notorious Haddock's Bagnio in Covent Garden and others, see E. J. Burford, *Wits, Wenches and Wantons* (London 1986), pp. 65–75. It should be noted that although most of the contemporary accounts from 1790 agreed that Pero's Bagnio was a respectable establishment, the bagnio in St. James's Street (probably Pero's Bagnio) had a resident prostitute in 1764, according to E. J. Burford, *Royal St. James's* (London 1988), pp. 144–46, quoting Jack Harris's *List of Cyprians* for that year. There is also a popular tradition that No. 63 St. James's Street had once been the site of a house of ill repute and that a murder had been committed there (Westminster Library Archives, Enquiries No. 6857).

20. Swift, *Monster at Large,* p. 99.

21. With regard to Rhynwick Williams's other alibis, he claimed that he was at work in the flower factory when Elizabeth Davis was attacked. When the Baughans were attacked, more than a year earlier, he had been at his lodgings, a fact he claimed could be proved by two people who remembered this particular day with unerring clarity. See Williams, *Appeal to the Public,* p. 10.

22. Frank McLynn, *Crime & Punishment in Eighteenth-Century England,* (Oxford 1991), pp. x, 125.

23. *Annual Biography and Obituary* 8 (1824): 275–98.

# INDEX